McGraw-Hill Construction Locator

Other Books in the McGraw-Hill Construction Series

Defect-Free Buildings: A Construction Manual for Quality Control and Conflict Resolution by Robert S. Mann

Building Anatomy: An Illustrated Guide to How Structures Work by Iver Wahl

Construction Safety Engineering Principles: Designing and Managing Safer Job Sites by David V. MacCollum

Solar Power Systems in Building Design: The Complete Photovoltaics Engineering Resource by Peter Gevorkian

McGraw-Hill Construction Locator

Building Codes, Construction Standards, and Government Regulations

Joseph A. MacDonald

McGraw Hill

New York   Chicago   San Francisco   Lisbon   London   Madrid   Mexico City
Milan   New Delhi   San Juan   Seoul   Singapore   Sydney   Toronto

The McGraw·Hill Companies

Library of Congress Cataloging-in-Publication Data

MacDonald, Joseph A.
    McGraw-Hill construction locator : building codes, construction standards, and
government regulations / Joseph A. MacDonald.
        p.   cm.—(McGraw-Hill construction series)
    Includes index.
    ISBN-13: 978-0-07-147530-3
    ISBN-10: 0-07-147530-3 (alk. paper)
    1. Building—Standards—United States—Information resources.   2. Building laws—
United States—Indexes.   3. Construction industry—United States—Directories.   I. Title.
II. Title: Construction locator.

    TH420.M33   2007
    690.02'1873—dc22

                                                                    2006036275

1 2 3 4 5 6 7 8 9 0   DOC/DOC   0 1 3 2 1 0 9 8 7 6

ISBN-13: 978-0-07-147530-3
ISBN-10: 0-07-147530-3

*The sponsoring editor for this book was Cary Sullivan, the editing supervisor was
David E. Fogarty, and the production supervisor was Richard C. Ruzycka. It was set in
Times by International Typesetting and Composition. The art director for the cover
was Anthony Landi.*

Printed and bound by RR Donnelley.

This book was printed on recycled, acid-free paper containing a minimum of 50%
recycled, de-inked fiber.

McGraw-Hill books are available at special quantity discounts to use as premiums and sales
promotions, or for use in corporate training programs. For more information, please write
to the Director of Special Sales, McGraw-Hill Professional, Two Penn Plaza, New York, NY
10121-2298. Or contact your local bookstore.

ABOUT THE AUTHOR

Joseph A. MacDonald, of Greenlawn, N.Y., has more than 40 years' editorial experience focusing on construction-related topics. In addition to 18 years with *Engineering New-Record* and *Construction Methods & Equipment*, Mr. MacDonald was the editor of *Information Display* and *Private Power Executive*; Editor-in-Chief of the *Encyclopedia of U.S. Building and Construction Technology* and the coeditor of both the *Handbook of Rigging and Scaffolding* and the *Directory of Worldwide Engineering & Construction Organizations*.

Contents

Appendices

Foreword

Although the Internet can help design-construction professionals locate and retrieve the documents that establish requirements for producing sound and safe buildings and structures—no matter where they are located—surfing the Web for a specific document needed often proves to be a complex, extremely time-consuming, and frequently frustrating process.

Currently available search engines are supposed to help you search through the myriad of documents available; however, they provide you no way of knowing that the information you're searching for is stored only in cryptically named files on a provider's server—at an unknown location, somewhere in the world.

The basic problem is that when you type a word into a search box, using one of the many readily available and most popular search engines—such as AOL, Google, and MSN—you still do not reach the actual file at a particular server. Instead, you're merely rifling through the search-company's index—a huge list assembled by software spiders that crawl through thousands of pages every second, copying keywords, phrases, titles/subtitles, link, and other descriptive information. Once a fragment of information lands in the server's index, it's usually compressed, assigned a weight of importance, and then stored in a database for supposedly quick retrieval. The search terms you enter are then compared against this index and linked to pages that contain one or more of your terms displaying the pages in order of sequence.

Inherently built-in flaws, however, can fool a search engine into finding pages peppered with thousands of key words in invisible white-on-white type. The problem is that although a legitimate page may perfectly match your search terms, it may get buried in search results—simply because there aren't enough other pages pointing to it. And also, if you enter the same search terms into ten different search engines, you're likely to get more than ten conflicting sets of results—partly because the search companies' spiders crawl different subsets of the Web.

Further complicating your surfing efforts are the unique principles at work in the various company-ranking algorithms. Each search engine is designed to identify the most popularly used sites, but a page's relevance to an individual user depends on more than its popularity.

The information industry's ultimate goal for improving search technology is to build software that is every bit as good at pointing users toward the specific resources they need—as would a well-trained reference librarian. In the meantime, today's McGraw-Hill Construction Locator attempts to fill the gap by putting, in the hands of design/construction professionals, a single reference tool that will enable them to quickly locate specific documents, identify their publishers, and retrieve document copies.

Preface

The *McGraw-Hills Construction Locator* is a single reference tool that identifies the most frequently referenced current codes, standards, specifications, and regulations, enabling users to quickly and easily locate and retrieve the numerous legal documents that govern the design/construction of safe and sound buildings and structures in all locations throughout the nation.

It is intended for use by architects, engineers, constructors, facility managers, planners, specifiers, estimators, and legal council counsel in the construction industry; and for building department and government agency officials to effectively administer and enforce ordinances and laws governing the construction methods, materials, and equipment used in their jurisdiction.

The locator lists over 400 professional societies, industry organizations, and government agencies that develop, as well as those that contribute to the development of these legal documents that comprise the minimum criteria for ensuring the public's safety, health, and welfare in the construction of new buildings, as well as the alteration and modification of existing structures. It follows a modified format of the Construction Specification Institute's new 50-topic masterformat, covering design and building specifications that are universally accepted and used by most practicing architects, engineers, and constructors in the United States.

Within this format, all documents pertaining to a specific construction subject are grouped together to eliminate the need for tedious cross-referencing. Topical listings under each section provide the complete title of a document, its ID number, and (wherever available) its publication date.

Appendices include:

- *Standards Writing Bodies*—List of principle standards documents publishers
- *Reference Publications*—Listing of books and other documents pertaining to codes, standards, and regulations
- *Document Distributors*—Listing of companies that distribute various standard documents
- *Keyword Index*—Alphabetical listing by building and construction topics of document producing organizations
- *Organization Acronyms*—Listing of acronyms for organizations named in the Locator

- *Organization Profiles*—Alphabetical index of document publishers (including names, addresses, telephone and fax numbers, website addresses, and information contacts) for retrieving selected documents

While the editor and the publisher have made every effort to be accurate and as comprehensive as possible in developing the listings, some documents may be missing due to the failure of a particular organization or agency to submit its information in time for publication. Any identified missing data, however, will be published in an updated version of the Locator.

Locator users are encouraged to notify the editor with information identifying errors or omissions to be corrected and included in future publications.

Joseph A. MacDonald

McGraw-Hill
Construction
Locator

1 Introduction

HISTORICAL PERSPECTIVE

From the days of antiquity, governments have exercised the right to regulate how buildings are designed and constructed to ensure the safety and health of the public. Today, they also regulate the welfare of the public with regard to proper building methods and materials.

Building and housing codes have existed in one form or another in urban cities for over 3000 years. During his reign as a king of ancient Babylonia, Hammurabi is often credited as having promulgated the first recorded building code about 1750 B.C. While basically being a humanitarian set of building restrictions, it also puts to death the architect of a building that collapsed, if the accident causes the building owner's death; and puts to death the architect's son, if the building's owner's son loses his life in the building collapse.

Roman laws, under Julius Caesar, regulated the heights of buildings, distances between them, and setbacks from thoroughfares, as well as party walls, light, ventilation, and sanitation. At that time, Greek laws also specified building inspection criteria.

It was not until the twelfth century A.D., however, that regulations on building construction addressed the problems created by rapid increase in urban area population density, focusing primarily on the potential for fire to spread between buildings. Criteria were established requiring construction of party walls between adjoining structures, as well as use of noncombustible roofing materials.

After the great fire of London destroyed much of the city in 1666, Parliament enacted the first regulations resembling a modern building code, to prevent repeating the dense congestion that had been a key factor in spreading the fire. But, it was not until the mid 1880s that Parliament passed the Metropolitan Building Act prescribing the regulations of construction type, building height, floor area, occupancy density, and fire resistance. The regulations also established the first need for a code administrator.

The legal concept of building codes was well established by the time America was settled, with the first building regulations in the New World[21] based on those brought from Europe by experienced builders and craftsmen who had settled in the colonies. Those early regulations, however, were developed primarily to protect the buyer from incompetent or unscrupulous builders.

New Amsterdam (New York City), as early as 1647, had promulgated the city's first building law regulating the construction and repair of chimneys, emission of smoke, prevention of fire, and other problems caused by poorly constructed chimneys. Other cities such as Boston, Philadelphia, and New Orleans, also facing rapid urban growth, were forced to quickly follow New York City's example, and develop their own building construction regulations. The Spanish Province of New Orleans in 1796 passed an ordinance prohibiting the use of wooden roofs.

With the end of the Revolutionary War, the states of the newly formed republic adopted a national constitution that relegated to the states and the local jurisdictions the power to regulate building design and construction within the states and the local jurisdictions. It took until the late 1860s, however, to develop and enact the first building code specifically for use in the states—the New York City Building Code. By the end of the nineteenth century, however, most major cities in the United States had enacted a building code to ensure the safety and protect the health of their citizens.

But, until the late 1890s, there was little development of building laws throughout the United States. The tremendous influx of immigrants, combined with the simultaneous Industrial Revolution triggering a movement of the labor force from rural to urban centers with their industrial plants. These developments created construction booms in major cities necessitating construction of multiple dwellings. Overcrowding and slum conditions then spurred the necessary remedial legislation.

Technological advances:

- Opened up new opportunities in building construction, such as the steel skeleton framing that permitted construction of multistoried buildings
- Introduced new complexities that necessitated imposing guidelines in the form of building codes

By 1901, New York City had enacted the Tenement House Law. The accelerated growth of the nation's cities and their housing problems rapidly accelerated new constructions, making it even more imperative to assure the protection of the public's health and safety, as well as that of the workers themselves. New building codes began including provisions for licenses or certificates of qualifications of architects, engineers, and contractors, as well as registration of various crafts such as plumbers, electricians, welders, and riggers.

After the turn of the twentieth century, even more building controls were imposed, primarily specifying fire protection because they were promulgated by insurance interests seeking to prevent payment of indemnities on fire risks.

The National Board of Fire Underwriters (forerunner of the American Insurance Association) published and promulgated the first model building code in 1905. Wisconsin, in 1914, developed what was to become the first statewide code (going into effect in 1920).

A not-for-profit service organization, the Building Officials & Code Administrators (BOCA), was formed in 1915 to advance the cause of professional code administrations and enforcement. Then in 1922, the International Conference of Building Officials (ICBO) was formed to develop the Uniform Building Code (published in 1927) that could be used by all state and local governments to develop their own building regulations. By the late 1930s, BOCA promulgated the National Building Codes, basic codes for state and local government adoption. Then in 1940, the Southern Building Code

Congress International (SBCCI) was formed to promulgate a set of model building codes for state and local governments—the Standard Building Code (first published in 1945).

By the 1950s, accelerated construction resulting from rapid population growth and expansion to the West and South, forced more cities and states to develop and implement construction regulations, with building laws inevitably focusing primarily on local conditions.

As a result, a National Academy of Science (NAS) report in 1960 recommended the development of a Uniform National Code to bring into concert the many variable standards and codes being promulgated by local and state regulatory agencies. In 1967, an advisory committee on intergovernmental regulations recommended that statewide building codes be adopted, and a national model code be developed. The threat of a possible federal code moved the governors of each of the 50 states and several territories to form the National Council of States on Building Codes and Standards (NCS/BCS), with a primary mission to coordinate a solution to the problem of multiple building codes, and to improve communications among the states.

During the 1970s and the 1980s, an increasing number of states began developing and adopting statewide building codes based on a Model Code. Although this regional code development proved effective and responsive to the country's needs, the Model Code groups recognized the need for a single building code without regional limitations. The three organizations jointly created the International Code Council (ICC) to jointly develop a single set of comprehensive and coordinated national Model Construction Code. The new code, adopted in 2000, now enables code enforcement officials, architects, engineers, designers, and contractors to work with a consistent set of requirements throughout the country, while manufacturers no longer need to design to three different sets of standards. In addition, the ICC code enables uniform education and certification programs.

DOCUMENT IDENTIFICATION

Regulation of construction practices has a valid public purpose—to protect against improper designs, poor workmanship, unsound practices, inadequate fire protection, and the use of inferior materials—thereby preventing both physical harm and financial tragedy. The terms—codes, standards, specifications, and regulations—are often mistakenly interchanged to describe the written requirements that states and localities use to control design and construction of buildings. In reality, these three sets of documents have very different technical, substantive, and legal meanings.

Building Codes

Building codes are established under the police powers of a state to provide safety, health, and welfare of the building occupants and the general public within a community. The codes are simple collections of standards or other conditions and requirements proposed by the sponsoring groups for adoption as building codes, and use as regulatory vehicles. A number of such codes fall into the broad category of building codes.

A true building code, however, is a comprehensive legal and technical document consisting of standards or other conditions and requirements that have been adopted by a government legislative authority. As a legal document, a code is used by building officials of the municipality or the state that adopts it to regulate the construction, alteration, repair, or modification of buildings and facilities. Compliance with the physical and the procedural requirements set forth in a building code, therefore, is mandatory. As a technical document, a building code makes reference to or includes portions of nationally recognized building standards that prescribe or proscribe various physical features or parameters, providing the basis for most of the code's technical requirements. Typically, a building code references between 300 and 400 standards.

Two types of building codes are in use today:

- *Specification*—Specifies acceptable materials and their minimum or maximum dimensions for specific applications.
- *Performance*—Specifies the end result to be obtained in terms of the required performance of the finished structure. This type of code focuses on such characteristics as strength, stability, permeability, hardness, and fire resistance—leaving selection of materials, methods, and dimensions to the designer. A catalog of acceptable materials and construction methods, shown by tests to meet the code requirements, usually supplements the codes.

Designers generally prefer performance-type codes because they provide greater flexibility in meeting a client's needs, while satisfying the intent of the code. In practice, however, most codes are combinations of specification and performance types.

More than 400 industry organizations, particular industries, and government agencies in the United States produce or promulgate (or both) standards regulating design and construction of buildings.

Construction Standards

As with building codes, there are two types of construction standards in use:

- *Prescriptive*—Defines an acceptable material, product, or process without stating the desired attributes. These types of standards are objective, and evaluation to determine whether or not they have been complied with is relatively straightforward. Prescriptive standards, however, may not necessarily satisfy the user's needs.
- *Performance*—Delineates the desired attributes of a material, product, or process permitting application of any scheme that results in achieving these attributes and meets the standards. Performance standards, however, are more difficult to evaluate and may require laboratory testing to determine whether they have been complied with. Because such standards focus on the user's requirements, they tend to promote economy and innovation.

Both forms of standards have their place in building design and construction requirements. Ideally, prescriptive standards will be related to performance standards so that the performance intended is explicit.

In addition, construction standards are categorized as reference, consensus, specification, and statutory standards.

Standard Categories

- *Reference standards*—These consist of voluntary rules or measures established and promulgated by various participants including professional societies, technical associations, industry groups, and government agencies. As recommended by these organizations, reference standards specify materials of construction and processes, setting forth detailed technical characteristics that must be met.

These standards are adopted as a basis for judging quality and quantity, forming the basis of current construction practice, especially with respect to quality of materials. They also frequently specify fabrication practices and construction methods as well. When used in building regulations and building contracts, compliance with these standards is mandatory.

- *Consensus standards*—These are generally more widely recognized and referenced by the building code and the government regulatory administrators because they are developed through broad participation and under rigorous review procedures. Specialized standard-writing organizations and some professional societies and technical associations develop and promulgate these standards that reflect the consensus of the members of the sponsoring groups.

- *Standard specifications*—In addition to voluntary standards, government agencies, and other public authorities sponsoring public works also publish standards specifying uniformity of administrative procedure and quality for constructed facilities including materials and workmanship. These standard specifications almost always require modifications and additions to ensure the particular contract specifications that are completely acceptable to the contract work.

- *Statutory standards*—The government at times develops statutory standards in response to a national need, such as exposure to hazardous materials in a building.

Project Specifications

Architects or engineers designing a building or structure for an owner imposes another set of restrictions on the building process in the form of three basic contract documents—drawings, conditions, and project specifications. The major contract document is the set of project specifications; the written or the printed descriptions of the work to be performed by a contractor that complements the design drawings by describing the qualities of materials, systems, and equipment; workmanship on-site and off-site fabrication; as well as installation and erection.

Project specifications are written not only to tell the contractor how to construct, manage, and direct the construction of buildings and structures, but also to provide specific information for other participants in successfully performing their particular roles in the construction process such as estimator, purchasing agent, project representative or inspector, owner, subcontractors, and manufacturers of building materials and installed equipment.

Four basic types of specifications are currently used in varying combinations in the construction industry:

- *Performance*—Specifies an end result by formulating the criteria for its accomplishment, with the criteria for materials established on the basis of physical properties of the end product; and for mechanical equipment by its operating characteristics.

- *Descriptive*—Describes in detail the materials to be used and the workmanship required to fabricate, erect, and install the materials.
- *Reference*—Refers to a standard established for a material, a test method, or an installation procedure, and can also be applied to workmanship standards.
- *Proprietary*—States outright the actual make, model, catalog number, and the like of a product or the installation instructions of a manufacturer.

Design Criteria

In addition to project specifications, design criteria add another layer of restrictions on building design and construction. The project owner imposes these criteria to help determine whether a building's design and construction are acceptable. They usually consist of a set of established precedents, rules, or measures upon which decisions are based; and may include, implicitly or by reference, applicable codes. In addition, they may also include many items not covered by the codes, or even standards exceeding levels adopted in building codes.

Government Regulations

Finally, government agencies at the federal, state, county, and municipal levels promulgate a variety of regulations, laws, and ordinances that address specific aspects of building design and construction. Among their considerations are public health and safety, fire protection, water and sewer, site access, adjoining streets, and so forth.

- *Federal*—A number of federal regulations apply to working conditions during construction as well as to the finished building such as Construction Health & Safety Regulations and Environmental Impact Statements required for all major projects. Other government agencies also issue regulations governing the design and the construction of buildings and structures such as minimum property standards, energy design criteria, construction specifications, as well as architect/engineer instructions and criteria, among other directives.
- *State*—At the state level, health and safety requirements are important considerations in designing buildings where workers will be employed, including lighting, toilet-fixture counts, ventilation, and noise levels, among other considerations.
- *Municipal*—Almost every municipality promulgates local ordinances to regulate zoning and property subdivisions, noise insulation and abatement, signage, building security, health, and housing, among others.

Miscellaneous Restrictions

Another set of construction restrictions includes statutory building laws, professional licensing and registration, occupational licensing and registration, and nonregulatory requirements.

- *Statutory building laws*—Unlike building codes and construction standards that are adopted by industry only after they have been formally developed through a consensus of all interested or affected parties, statutory building laws are frequently developed on a crash basis. As a result, they lack the comprehensive research or the professional and industry input to ensure their promulgation and use within a rational and orderly framework of existing regulations.
- *Zoning ordinances*—A single set of maps for the entire local entity establishes districts in which various specific regulations prevail, including uses permitted as of right,

uses permitted by a special permit, supplementary use regulations, performance standards, signage, bulk restrictions, and off-street parking/loading.

- *Nonregulatory restrictions*—These include insurance, financing, and public agency influences on the design and construction processes.
- *Building permits*—These cover new buildings, foundations and earth work, demolition and removal/disposal, as well as equipment use and work.
- *Occupational licensing and certification*—To protect workers and suppliers on a project site and the public exposed to the construction, building codes include provisions for licenses, certificates of qualification, or registration of various crafts such as plumbers, electricians, welders, riggers, and others. In addition, many states and large municipalities require that general contractors also to be licensed.
- *Professional licensing and registration*—Registration laws of the US states, territories, possessions, and districts for architects and engineers are predicated on protecting the public health, safety, and welfare.

Although overly numerous, extremely complicated, and severely constraining, the body of codes, standards, specifications, and regulations nevertheless are necessary to ensure the health, safety, and welfare of the public. Normally, these publications express only basic or legally accepted standards of design and construction. They must never be considered as optimum standards of good practice. And, they certainly should not be used as design or construction handbooks. They are society's laws to be obeyed or changed by due process.

REGULATIONS KNOWLEDGE

Although the regulation of building construction, renovation, and demolition is one of the primary activities of the states, implemented through promulgation and enforcement of building codes and regulations, the building code itself traditionally is administered by a local building department, and generally applies only to constructions within the boundaries of a lot or a parcel of land. Building regulations, on the other hand, are under the jurisdiction of various other local or state government departments, which usually control construction of sidewalks or streets, curbing openings, driveway extensions, water and sewer connections, and other works on public property.

Projects that are independently funded and built for private owners within municipal jurisdictions, however, are usually regulated by a combination of local building and zoning ordinances that cover all aspects of construction as well as electrical, mechanical, and plumbing systems; and elevators, boilers, and refrigeration installations, among other services. (Locally enacted codes can exceed mandatory statewide building codes or minimum state codes.)

Even the federal government is involved, although in a much more limited way, such as HUD's mobile home-building code that pre-empts any state or local code applicable to mobile homes. Any government-promulgated regulation represents a legislative response, at both the state and the federal levels, for both implementation and increased productivity in the construction industry.

Many urban and rural localities, though, are still governed by building codes that are adopted predominantly by local legislation. And, almost all enforcements—whether the code is enacted locally or is state mandated—are still vested at the local level. Municipal regulations, however, can be pre-empted by the State or Federal Regulations Standards (or both) when projects are being developed for a government client—or when they involve public funding.

- *Safety & health*—On all construction projects, the safety and the health of both employees and the public exposed to the construction work are subject to federal or state requirements (or both). These requirements, of course, are based on the federal Occupational Safety and Health Act (OSHA) of 1970 that governs conditions under which employees may work on a construction site.

The OSHA regulations (1926) contain detailed construction standards that contractors and subcontractors must comply with during construction operations. Architects, engineers, and project owners may also be held accountable under OSHA for any unsafe conditions that might endanger a building's occupants once it is completed.

Architects and engineers, therefore, must take every precaution to ensure that the building or facility they design provides a safe and healthy environment for its occupants (both employees and visitors) that are acceptable under OSHA. Owners, in turn, should maintain the same level of safety and health conditions, as specified by OSHA, once the structure is in place and operating.

As promulgated and enforced, OSHA makes no provisions for reviewing design plans before construction starts. Only after the Occupational Safety & Health Administration or the state agency counterpart receives a complaint, the appropriate government agency inspects a building or facility. Therefore, it is imperative for all members of the building team—project designers, constructors, and owner alike—be thoroughly familiar with the law and its most current interpretations and make every effort to comply with it.

- *Environmental protection*—Federally funded, as well as very large, projects usually also will require the project's architect/engineer to file an Environmental Impact Statement (EIS) with the federal Environmental Protection Agency (EPA) or with a state agency counterpart (or both) before construction is allowed to start.

The EIS for a proposed project must provide an analysis of the site and its surrounds, an evaluation of the project's impact on the environment and the recommendations for abating or eliminating any adverse impacts. It must outline in detail the proposed actions, alternative actions (including no action), their probable environmental ramifications, as well as the probable impact of alternative actions outside the jurisdiction of the responsible agency.

Although requirements differ from situation to situation, a responsible project official must provide EPA with a detailed statement that includes:

- Direct and indirect effects of the project
- Interference with other activities

- Energy and resource requirements
- Conservation and reparation of potential
- Preservation of urban, historic, and cultural qualities
- Ways to minimize damage

DEVELOPMENT PROCEDURES

Whether promulgated by local or state authorities, all building codes formerly were based on one of the three model codes—National (BOCA), Standard (SBCCI), and Uniform (ICBO)—with modifications and amendments made to them to satisfy specific local conditions. Since 2000, however, the International Building Code, developed and promulgated the International Code Conference (ICC), has been the basic code for all construction projects in the country.

Although public agencies adopt the codes through legislative enactment, the agencies themselves do not develop the standards comprising the code, but rather rely on private organizations to develop the actual standards. Thousands of nongovernment and commercial standards used in the construction industry today represent the output of more than 500 private organizations and government agencies that either develop or sponsor standards, or work closely with the standards writers to develop their documents.

These organizations include private standards developers, professional societies, trade associations, and product certifiers that conduct the basic research, testing, and measurement of materials, products, and systems; and provide a means for achieving consensus from a broad cross-section of private and public interests in determining what constitutes appropriate standards. The American National Standards Institute (ANSI) has established and certified the process whereby a "consensus" agreement is reached through formal notification, participation, and review procedures that must be followed in the development of a standard. Once a voluntary consensus is achieved, and the standards are formally adopted, they are promulgated for incorporation into the model code, which then is adopted by the state and the local governments as their own codes.

Building codes essentially are compilations of accepted good practices and minimum standards, promulgated and enforced to ensure the safe design and construction of a building or facility and the protection of public health, safety, and welfare. They should not be considered aggravating nuisances or necessary evils that inhibit building design concepts and construction methods.

The codes ordinarily incorporate, by reference, the latest version of existing construction standards or specifications for materials and methods, as promulgated by the American Society for Testing and Materials (ASTM); structural design and construction standards promulgated by the American Institute of Steel Construction (AISC), the American Concrete Institute (ACI), and the American Institute of Timber Construction (AITC); or fire protection standards as promulgated by the National Fire Protection Association (NFPA).

Architectural and structural constraints that these codes impose on the design and construction of buildings and facilities are generally determined by the code's classification of various types of buildings. Classifications typically are based on:

Fire zone rating—Building construction and occupancy type permitted or prohibited in a particular zone

Occupancy group—Intended use of building
Assembly areas—Theaters, concert halls, auditoriums, stadiums
Educational—School, colleges, universities
Health care—Hospitals, nursing home, sanitariums
Storage—Combustible materials
Manufacturing—Noncombustible materials
Multiple residential—Apartments, hotels, dormitories, convents, monasteries, one- and two-story dwellings

Construction type—Degree of public safety and fire resistance
Airport terminals
Auditoriums, theaters, concert halls
Banks, vaults
Commercial, retail buildings
Convention halls, arenas
Correctional facilities, prisons, jails, detention centers
Dining facilities, restaurants
Educational facilities, schools, colleges, universities
Farm buildings
Fire Stations
Food processing, storage
Garages, vehicle maintenance facilities
Health care facilities
Hotels, resorts
Housing, high-rise
Industrial, manufacturing facilities
Judicial, courtroom facilities
Laboratories, research facilities
Libraries
Municipal buildings
Museums, galleries
Offices, low- and high-rises
Parks, playgrounds, zoos, conservatories
Police stations
Postal facilities
Railroad stations, transit facilities
Recreational facilities, clubhouses, gymnasiums, stadiums
Religious structures, churches
Roads, driveways, parking lots
Utilities, power plants, substations
Warehouses

APPLICATION PROBLEMS

Problems in using standards arise from three basic sources:

- *Failure to understand the system*—Some design professionals believe that standards are issued by government agencies—in part because their companies do business with the government, or in doing so they come face-to-face with Military Specifications and Standards, Federal Specifications and Standards issued by various federal agencies. These, however, are either procurement documents or regulations, and not industry consensus standards.

Major problems in using obsolete standards include:

- *Driving costs up and leaving a producer wide open to product liability*—Very often a specification is changed as a result of the knowledge obtained from its failure. The revised specification seeks to avoid the cause of the failure. Using obsolete documents simply repeats the failure.

- *Rote use of standards*—Documentation of a product or service often repeats and compounds errors by referring either to a nonexistent or an obsolete document. Sometimes, standard requirements are listed, and then totally ignored as just to do much more paper work.

- *Identification of documents*—Over 400 organizations issue construction standards, and each has its own numbering and designation system. In addition, sometimes a designation coincides with the designation from another organization.

- *Difficulty in acquiring documents*—An organization producing standards goes out of business and references to those standards are never revised or updated. More often the organization ceases to issue the standards transferring the activity to another organization.

- *Keeping abreast of new and revised standards*—Only methods include serving-on a particular standards committee, be on an organization's mailing list, or subscribe to the service of private document distributors. CDs make it easy, today, to handle standards revisions with organizations able to reprint an entire document including all revisions.

REFERENCES

American Institute of Architects, Washington, DC (www.aia.org).
American National Standards Institute, Washington, DC (www.ansi.org).
ASTM International (American Society for Testing & Materials), Conshohocken, PA (www.astm.org).
Construction Specifications Institute, Alexandria, VA, (www.csinet.org).
National Conference of States on Building Codes & Standards, Herndon, VA (www.ncsbcs.org).
National Institute of Standards & Technology, Gaithersburg, MD (www.nist.gov).

2 Building Codes

INTERNATIONAL CODES

Building codes regulate the arrangement of building, material performance, and structural requirements. They establish the minimum criteria that designers and constructors must meet to satisfy the code's requirements for protecting the building's occupants and the general public.

These criteria, however, are not intended to assure efficient, convenient, or adequately equipped buildings. In fact, architects and engineers often must design buildings more conservatively to

- Meet a client's needs.
- Produce a more efficient building system.
- Take into account conditions not covered fully by the code provisions.

Authority for code enforcement varies from state to state, depending on whether there is a statewide code with an ultimate central authority, or if codes are the purview of local authorities. Although the state holds the ultimate power to enforce building codes, traditionally these regulations have been adopted and enforced at the municipal and the county levels to meet local conditions. These local jurisdictions may write their own codes or may legally adopt other codes, such as the State Building Code or the International Building Code.

- **Building Code, International (IBC)—***ICC*
  Covers means of egress and interior finish requirements, comprehensive roof provisions, seismic engineering provisions, innovative construction technology, revamped structural provisions, reorganized occupancy classifications, and the latest industry standards in material design.

- **Electrical Code, ICC (ICCEC)—***ICC*
  Features all electrical criteria found in the International Code Series in one convenient location. Includes administrative provisions.

- **Energy Conservation Code, International (IECC)—***ICC*
  Addresses the design of energy-efficient building envelopes and the installation of energy-efficient mechanical, lighting, and power systems; through requirements emphasizing performance. Establishes minimum regulations for energy-efficient buildings using prescriptive and performance-related provisions.

- **Fire Code, International (IFC)—***ICC*
  Based on a solid foundation of proven fire-code provisions and standards. Developed by a broad-based committee of fire chiefs, fire marshals, and members of the fire-service/protection industry.

- **Fuel Gas Code, International (IFGC)—***ICC*
  Addresses the design and the installation of fuel gas systems and gas-fired appliances through requirements that emphasize performance. Provides model code regulations that safeguard public health and safety in both large and small communities.

- **Housing Accessibility, Requirements for (RHA)—***ICC*
  Provides an opportunity for safe harbor in compliance with accessibility requirements in the federal Fair Housing Act. This publication can be used by states, jurisdictions, builders and architects to design and construct new multifamily housing

that meets accessible facilities as covered under the Fair Housing Act. The publication brings together contemporary and up-to-date provisions from model codes and consensus national standards that meet or exceed the minimum requirements of the Fair Housing Act.

- **Mechanical Code, International (IMC)**—*ICC*
  Developed by the International Code Council, the International Mechanical Code (IMC) establishes minimum regulations for mechanical systems using prescriptive and performance-related provisions. It is founded on broad-based principles that make possible the use of new materials and new mechanical designs.

- **Performance Code for Buildings and Facilities (PCBF)**—*ICC*
  Defines the objectives for achieving the intended outcomes regarding occupant safety, property protection, and community welfare.
  Provides a framework to achieve the defined objectives in terms of tolerable levels of damage and magnitudes of design events, such as fire and natural hazards.

- **Plumbing Code, International (IPC)**—*ICC*
  Provides consistent requirements that can be used across the country to provide comprehensive regulation of plumbing systems setting minimum regulations for plumbing facilities in terms of both performance and prescriptive objectives.
  Provides the acceptance of new and innovative products, materials, and systems.

- **Private Sewage Disposal Code, International (IPSDC)**—*ICC*
  Provides flexibility in the development of safety and sanitary individual sewage-disposal systems, and includes detailed provisions for all aspects of design, installation, and inspection of private sewage disposal systems.
  Companions the document to the International Plumbing Code.

- **Property Maintenance Code, International (IPMC)**—*ICC*
  Addresses the need in communities for a modern and up-to-date property maintenance code governing the maintenance of existing buildings.
  Includes clear and specific property maintenance requirements that regulate interior and exterior building facilities.

- **Residential Code, International (IRC)**—*ICC*
  Covers the latest technological advances in building design and construction, including provisions for steel framing and energy savings.
  Contains mechanical, fuel gas and plumbing provisions that coordinate with the International Mechanical Code and the International Plumbing Code.
  Replaces the CABO One- and Two-Family Dwelling Code.

- **Zoning Code, International (IZC)**—*ICC*
  Provides jurisdictions with a means of promoting uniformity and consistency in zoning laws and their enforcement. (An excellent resource for jurisdictions that do not currently have a zoning code, or are operating with one that is outdated.)

CODE COMMENTARIES—*ICC*

- **Accumulative Supplement to the International Building Codes**—*ICC*
  Contains all code changes voted on and approved by the membership since the release of the 2000 International Codes—*ICC*.

- **Inspection Workbooks, IBC**—*ICC*
  Explains the steps of rough-in and final inspection and the tasks an inspector performs to verify compliance with the code.
- **ASTM Reference Standards in the International Building Code**—*ICC*
  Contains all ASTM Standards that are referenced by, but not included in, the International Building Code. (More than 200 standards in over 1300 pages.)

SPECIALTY INDUSTRY CODES

- **Accessibility & Usability for Physically Handicapped People, Providing**—*AB/ANSI 117.1*
  The code is designed to ensure that persons with disabilities have access to public accommodations throughout the United States. Facilities covered by this code, but not limited to, are hotels, restaurants, theaters, retail stores, museums, parks, transportation terminals, and other facilities open to the public.
- **Boiler & Pressure Vessel Code (BPVC)**—*ASME*
  The ASME Boiler Code is an American National Standard, affecting industries such as public utilities, construction, materials engineering, chemical and food production, nuclear power generation, petroleum processing, and industrial manufacturing.

Since it was first proposed in 1911, BPVC has influenced public safety, product reliability, and industrial efficiency. It reflects, and has spurred, the growth of cooperation and research efforts among industrial groups, as well as has contributed to the stability of contractual relations, certification, and the insurance industry. Since 1972, it has been a de facto International Standards, and the basis of an international accreditation program.

- **Concrete & Masonry**
  Building Code Requirements for
    Masonry Structures—*ACI*
    Reinforced Concrete—*ACI*
    Structural Concrete—*ACI*

- **Dwelling Requirements Plumbing Code**—*IAPMO*
- **Elevators & Escalators, Safety Code for**—*ASME/ANSI 17.1*
- **Fire Prevention Code**—*NFPA*
  Consists of some 270 codes and standards covering air conditioning and ventilating systems, boilers and furnaces, chimneys and vents, and dry cleaning operations; fire-extinguishing equipment, flammable and combustible liquid storage; compressed gas, fire extinguishing systems that use halons, and liquefied natural and petroleum gases, among others.
- **Life Safety Code**—*NFPA*
  Establishes minimum requirements to ensure a reasonable degree of safety from fire in both new and existing buildings and structures, covering construction, protection, and occupancy features necessary to minimize danger to life from fire, smoke, and panic.

Includes requirements for means of egress, fire protection features, assembly and educational occupancies, amusement buildings, health care facilities, residential occupancies, and board and care facilities, among others.

- **Lighting Code**—*IDA/IEEE*
  May be enacted at different government levels, from states to counties or townships, to cities, and even to development projects or neighborhoods. State level codes usually address only very general issues, such as lighting built with state funding. State laws also enable the adoption of more comprehensive codes at local levels.

Different areas with different developed and natural conditions have differing levels of appropriate light usages, and different sensitivities to the various obtrusive aspects of outdoor lighting. Because of this, five lighting zones were redefined in the US Pattern Lighting Code, with lighting standards appropriate to those zones established. The zones are based on the CIE Environmental Zones and range from areas with intrinsically dark landscapes such as national parks and other areas set aside as dark-sky preserves, through rural and urban residential areas to areas of relatively high ambient brightness in the most highly developed urban areas.

The International Dark-Sky Association (IDA) together with the Illumination Engineering Society of North America (IESNA) have developed a Model Lighting Ordinance (MLO) and Companion Design Guidelines—intended for use by cities and municipalities that want to provide a regulatory strategy for outdoor lighting, to require outdoor lighting appropriate to communities, the environment, and the natural habitat.

Most cities are already familiar with classifying different areas into zoning districts for other regulatory purposes, and the MLO will recommend Lighting Zones (LZs) that correspond to those districts, typically based on population or use type, or both. Each LZ (from 0 to 4) will provide a recommended upper limit on the amount of light. A community will be able to assign a different LZ to an area, preferably lower, to align with its existing districts.

- **Lightning Protection Code**—*NLSI*
  The National Lightning Safety Institute (NLSI) makes a number of lightning protection codes and standards available, including:

  Electrical Storms & Lightning Protection—*DOE M440.1-1*

  Grounding, Bonding & Shielding for Electronic Equipment & Facilities—*MIL-HDBK 419A*
  - Vol. I—Basic Theory (1987)
  - Vol. II—Applications (1987)

  Lightning Protection, Grounding, Bonding & Shielding
  - Requirements for Facilities—*FAA 019d*
  - Surge Protection Requirements (2004)—*NWS 30-4105*

  Lightning Safety
  - *DDESB 6055.9*
  - *DOE/EH 0530*

  Practices & Procedures for Lightning Protection, Grounding, Bonding & Shielding
  - Implementation (1996)—*FAA 6950.19A*

Protection against ignitions arising out of Static, Lightning & Stray Currents (2003)—*API*

- **Mechanical Refrigeration, Safety Code for**—*ASHRAE*
- **National Electrical Code (NEC)**—*NFPA*

  Contains provisions covering the electrical power systems and wiring for the building, as well as such items as electrical equipment, motors, fans, and pumps. The code addresses how systems must be designed to meet various electrical power demands throughout the building and how they must be installed to prevent fire and ignition in the building.

- **National Electrical Safety Code (NESC)**—*IEEE*
- **Structural Welding Code**—*AWS*
- **Minimum Property Standards (MPS)**—*HUD*

  Supplements the International Building Code.

  Establishes certain minimum standards for buildings constructed under HUD housing programs, and covers new single-family homes, multifamily housing, and health care type facilities. Includes:

  Minimum Design Standards for Community Sewerage Systems

  Minimum Property Standards for Housing

  Permanent Foundations Guide for Manufactured Housing

Although HUD has accepted the model building code, including over 250 referenced standards, and local building codes, in lieu of separate and prescriptive HUD standards, one major area of difference exists between the MPS and other model building codes. Model codes do not contain any minimum requirements for the durability of such items as doors, windows, gutters and downspouts, painting and wall coverings, kitchen cabinets, and carpeting, while the MPS includes minimum standards for these, and other items, to ensure that the value of an FHA-insured home is not reduced by the deterioration of these components.

HUD requires that each property insured with an FHA mortgage meets one of the nationally recognized building codes of a state, or the local building code based on the International Building Code (IBC). In areas where such state or local codes are used, HUD determines if the state or the local code is comparable to the IBC.

If no state or local building code has been adopted, the appropriate HUD Field Office will specify the IBC.

3

Construction Standards

FACILITY CONSTRUCTION

General

Safety & health

AC Substation Grounding, Guide for, Safety in (3rd Ed.)—*ANSI/IEEE 80*

Accepted Practice, Criteria for, in Safety, Health & Environmental Training—*ANSI Z490.1*

Accident Prevention in Construction

    Manual—*AGC*

    Tags—*ANSI Z 535.5*

Adjustable Drive Systems, Safety Standards for Construction & Guide for Selection, Installation & Operation of—*NEMA ICS 7.1*

Aerial Tramway, Aerial Lifts, Surface Lifts & Tows, Safety Requirements—*ANSI B77.1*

Barrier Materials, Flexible—*ASTM 15.09*

Belt Manlifts, Safety Standards for (2000)—*ASME A90.1*

Color Chart, Safety—*ANSI Z535 COLOR CHART*

Combustion Safeguards & Flame Sensing Systems—*FMRC 76610*

Construction Safety—Occupational Safety & Health, Code of Federal Regulations—*29 CFR 1926*

Confined Spaces, Safety Requirements for—*ANSI Z117.1*

Conveyors & Related Equipment, Safety Standard for—*ASME B20.1*

Earthquake Activated Safety Devices—*FMRC 7431*

Electric Motors & Generators, Safety Standards for Selection, Installation & Use of—*NEMA MG 2*

Electrical Construction Workers, Safety & Health Standards Digest for—*OSHA*

Electronic Apparatus, Safety Requirements, Audio, Video & Similar—*IEC 60065*

Elevators & Escalators

    Handbook—*ASME A17.1 HDBK*

    Safety Code for—*ASHRAE; ASME 17.1*

    Safety Code for Existing—*ASHRAE; ASME A17.3*

Employee Workplaces, Electrical, Safety Requirements for—*NFPA #70E*

Engineering & Management, System, Safety (2nd Ed.)

Environmental Control, Safety, Health &

Eye & Face Protection, Practice for Occupational & Educational—*ANSI Z87.1*

Floor & Wall Openings, Stairs & Railing Systems, Safety Requirements for Workplace—*ASNI A1264.1*

Hazardous Industrial Chemicals—Material Safety Data Sheets—*ANSI Z400.1*

Health

    Construction—*29 CFR 1926*

    Industrial—*29 CFR 1900–1910*

Emergency/disasters
Emergency Management & Assistance—*44 CFR*

Ergonomics
Ergonomic Design for People at Work, Vol. 1 (1984)

Ergonomic Design for People at Work, Vol. 2 (1986)

Human Factors Design Handbook

Inspection—building/construction
Building Inspection Manual & Study Guides—*SBCCI*

Concrete, Inspection, Guide for—*ACI-311.4R*

Construction Inspection Manual (5th Ed.)—*CSI MASTERFORM*

Concrete Inspection, Manual of (7th Ed.)—*ACI-SP-2*

Electrical Inspections, Basic Checklist for Building

    Elevators & Escalators (2000)—*ASME A17.2.1*

    Escalators & Moving Walks (2000)—*ASME 17.2.3*

    Hydraulic Elevators (2000)—*ASME 17.2.2*

Electrical Inspection & Plan Exam Manual—*SBCCI*

Inspector's Handbook, Reinforced Concrete Masonry Construction—

Inspection

    Isolated Lots by Attributes, Sampling Procedures & Tables for—*ASQ Q3*

    Planning, Guide to—*ASQ E2*

Plumbing Inspector's Manual—*SBCCI*

Sprinkler Systems, Inspection Testing & Maintenance of—*NFPA #13A*

Welds, Guide for Visual Inspection of—*B1.11*

Information technology systems
Configuration Management, National Consensus Standard for—*EIA 649*

Engineering & Systems, Processes for—*EIA 632*

Information Technology—*ISO ICS 35*

    Interference, Physical & Signaling, Fiber Channel, FC-PH—*ANSI INCITS 230*

    Protection of—*ANSI//NFPA 75*

    Software Life-Cycle Processes

        Implementations Considerations, Guide for—*IEEE/EIA 12207.3*

        Industry Implementation of International Standard—*ISO/IEC 12207.0—IEEE/EIA12207 SET*

        Life-Cycle Data, Guide for—*IOS/IEC 12207.1*

Records, Protection of—*ANSI/NFPA 232*

Safety—Information Technology Equipment

Part 1: General Requirements—*BS EN 60950-1*

Instruments/instrumentation

Instrumentation, General Methods &, Temperature Measurement—*ASTM 14.03*

Laboratory Apparatus, General Methods & Instrumentation—*ASTM 14.04*

Lasers

    Safe Use of, ANS for—*ANSI Z136.1*

    Safety of, Products—*IEC 60815-1*

        Part 1: Equipment Classification, Requirements & User's Guide

Measuring Equipment, Quality Assurance Requirements for

        Part 1: Metrological Confirmation System for Measuring Equipment—*ISO 10012-1*

        Part 2: Control of Measurement Process—*ISO 10012-2*

Safety Requirements for Electrical Equipment for Measurement, Control & Laboratory Use

        Part 1: General Requirements—*BS EN 61010-1*

Temperature Measurement, Medical—*ASTM 14.-3*

Quality

Auditing, Fundamentals of Quality—*ASQ H0794*

Audits for Improved Performance, Quality (2nd Ed.)—ASQ H0844

Configuration Management, Quality Management, Guidelines for—*ASQ Q10007; ISO 10007*

Constructed Project, Quality in the—*ASCE*

Control Charts, Quality, Guide for—*ASQ B1, B3*

    Analyzing Data, Method of, Control Chart

    Controlling Quality During Production, Method of, Control Chart

Economics of Quality, Guidelines for Managing—*ISO TR 10014*

Management & Environmental Management Manuals, Guidelines for Developing Quality—*ISO 10013; ISO 9000*

Management System Approach, A Quality:

    Eight-Step Process to Successful ISO 9000 Implementation—*ASQ H0878*

Management Systems, Quality

    Fundamentals & Vocabulary—*ASQ Q9000; ISO 9000*

    Guidelines for Performance Improvement—*ASQ Q9004—ISO 9004*

    Requirements—*ASQ Q9001; ISO 9001*

Managing Work Processes—*ASQ H0822*

Measuring Equipment, Quality Assurance Requirements for—*ISO 10012 SET*

    Part 1: Metrological Confirmation System for Measuring Equipment—*ISO 10012-1*

    Part 2: Control of Measurement Process—*ISO 10012-2*

Organizational Performance Excellence, Principles & Practice of—*ASQ H0995*

Probability & General Statistical Terms: Statistics—Vocabulary & Symbols—*ASQ A3534-1*

Project Management, Guidelines to Quality in—Quality Management—*ASQ Q10006; ISO 10006*

Quality

    Assurance Standards, Quality Management &

        Guidelines for Selection & Use—*ASQ Q9000 -1*

        Vocabulary—*ASQ Q9004; ISO 9004*

    Management & Assurance—*ISO ICS 03 120.10—ISO 9000 & 10000*

    Management, International Standards for—*ISO 9000 COMPENDIUM*

    Manuals, Guidelines for Developing—*ISO 10013*

    Operations, TQM: Management Processes for—*ASQ HO732*

    Program, General Requirements for—*ASQ C1*

System

    Auditing, Quality Management & Environmental Management—*ISO 19011*

    Elements, Quality Management & Quality, Guidelines for

        Performance Improvements—*ISO 9004*

    Documentation, Guidelines for Quality Management—*ISO TR 1001.3*

    Guidelines for Auditing—*ASQ Q10011 SERIES; ISO 10011 SET*

      Part 1: Auditing—*ISO 10011-1*

      Part 2: Qualifications Criteria for Quality Systems Auditors—*ISO 10011-2*

    Manual

      ISO 9001–*QCSS ISO 9001 MANUAL*

      Policies, Objectives, Procedures, Control Forms, Work Instructions,

        Audit Checklists & Support Standards (2000)—*QCSS ISO 9001 MANUAL*

        Self Implementation Package &—*QCSS ISO 9002 SET*

      ISO 9002—*QCSS ISO 9002 MANUAL*

        Manual & Inspection System Package—*QCSS ISO 9002 SET*

      ISO 9003—*QCSS ISO 9003 MANUAL*

        QC Manual & Inspection System Package—*QCSS ISO 9003 SET*

    Requirements, Quality—*ASQ QS9000*

Sampling

    Attribute, Introduction to—*ASQ 72*

    Attribute Skip-Lor Program, An—*ASQ S1*

    Inspection by Attributes, Procedures & Tables for—*ASQ Z1.4; MIL STD 1058*

    Variables for Percent Nonconforming, Procedures & Tales for—*ASQ Z1.9; MIL STD 414*

      (Interchangeable with ISO 3951)

Statistical Techniques for ISO 9001, Guidance on—*ISO 10017*

Training

Practices, TQM: Quality—*ASQ HO734*

Quality Management Guidelines for—*ISO 10015*

Standards

ASQ Standards—*ASQ Q9000 SET*

Book of Standards: Complete Set of NACE RPs, MRs, and TMs—*NACE*

Building Codes, ASTM Standards in (2002, 4 Vol. Set0—*ASTM BUILDING CODES*

Canadian Standards, Canadian Standards Association Guide to—*CSA PLUS 4000*

Quality Management, International Standards for—*ISO 9000 COMPENDIUM*

Quality Standards, ISO

    1. Revisions of 9000, 9004—*ISO 9000 COLLECTION 1*

    2. Series Documents—*ISO 9000 COLLECTION 2*

Standards

    Catalog—*ASQ T62*

    Quality Management, International—*ISO 9000 COMPENDIUM*

    Quality ISO

        Revisions of 9000, 9004—*ISO 9000 COLLECTION 1*

        Series Documents—*ISO 9000 COLLECTION 2*

Time Saver Standards

    Architectural Design Data

    Building Types

    Housing & Residential Development

    Interior Design & Space Planning

    Standardization Documentation, Generalities, Terminology—*ISO ICS 01*

Tests/testing

Acceptance Testing Specifications—*NETA*

Testing & Calibration Laboratories, General Requirements for the Competence of—*ISO/IEC 17025*

Metals Test Method & Analytical Procedures

    Mechanical Testing: Elevated & Low Temperature Metals—*ASTM 03.01*

    Metallography Tests—*ASTM 03.01*

Nondestructive Examination

    BPVC Section V—*ASME S00050, S00050 ADDENDA*

    Welding, Brazing &, Standard Symbols for—*AWS A2.4*

Nondestructive Testing—*ASTM 03.03*

    Wear & Erosion, Metal Corrosion—*ATM 03.02*

    Recommended Practice, Personnel Qualification & Certification—*ASNT TC 1A*

Radiographic Examination

Standard Practice for—*ASTM E11742*

Weldments, Standard Test Method for—*ASTM E1032*

Radioscopic Examination of Weldments, Standard Test Method for—*ASTM E1416*

Surface Burning Building Materials, Test Methods—*NFPA 255*

Testing Specifications, Maintenance—*NETA*

Testing & Calibration Laboratories, General Requirements for the Competence of—*IAO/OEC 170525*

Welding, Brazing & Nondestructive Examination, Standard Symbols for—*AWS A2.4*

Existing Conditions

Accessibility
Accessible

    Design, Minimum Guidelines & Requirements for—*ATBCB*

    Housing Design File—*NACE*

Accessible & Usable Buildings & Facilities

    Guidelines for—*ANSI 117.1*

Accessibility

    Guidelines for Building—*ICBO/ANSI*

    Code Requirements for Housing—*ICC*

Standards, Uniform Federal—*ATBCB*

    Usability for Physically Handicapped People, Providing—*ANSI 117.1*

ADA (Americans with Disabilities Act)

    Accessibility Guidelines: Checklist for Buildings & Facilities—*ADAAG*

    Compliance Evaluation Survey—*ATBCB*

    Compliance Guidebook—*BOMA*

    Documents & Fair Housing Amendments Act—*ATBCB*

    Fair Housing

      Act—HUD

      Manual—HUD

    Guidelines/Documents & Fair Housing

    Handbook—*EEOC/DoJ*

    Public Law 101-336

ADAAG Guide to the ADA—Accessibility Guidelines—*US Access Board*

Code Requirements for Housing Accessibility—*ICC*

Fair Housing Act—*Public Law 100—430*

    HUD Development

Fair Housing Manual—*HUD*

Guidelines/Requirements for Accessible Design, Minimum—*ATBCB*

Nondiscrimination/Disability

    Public Accommodations and in Commercial Facilities—*DOJ*

    State/Local Government Services—*DOJ*

Building/facility construction

Amusement Rides & Devices—*ASTM 15.08*

Aging, Architect's Design Guide for

Airport Terminal Buildings, Fueling Ramp Drainage & Loading Walkways—*ANSI/NFPA 415*

Buildings & Other Structures

  Minimum Design Loads for—*ASCE 7*

  Minimum Design Loads for—*ANSI A58.1*

Building & Safety Codes for Industrial Facilities

Building

  Alteration & Demolition Operations, Safeguarding—*ANSI/NFPA 241*

  Construction

    I: E 72– E 1670—*ASTM 04.11*

    I: E 72– E 1670 (116)—*ASTM 04.11*

    II: E 1671– Latest—*ASTM 04.12*

    Standards, Fire—*ANSI/NFPA 04.07*

  Elements of Fire Resistance Tests, Part 1: General Requirements—*ISO 834.1*

  Groups, Fire Protection in Planned—*ANSI/NFPA 1142*

  Materials—*UL 263*

  Standards, Constuction, Fire

  Systems Integration Handbook—*AIA*

  Test for Surface Products, Full Scale Room—*ISO 9705*

Correctional Facilities, Design for Contemporary—*NICSF*

Detention Facilities—*ASTM 15.08*

Dry Cleaning Plants—*NFPA 32*

Exterior Fire Exposure, Protection of Buildings from—*ANSI/NFPA 80A*

Grandstands, Folding & Telescopic, Tents & Membrane Structures—*ANSI/NFPA 102*

Health Care Facilities—*ANSI/NFPA 99*

  Handbook—*ANSI/NFPA*

Heliports—*ANSI/NFPA 418*

Homes

  Installation Standard, Manufactured, Model—*ANSI/NFPA 225*

  Installations, Sites & Communities Manufactured, Fire Safety Criteria—*ANSI/NFPA 501 A*

Housing—*ANSI/NFPA 501*

Hypobaric Facilities—*ANSI/NFPA 99B*

Laboratories

  Apparatus—*ASTM 14.03*

Fire Protection for, Using Chemicals—*ANSI/NFPA 45*

Instrumentation, Temperature Measurement—*ASTM 14.03*

Incinerators & Waste & Linen Handling Systems & Equipment—*ANSI/NFPA 82*

Malls, Atria & Large Spaces, Smoke Management in—*ANSI/NFPA 92B*

Marinas & Boatyards—*ANSI/NFPA 309*

Marine Terminals, Piers & Wharves, Construction & Fire Protection of—*ANSI/NFPA 307*

Minimum Design Loads for Buildings & Other Structures—*ASCE 7*

Motor Fuel Dispensing Facilities & Repair Garages—*FMRC 4910*

Parking Structures—*ANSI/NFPA 88A*

Petroleum Industry, Fire Protection in the, Application of Fixed Water Spray Systems for—*API PUBL 2030*

Plant Safety

OSHA Compliance Manual—*29 CFR 1910*

Regulations & Index, Guide—*OSHA 1910*

Refineries, Fire Protection in—*API-RP*

Residential Construction, Principles & Practices of

Service Station Code, Automotive & Marine—*NFPA 30A*

Solvent Extraction Plants—*ANSI/NFPA 36*

Sports

Facilities, Equipment &—*ASTM 15.07*

Pedestrian Walkways Safety & Footwear—*ASTM 15.07*

Subterranean Spaces—*ANSI/NFPA 520*

Bathroom appurtenances

Plastics

Bathtub Units—*ANSI Z124.1*

Lavatories—*ANSI Z124.3*

Shower Units—*ANSI Z124.2*

Sinks—*ANSI Z124.6*

Water Closet, Toilet Seats—*ANSI Z124.5*

Water Closet Bowls & Tanks—*ANSI Z214.4*

Chimneys/fireplaces

Ceiling Dampers—*UL 555C*

Chimneys, Fireplaces, Vents & Solid Fuel Burning Appliances—*NFPA 211*

Fire Dampers—*UL 555*

Mechanical—Chimneys & Stacks—*CSI SPECTEXT—S15000*

Smoke Dampers—*UL 555S*

Clean rooms

Materials Flammability Test Control, Clean Room—*FMRC 4910*

Controlled Environments, Cleanrooms & Associated—*ISO 14644 SET*

Part 1: Classification of Air Cleanliness—*ISO 14644-1*

Part 2: Testing & Monitoring to Prove Continued Compliance, Specifications for—*ISO 14644-2*

Part 4: Design, Construction & Start-Up—*ISO 14644-4*

Part 5: Operations—*ISO 14644-5*

Part 7: Clean Air Hoods, Gloveboxes, Isolators, Mini-Environments, Separative Enclosures—*ISO DIS 14544-7*

Products & materials

Accessible & Usable Buildings & Facilities, Guidelines for—*ANSI 117.1*

Building Materials Directory—*UL BMD*

Construction

Materials & Building—*ISO ICS*

Materials Directory, Electrical—*UL ECMD*

Detention Facilities, General Products, Chemical Specialties & End Use Products—*ASTM 15.08*

Ladders, Fixed, Safety Requirements—*ANSI A14.3*

Materials & Methods, Fundamentals of Building Construction

Materials, Test Methods—Surface Burning Building—*NFPA 255*

Plastic Pipe, Building Products:—*ASTM 08.04*

Rehab of Existing Buildings, Guidelines for—*ICC*

Sheet Metal Manual, Architectural—*SMACNA*

Building constructions

(I) E 72–E 1670—*ASTM 04.11*

(II) E 1671–Latest—*ASTM 04.12*

Demolition

Demolition Operations, Construction &—*ANSI A10.4*

Maintenance

Facilities Maintenance Standards, 1988

Maintenance of Buildings, Preventive (1991)

Maintenance Testing Specifications (1989)—*NETA*

Property Maintenance Code, BOCA National—*BOCA*

Scaffolds/scaffolding

Scaffolding, Safety Requirements for (NSC)—*ANSI A10.8*

Signs/signage

Color Code, Safety—*ANSI Z353.1-5 SERIES*

   Accident Prevention Tags

   Color Chart

   Environmental Facility Safety Signs

   Safety Symbols, Criteria for

   Product Safety Sign & Label

Highway Signs, Structural Support for, Standards Specifications—*AASHTO—LTS-4*

Safety Sign & Label, Product—*ANSI Z353.4*

Sign Code, Uniform—*ICBO*

Concrete & cement   **Concrete**

   ASTM Standards—*ASTM 04.01*

   Concrete

   Cement; Lyme; Gypsum

   Concrete Curing & Miscellaneous Materials: Expansion Joint Fillers

   Concrete Reinforcing Steel

   Gypsum Related Building Materials & Systems

   Paving Brick & Bock

   General Methods of Testing

Building Code Requirements:

   Reinforced Concrete—*ACI 318*

      Commentary—*ACI 318R*

   Structural Concrete—*ACI 318*

      Commentary—*ACI 318R*

Cast-in-Place Concrete in Tall Buildings Design & Construction

   Council on Tall Buildings & Urban Habitat

Cement, Lime, Gypsum (132)—*ASTM 04.01*

Chemical Resistant Materials: Vitrified Clay, Concrete, Fiber-Cement Products, Mortars, Masonry—*ASTM 04.04*

Cold Weather Concreting—*ACI 306R*

Cold Weather Concreting, Standard Specifications for—*ACI 306.1*

Concrete

   CSI SPECTEXT—*S03000*

   Practice, Manual of (2003, 6 Vol. Set)—*ACI*

   Principles—*ATP*

   Slabs on Grade, Design & Construction—*ACI*

Concrete & Aggregates (176)—*ASTM 04.02*

Concrete for Buildings, Specifications for Structural—*ACI*

Construction & Materials, Standard Tolerances for Concrete—*ACI 117-199*

Cracking in Concrete Structures, Control of—*ACI 224R*

Design Handbook—*PCI*

Design Handbook, Concrete—*ACI AP-17*

    Vol. 1: Beams, Slabs, Brackets, Footings, Pile Caps—*ACI 17SP-17*

    Vol. 2: Columns—*ACI SP-17A*

Design Loads for Buildings & Other Structures, Minimum—*ANSI A58.1*

Detailing Manual—*ACI*

Fiber-Reinforced Cement Products—*ASTM 04.05*

Fiber Reinforced Concrete

Hot Weather Concreting—*ACI 305.R*

Inspection, Guide for Concrete—*ACI 311.4R*

Inspection, Manual of Concrete—*ACI SP-2*

Mixtures, Design & Control of Concrete (2000, 14th Ed.)—*PCA*

Precast & Prestressed Concrete Design Handbook—*PCI*

Precast Concrete, Chemical-Resistant Nonmetallic Materials (271)—*ASTM 04.05*

Post Tensioning Manual

Quality Concrete Construction, Contractor's Guide to—*ASCC/ACI*

Roof Deck & Loose Fill Insulation, Concrete, Perlite

Ready-Mixed Concrete, Standard Specifications for—*C-94-9*

Reinforced Concrete, Building Code Requirements for, Plus Commentary—*ACI*

Reinforced Concrete Handbook—*CRSI*

Reinforced Concrete Plus Commentary, Building Code Requirements for—*ACI*

Reinforcing Bars, Placing—*CRSI*

Reinforcing Steel

    Concrete—*ASTM 01.04*

    Institute, Manual, Concrete—*CRSI*

Fiber Reinforced Concrete (1991)

Slabs on Grade, Design & Construction of Concrete—*SCM 11; ACI*

Concrete, Guide to—*ACI 506R*

Structural Concrete for Buildings, Specifications for—*ACI 301*

Structural Concrete, Commentary, Building Code Requirements for (2002)—*ACI 318*

Tilt-Up Concrete Design & Construction Manual (2000)—*TCA*

Tolerances for Concrete Construction & Materials, Standard—*ACI 117*

(Tilt-Up Concrete Association)

Aggregates

Concrete & Aggregates—*ASTM 04.02*

Forms/formwork

Form Construction, Concrete

Formwork for Concrete—*ACI SP-4*

Formwork for Concrete, Guide to—*ACI 347R*

Pipe

Concrete Pipe, Chemical-Resistant Nonmetallic Materials—*ASTM 04.05*

Concrete Practice, Manual of (1992-5 Vols)—ACI

Concrete Pressure Pipe (1979/88)—M-9

Pipe Handbook, Concrete

Pressure Pipe

   Asbestos Cement Standard for Installing—*AWWA C-603*

   Concrete—*M-9*

Asphalt

Asphalt Handbook (1990)—*Series 4*

Emulsion Manual, Basic Asphalt (1987-2nd Ed)—*MS*-19

Introduction to Asphalt (1986, 8th Ed.)—*MS-6*

Pavement Maintenance, Asphalt in (1983-2nd Ed)—*MS-16*

Paving Manual, Asphalt (1978/87-3rd Ed—*MS-8*

Roofing Manual, Residential, Asphalt (1988)

Surface Treatments & Construction Techniques, Asphalt—*ES-12*

Surface Treatments Specifications, Asphalt—ES-11

Bricklaying, Brick & Block Masonry—*BIA*

Masonry

Codes & Specifications, Masonry

Concrete

   Handbook for Architects, Engineers & Builders—*PCA*

   Masonry Structures & Commentary, Building Coder Requirements for—*ACI 531-079*

Designer's Guide, Masonry (2002)

Dimension Stone—*ASTM 04.07*

   Soil & Rock, Geotextiles—*ASTM 04.08*

Masonry—*ASTM 04.05*

Masonry—*CSI SPECTEXT S04000*

   Structures & Specifications, Building Code Requirements for (2002)—*ACI 530 & 530.1*

Standards on Masonry—*ASTM 04.05*

   Fiber-Reinforced Cement Products

   General Methods of Testing

   Manufactured Masonry Units

     Chemical-Resistant Masonry Units

Clay or Shale Masonry Units

Concrete Masonry Units

Flue & Chimney Linings

Sand-Lime Masonry Units

Structural Tile & Filter Rock

Vitrified Clay Filter Block

Vitrified Clay Liner Plates

Masonry Construction

Precast Concrete Products

Terrazzo, Finishes—*CSI SPECTEX—S0900*

Mortars & grouts

Cementitious Grouts & Grouting, Chemical-Resistant Nonmetallic Materials

Mortars & Grouts, Masonry (271)—*ASTM 04.05*

Standards on Masonry

Mortars & Grout for Unit Masonry (271)—*ASTM 04.05*

Mortar, Grouts, Monolithic Surfacings & Linings

Concrete block & pipe

Concrete Pipe, Chemical-Resistant Nonmetallic Materials (271)—*ASTM 04.05*

Clay brick & pipe

Chemical-Resistant Nonmetallic Materials—*ASTM 04.05*

Vitrified Clay Pipe

Brick Flooring, Finishes—*CSI SPECTEXT S09000*

Bricklaying, Block & Block Masonry—*BIA*

Vitrified Clay Pipe, Chemical-Resistant Nonmetallic Materials (271)—*ASTM 04.05*

Gypsum & stucco

Adhesives for Fastening Gypsum Wallboard to Wood Framing, Standard Specification for—*C 557*

Application of Gypsum Base to Receive Gypsum Veneer Plaster, Standard Specification for—*C 844*

Application of Interior Gypsum Plaster, Standard Specification for—*C 842*

Application & Finishing of Gypsum Board, Recommended Specifications for—*GA 216*

Exterior Gypsum Soffit Board, Standard Specification for—*C 931*

Gypsum

Backing Board & Coreboard, Standard Specification for—*C 442A*

Backing Board, Standard Specification for Water Resistant—*C 630*

Base to Receive Gypsum Veneer Plaster, Application of, Standard Specification for—*C 844*

Board, Standard Specification for Application & Finishing of—*C 840*

Board, Standard Specification for Nails for the Application of—*C 514*

Sheathing Board, Standard Specification for—*C 79*

Wallboard & Gypsum Veneer Base, Accessories, Standard Specification for—*C 1047*

Wallboard, Standard Specification for—*C 36*

Joint Compound & Joint Tape for Finishing Gypsum Board, Standard Specification for—*C 475*

Lathing & Furring, Standard Specification for Installation of Interior—*C 841*

Plaster (Stucco) Manual, Portland Cement—*PCA*

Screw Attached Installation of Steel Framing Members to Receive Gypsum, Standard Specifications for—*C 754*

Tile & ceramics
Advanced Ceramics—*ASTM 15.01*

Ceramic Tile, American National Standard Specifications for—*ANSI 137.1*

Ceramic Tile, American National Standard Specifications for Installation of—*ANSI 108.1*

Ceramic Tile Installation, Handbook for

Finishes: Ceramic Tiles—*CSI SPECTEXT S09000*

Terrazzo & mosaic

Ceramics
Advanced Ceramics

Ceramics, Glass &—*ISO ICS 81*

Ceramic Tile, Installation of—*ANSI A108.1*

Metals

Ferrous
Architectural Sheet Metal Manual (2000)—*SMACNA 1013*

ASTM Standards—*ASTM 01.04*

    Boilers & Pressure Vessels, Plate & Forgings for

    Concrete Reinforcement & Prestressed Concrete, Steel for

    Rails & Accessories, Wheels, Axels & Tires, Steel

Bars, Forgings, Bearings, Chain & Springs—*ASTM 01.05*

Coated Steel Products (116)—*ASTM 01.06*

    Structures,

Steelwork in Building, Structural Use of

    Part 1:

Code of Practice for

    Rolled & Welded Sections, Design of, Structural Use of Steelwork in Building—*BS 5950-1*

Reinforcing steel

Corrosion/erosion

Passive Treatments for—*SAE AMS QQ-P-35*

Sheet, Strip & Plate, Corrosion & Heat Resistant—1.5 CR-25.5NI-1.2 0-2.1 ITI

0.0006B-0.30v 1800F (982C) Solution Heat-Treated—*SAE AMB 552.5*

Wear & Erosion; Metal Corrosion

Metals Test Methods & Analytical Procedures—*ASTM 03.02*

Refractories

Activated Carbon; Advanced Ceramics, Refractories (147)—*ASTM 15.01*

Metals & Alloys, Reactive Refractory—*ASTM 02.04*

Metal test methods

Analytical Chemistry for Metals, Ores & Related Materials (I): E 32-Latest—*ASTM 03.05*

Magnetic Properties—*ASTM 03.04*

Mechanical Testing, Elevated Temperature Tests, Metallography—*ASTM 03.01*

Metals—Mechanical Testing (125)—*ASTM 03.01*

Nondestructive Testing (177)—*ASTM 03.03*

Spectroscopy, Molecular, Surface Analysis—*ASTM 03.06*

Wear & Erosion: Metals Test Methods & Analytical Procedures Corrosion—*ASTM 03.02*

Fasteners

Acceptance Inspection, Fasteners—*ISO 3269*

Bearing, Rolling Element—*ASTM 01.08*

Bolting

High Strength Structural (Fasteners Standards Book—Sec. E)—*IFI*

Materials for High-Temperature Service, Standard Specifications for
Alloy-Steel & Stainless Steel—*ASTM A193/A193M*

Bolts

Nuts, Screws & Studs; Washers; Pins, Rivets, & Keys; Adjusting & Retaining Rings
Standards on Fasteners—*ISO; DIN*

Studs & Bent—*IFI 136*

Fastener Quality Act—*NIST—15 CFR 0-299*

Fastener Standards

Steel Products—*ASTM 01.08*

Washers & Rivets, Externally & Internally Threaded, Standard Method for
Determining the Mechanical Properties of—*ASTM F 60G*

Fasteners, Rolling Element, Bearings—*ASTM 01.08*

Hex

Coupling Nuts—*IFI 126*

Screws, Large Size—*IFI 149*

ISO Standards Handbook

Vol. 1—Terminology & Nomenclature

General Reference Standards Handbook—*ISO HDBK FASTENERS*

Vol. 2—Product Standards—*ISO HDBK FASTENERS*

Joints Using ASTM A325 or A490 Bolts, Specification for Structural—*ASTM*

Mechanical Fasteners: Carbon & Alloy Steel Wire, Rods & Bars for—*IFI-140*

Mechanical Properties of Fasteners Made of Carbon Steel & Alloy Steel

Part 1: Bolts, screws & Studs—*ISO 898-1*

Part 2: Nut with Specified Proof Load Values, Course Thread—*ISO 898-2*

Part 7: Tensional Test & Minimum Torques for Bolts & Screws with

Nominal Diameters 1 mm to 10 mm—*ISO 898-7*

Metric Fastener Standards: A Simplified Standards System for Metric Mechanical Fasteners—*IFI-0100*

Metric Screw Threads—General Purpose—*ISO 261*

General Purpose—Tolerances

Part 1: Principles & Basic Data—*ISO 965/1*

Nuts for Bolts for High Pressure or High-Temperature Service (or both), Standard Specifications for Carbon & Alloy Steel—*ASTM A194/A194M*

Roof & Rock Bolts & Accessories, Standard Specifications for—*ASTM F432*

Screw Thread Standards for Federal Services Set—*FED-STD H28 SET*

Socket Cap Shoulder & Set Screws Hex & Spine Keys (Inch Series)—*ASTM B18.3*

Square & Hex

Bolts & Screws (Inch Series)—*ASTM/ANSI B18.2.1*

Nuts (Inch Series)—*ASTM/ANSI B18.2.2*

Steel & Nonferrous—*ASTM 15.08*

Structural Bolts, Steel, Heat Treated 120/105 KSI Minimum Tensile Strength, Standard Specifications—*ASTM A 325*

Tapered & Reduced Cross Section Retaining Rings (Inch Series)—*ASME B18.27*

Tolerances for Fasteners

Part 1: Bolts, Screws, Studs & Nuts—Product Grades A, B & C—*ISO 4759-1*

Torque Screws, Test Procedures for the Performance of Nonmetallic Resistant Element Prevailing—*IFI-124*

Chain & wire

Steel

Chain—ASTM 01.05

Wire—ASTM 01.3

Storage tanks

Cathodic Protection of Underground Petroleum Storage Tanks & Piping Systems

Combustible Liquids, Underground Leakage of Flammable &—*NFPA 329*

Cleaning, Underground Storage Tanks—*API 2015*

Fire-Protection, Considerations for Design & Operation of
Liquefied Petroleum Gas (LPG) Storage Facilities—*API PUBL 2510A*

Storage Tanks

Abandonment or Removal of Used Underground Service Station Tanks, Recommended Practice for the—*API 1604*
Aluminum Alloy, Welded—*ASME B96.1*

Large Aboveground Atmospheric, Prevention & Suppression of Fire—*API PUBL 2027A*

Large Welded, Low-Pressure, Design & Construction—*API STD 620*

Steel, Welded, for Oil Storage—*API STD 650*

Underground Liquid Storage Systems

Flammable & Combustible Liquids, Steel—*UL 58*

Installation Instructions for—*STI-P3*

Installation of, Recommended Practice for

Petroleum, Installation of—*API 1615*

Tubes/tubing

Piping Tubing, Fittings, Steel—*ASTM 01.01*

Sanitary Hygienic Applications, Austenitic Stainless Steel Tube & Pipe Systems Specifications for Welding of—*AWS DD18.1*

Structural Tubing in Rounds & Shapes, Cold-Formed Welded & Seamless Carbon Steel, Standard Specifications for—*ASTM A 500*

Stainless Steel Tubing for General Service, Seamless & Welded Austenitic, Standards Specifications for—*ASTM a 269*

Welding & brazing

Automatic Welding Installations, Robotic &,
Guide for Components of—*AWS/NEMA D16.2/D16.2M*

Boiler & Pressure Vessel Code: Qualification Standards for
Welding & Brazing—*ASME S00090/S00090 ADDENDUM*

Code, Welding

Sheet Metal—*AWS D9.l./D9.1M*

Sheet Steel, Standard—*AWS D1.3*

Stainless Steel—*AWS D1.6*

Structural Steel—*AWS D1.1/D1.1M*

Reinforcing Steel, Structural—*AWS D1.4*

Copper Tubing & Fittings for Medical Gas Systems, Recommended Practices for the Brazing of—*AWS D10.13/D10.13M*

Cost Effective Welding, Design & Planning Manual for—*AWS DPW*

Brazing Procedure & Performance Qualifications—*AWS B2.2*

Bridge Welding Code—*AASHTO/AWS D1.5/D1.5M*

Electrodes for

Nickel and Nickel Alloy Welding, Specifications for Shielded Metal Arc Welding—*AWS A5.11/A5.11M*

Tungsten & Tungsten Alloy, Specifications for Arc Welding & Cutting,—*AWS A5.12/A5.12M*

Examination of Welds, Guide for the Visual—*ASW B1.11*

Fluxes, Electrodes &, for

Carbon & Low Alloy Steel, Arc Welding & Cutting, Specifications for—*AWS A5.25/A5.25M*

Handbook, Everyday Pocket, for

Aluminum, Gas Metal Arc Welding of—*AWS PHB-8*

Gas Metal Arc & Flux Cored Arc Welding—*AWS PHB-4*

Metric Practices for the Welding Industry—*AWS PHB-5*

Shielded Metal Arc Welding—*AWS PHB-7*

Steel Arc Welding—*WS PHB-1*

Inspection, Visual, & Weld Discontinuities, Visual—*AWS PHB-2*

Inspection, Visual, of AWS D1.1 Structural Welding Code

Fabrication & Welding Requirements—*AWS PHB-6*

Welded Joint Details for Structural Applications—*AWS PHB-3*

Handbook, Welding

Materials & Applications, Vol. 3-Part 1—*AWS WHB-3.8*

Materials & Applications, Vol. 4-Part 2—*AWS WHB-4.8*

Welding Processes, Vol. 2-*AWS WHB-2.18*

Welding Science & Technology-*Vol. 1*—*AWS WHB-1.9*

Inspection Handbook, Welding—*AWS WI*

Inspection of Welds, Guide for Visual—*AWS B1.11*

Inspector's Manual, Welding, Certification Manual for—*AWS CM*

Manager's guide for Welding—*SMACNA*

Metallurgy, Fundamental of Welding (Vol. 1)—*AWS WM1.4*

Mill Cranes & Other Material Handling Equipment, Welding of—*AWS D14.1*

Nondestructive Examination of Welds, Guide for—*AWS B1.10*

Qualification Standards for Welding & Brazing Procedures, Welders, Brazers & Welding & Brazing Operators, Welding & Brazing—Boiler & Pressure Vessel Code—*ASME S00090; ASME S00090 ADDENDA*

Procedure & Performance Qualification, Welding & Brazing,
  Requirements for—*NA VSEA S9074-AQ-GIB 010*

Procedures & Performance Qualifications, Welding, Specifications for—*AWS B2.1*

Radiographic Examination of Weldments, Standard Test Method for—*ASTM E1032*

Radioscopic Examination of Weldments, Standard Test Method for—*ASTM 1416*

Robotic & Automatic Welding Installations, Guide for Components of—*AWS/NEMA D16.2/D16.2M*

Tube & Pipe Systems in Sanitary (Hygienic) Applications, Specifications for Welding Stainless Steel—*AWS D18.1*

Safety in Welding & Cutting & Allied Processes—*AWS Z-49.1*

Specification for, Standard Welding Procedure—*AWS D9.1/D9.1M*

  Carbon Steel (M-1) Group, 18 through 10 Gauge, Gas Metal Arc Welding (Short Circuiting Transfer Mode) of, in As-Welded Condition, with or without Backing—*AWS B2.1-1-004*

Galvanized Steel (M-1 Group), 18 through 10 Gauge, Gas Tungsten Arc Welding of, in the Arc-Welded Condition, with or without Backing—*AWS B2.1-1-007*

Carbon Steel (M-1/P-1/S-1 Group 1 or 2), 1/8-in through 1-1/2-in Thick, E7018, As-Welded or PWHT Condition—*AWS B2.1-1-016*

Carbon Steel (M-1/P-1/S-1 Group 1 or 2), 1/8-in through 1-1/2-in Thick, E6010, (Vertical Uphill) Followed by E7018, As-Welded or PWHT Condition—*AWS B2.1-1-022*

Austenitic Stainless Steel (M-8/P-8/S-8, Group 1), 1/16-in through 1-1/2-in Thick, Er.3xx, As-Welded Condition, Primarily Plate & Structural Applications—*AWS A3.0*

Symbols for Brazing, and Nondestructive Examination of Welds, Standard—*AWS A2.4*

Terms & Definitions: Standard, Including Terms for Adhesive Bonding, Brazing, Soldering, Thermal Cutting & Thermal Spraying—*AWS A3.0*

Terms & Definitions: Structural, Including Terms for Adhesive Bonding, Brazing, Soldering, Thermal Cutting & Thermal Spraying—*AWS A3.0*

Welding

  Brazing Qualifications—Boiler & Pressure Vessel Code, Section IX—*ASME*

  Cutting & Allied Processes (Other Hot Works)

    Design & Installation of Oxygen-Fuel Gas Systems for—*ANSI/NFPA 51*

    Fire Prevention During—*ANSI/NFPA 5B*

Nonferrous

Aluminum & Magnesium Alloys—*ASTM 02.02*

Design Manual: Specifications & Guidelines for Aluminum Structures—*AA ASDI:ASDI M*

Cadmium Plating—Electrodeposited—*SAE ASM QQ-P-416*

Coatings, Metallic & Inorganic, Metal Powders, Sintered P/M Structural Parts—*ASTM 02.05*

Copper & Copper Alloys—*ASTM 02.01*

Electrical Conductors—*ASTM 02.03*

Electrical Heating & Resistance, Alloy Materials for Thermostats, (258)—*ASTM 02.04*

Nickel, Cobalt, Lead, Tin, Zinc, Cadmium—*ASTM 02.04*

Nonferrous Metal

 Alloys Worldwide Guide to Equivalent—*ASTM WWDG NONFERROUS*

 Products, Book of Standards-Section 3—*ASTM*

Siding, Aluminum

 Application Manual

 Residential, Installation Specifications for

Standards & Data, Aluminum—*AA ASDI; ASDI M*

Welding Code for Structural Aluminum—*AWS D1.2*

Wood, Plastics & Composites

Wood & wood products

Architectural Woodwork Quality Standards—*AWI*

Design Specifications for Wood Construction, National

Heavy Timber Construction Details—*WCD 5*

Standards

 Wood—*ASTM 04.09; 04.10*

  Building Construction & Structural Units

  Fire Tests of Building Materials & Construction

  Methods for Chemical Analysis of Wood

  Methods for Evaluating Mechanical & Physical Properties

  Preservatives (117)—*ASTM 04.10*

Structural Design Data, Wood—with Supplement & Revisions

Timber Construction

 Details, Heavy—*WCD 5*

 Manual—*AITC*

Trusses

 Design Specifications for Metal Plate Connected to Wood—with Supplement

Wood & Plastics—*CSI SPECTEXT S06000*

Wood—*ASTM 04.10*

 Structural Design Data—with Supplement & Revisions

 Technology—*ISO ICS 79*

Woodworking Facilities, Prevention of Fires & Explosions in—*ANSI/NFPA 664*

Plastics/composites

Plastics

    (I): D 256–D 3159—*ASTM 08.01*

    (II): D 3222–D 5083—*ASTM 08.02*

Plastics Standards—*ASTM 08.04*

  General Test Methods

  Building Products

  Classification, Plastic Pipe Systems

    Conduit & Fittings

    Drain, Waste & Vent (DWV) Pipe & Fittings

    Sewer Pipe & Fittings

    Water Pipe

  Installation, Components & Procedures, Plastic Pipe

    Fittings

    Joints & Seals

    Solvent Cement

    Underground Installations

  Pipe

    ABS Plastic Pipe & Fittings

    CPVC Plastic Pipe, Tubing & Fittings

    PB Plastic Pipe & Tubing

    Polyethylene Plastic Pipe, Tubing & Fittings

    Styrene-Rubber Plastic Pipe & Fittings

    Fiberglass Pipe & Fittings

    Fiberglass Tanks & Equipment

    Metal Pipe & Fittings, Plastic Lined

  Standards, Plastic Piping

Composite Materials—General Products, Chemical Specialties & End-Use Products—*ASTM 15.03*

Corrosion of Plastic & Rubber in Process Equipment

  Experiences from the Pulp & Paper Industry—*NACE 37769*

Corrosion with Plastics, Managing

    Vol. X—*NACE 31368*

    Vol. XI—*NACE 31382*

Electric Connector, Cap, Dust, Plastic—*SAE AS 90376*

Engineering Plastics—*ASME ENGINEERING PLASTICS*

Fire Protection Service PVC Pipe & Fittings for Underground—*FMRC 1635*

Flexural Properties, Plastics, Determination of—*ISO 178*

Foamed Plastics Used for Decorative Purposes, Fire Tests for—*UL*

Handbook, Plastics Engineering, Society of the Plastics Industry—*SPI PLASTICS HDBK*

Identification & Marking of Plastic Products, Generic—*ISO 11469*

Thermoset Plastics, Furan Reinforced, for Chemical Processes—*SAE AS 90376*

Piping Systems, Plastic, Components & Related Materials—*NSF 14*

Pipe &

 Building Products, Plastics (233)—*ASTM 08.04*

 Plastic Pipe & Fittings for Automatic Sprinkler Systems—*FMRC 1635*

Plastic Parts, Marking of—*SAE JI344*

Plastics—*ASTM SECTION 8*

 I. D 256–D 2343—*ASTM 08.01*

 II. D 2383–D 4322—*ASTM 08.02*

 III. D 4329–Latest—*ASTM 08.03*

 Flammability of Plastics Materials, Tests for—*UL SET 15*

 Parts in Devices & Appliances, Plastics, Tests for—*UL 94*

 Pyroxylin, Storage of—*ANSI/NFPA 42*

 Rubber &—*ISO ICS 83*

 Surface Burning Characteristics of Building Materials, Tests for—*UL 723*

Polymeric Materials

 Coil Forms—*UL 1692*

 Fabricated Parts—*UL 746D*

 Long Term Property Evaluation—*UL 746B*

 Short Term Property Evaluation—*UL 746A*

 Use in Electrical Equipment Evaluation—*UL 746N*

Polymeric Component Materials, Small Test for Flammability of—*UL 1694*

Safety Signs for Plastic Machinery & Related Equipment, Recommended Guidelines—*SPI AN131*

Symbols & Abbreviated Terms, Plastics

 Part 1: Basic Polymers & Their Special Characteristics—*ISO 1043-1*

 Part 2: Filter & Reinforcing Materials—*ISO 1043-2*

 Part 3: Plasticizers—*ISO 1043-3*

 Part 4: Flame Retardants—*ISO 1043-4*

Tensile Properties, Plastics, Determination of

 Part 1: General Principles—*ISO 527-1*

 Part 2: Molding & Extrusion Plastics, Test Conditions for—*ISO 527-2*

Wood & Plastics—*SPECTEXT CSI S09000*

Vinyl

Siding, Rigid Vinyl, Application Instructions

Acoustical

Acoustical

Calibrations—*ANSI S1.40*

Measuring, Design Response of Weighting Networks for—*ANSI S1.42*

Terminology—*ANSI S1.1*

Ceilings Finishes, Acoustical—*CSI SPECTEXT S0900*

Computer & Business Equipment, Measurement & Designation of Noise Emitted by—*ASA/ANSI 12.10*

Environmental Acoustics: Thermal Insulation (2000)—*ASTM 04.06*

Sound

Attenuators, Mechanical—*CSI SPECTEXT—SI5000*

Level Meters—*ASA/ANSI S1.4*

Power Levels of, Precision Methods for the Determination of:

Broadband Noise Sources in Reverberation Rooms—*ASA/ANSI S12.31*

Discrete-Frequency & Narrow-Band Noise in Reverberation Rooms—*ASA/ANSI S12.32*

Noise Source, Survey—*ASA/ANSI S12.33*

Pressure Levels in Air, Methods for the Measurement of—*ASA/ANSI S1.13*

Weighting Networks for Acoustical Measuring, Design Response—*ANSI S1.42*

Moisture

Building Seals & Sealants: Fire Standards; Dimension Stone (191)—*ASTM 04.07*

Humidity Control Design Guide (2001)—*ASHRAE 1*

Moisture

Control for Residential Roofing, Ventilation & (1986)

Migration in Buildings

Protection, Thermal &—*CSI SPECTEXT—S07000*

Mold a Growing Concern—*ASPREI*

Perlite Concrete Roof Deck & Loose Fill Insulation (1991)

Roofing & Waterproofing (150)—*ASTM 04.04*

Bituminous Materials—*ASTM 04.04*

Manual—*NRCA*

Rubber (Products)

Natural & Synthetic General Test Methods—*ASTM 09.01*

Industrial Specifications & Related Test Methods—*ASTM 09.02*

Waterproofing, Roofing &—*ASTM 04.04*

Thermal

Concrete Roof Deck, Lightweight Insulating—*FMRC 4454*

Insulation Standards, National Commercial & Industrial (1988-3rd Ed.)

Perlite Concrete Roof Deck & Thermal & Moisture Protection, Loose Fill Insulation—*CSI SPECTEXT S07000*

Thermal & Moisture Protection—*CSI SPECTEXT S07000*

Thermal Insulation, Environmental Acoustics (200)—*ASTM 04.06*

Vibration & shock

Vibration Isolation, Mechanical—*CSI SPECTEXT S15000*

Roof/roofing & decks

Asphalt Roofing Manual, Residential

Asphalt Shingles to Steep Slope, Application of, Recommendations for

Built-Up Roofing Systems Design Guide

Composite, Form & Roof Decks, Design Manual for—*SDI*

Concrete Roof Deck

Perlite Concrete Roof Deck & Loose Fill Insulation

Concrete Roof Deck—Lightweight Insulating—*FMRC 4454*

Panel Roofs—*FMRC 4471*

Loss Prevention Data—*Constructor 1-28*

Maintenance & Repair, Manual of Roof—*NRCA*

Manual, Roofing, Residential Asphalt

Materials & Systems Directory, Roofing (2001)—*US ROOF*

Roof Covers; Class 1—*FMRC 4470*

Roof Insulated Steel Deck—Loss Prevention Data—*C 1-28*

Roofing & Waterproofing—*ASTM 04.04*

Ventilation & Moisture Control for Residential Roofing—*ARMA*

Waterproofing & Bituminous Materials Roofing—*ASTM 04.04*

Waterproofing Manual Roofing &—*NRCA*

Rubber

General Test Methods, Rubber, Natural & Synthetic General—*ASTM 09.01*

Industrial Specifications & Related Test Methods, Rubber Products—*ASTM 09.02*

Rubber & Plastics—*ISO ICS 83*

Openings

Doors & windows

Aluminum Installation Manual

Assemblies, Smoke Door, Installations of—*ANSI/NFPA 105*

Controls, Closets, Door—*ANSI A156.4*

Doors & Windows, Fire (1990)—*NFPA 80*

Doors & Windows—*CSI SPECTEXT S08000*

Egress for Buildings & Structures, Means of—*ANSI/NFPA 101B*

Fire Doors & Fire Windows—*ANSI/NFPA 79*

Power-Operated Doors, Power Assist & Lower Energy—*ANSI 156.19*

Pedestrian Doors, Power-Operated—*ANSI A156.10*

Glass

Glass (117)—*ASTM 15.02*

Glass & Ceramics—*ISO ICS 81*

Glazing Manual

Ceramics

Ceramic Tile, Installation—*ANSI A108.1*

(Includes *A108.1A-C; A108.4-13; A108.1-.10; ANSI A136.1*)

Adhesives & sealants

Finishes

Adhesives (130)—*ASTM 15.05*

Building Seals & Sealants; Building Construction—*ASTM 04.7*

Fastening Gypsum Wallboard to Wood Framing, Standard Specifications for Adhesives for—*C557*

General Products, Chemical Specialties & End Use Products, Adhesives:—*ASTM 15.06*

Metallic, inorganic, organic

Anodic Coatings for Aluminum & Aluminum Alloys—*MIL A-8625*

Chemical Conversion Coatings & Pretreatment for Ferrous Surfaces, Base of Organic Coatings—*TT C-490*

Chemical Conversion Coatings on Aluminum & Aluminum Alloys—*MIL C-5541*

Coatings, Oxide, Black for Ferrous Metal—*MIL DTL-3924*

Finishing of Metals & Wood Surfaces—*MIL-STD-171*

Metallic & Inorganic Coatings; Metal Powders, Sintered P/M Structural Parts—*ASTM—02.05*

Paint, varnish, lacquer

Paint

    Fatty Oils & Acids—*ASTM 06.03*

    Pigments, Drying Oils; Cellulose—*ASTM 06.03*

    Polymers, Resins & Naval Stores—*ASTM 06.03*

    Tests for—*ASTM 06.02*

        Appearance

        Chemical, Physical & Chemical Properties

        Varnish, Lacquer & Related Materials, Methods of Inspection, Sampling & Testing—*FED STD-141*

Paint & Color—*ISO ICS 87*

Pipeline Coatings, Paint-Products & Applications (246)—*ASTM 06.02*

Protective Coatings, Paint-Products & Applications (246)—*ASTM 06.02*

Specialties

Solvents, Aromatic Hydrocarbons—*ASTM 06.04*

Laboratory Apparatus; Degradation of Materials; Si; Oxygen Fire Safety (131)—*ASTM 13.04*

Equipment

Temperature Measurements (44)—*ASTM 14.03*

Ladders, Safety Requirements

    Fixed—*ANSI A14.3*

    Portable Metal—*ANSI A14.2*

Laser Products, Safety

    Part 1: Equipment Classification, Requirements & User's Guide—*IEC 60625-1*

Materials Handling Equipment—*ISO ICS 53*

Safety Requirements for

    Personnel Hoists & Employee Elevators for Construction & Demolition Operations—*ANSI A10.4*

Scaffolding, ANSI Construction & Demolition Operations—*ANSI A10.8*

Special Construction

Clean rooms

Clean Rooms & Associated Controlled Environments

Part 1: Classifications of Air Cleanliness—*ISO 14644-1*

Part 2: Specifications for Testing & Monitoring to Prove Continued Compliance with ISO 14644-1—*ISO 14644-2*

Confined spaces

Safety Requirements for Confined Spaces—*ANSI Z117.1*

Swimming pools, spas & hot tubs

Above-Ground/On-Ground Residential Pools

Bathing Places—*CHAPTER 10-D-5*

Circulation System Components for Swimming Pools, Spas or Hot Tubs—*STD 50*

Fountains & Pools: Construction Guidelines & Specifications

Heater, XE Pool/Spa, Installation, Operating & Servicing Manual for—*TYPE EG*

Hot Tubs, Understanding NEC Rules on Swimming Pools, Spas &

Minimum Standards for

    Public Spas

    Residential, Spas & Hot Tubs

NEC Rules on Swimming Pools, Spas & Hot Tubs, Understanding

Pool/Spa Operators Handbook

Pool Heating Manual, Solar Water & (Vols. I & II)

Spas or Hot Tubs

   Circulation System Components for—*STANDARD #50*

   Understanding NEC Rules on—*NEC*

Swimming Pool

   Code, Standard—*ICC*

   Design Compendium, Official

Swimming Pools

   Public, Standard for—*ANSI*

   Residential, Standard for

   Solar Heating for

Recreational facilities

Sports Facilities; Pedestrian/Walkway Safety; Amusement Rides & Devices (308)—*ASTM 15.07*

Conveying Systems—*CSI SPECTEXT—S014000*

   Electric Elevators

   Escalators

   Hydraulic Elevators

Conveyors & Related Equipment, Safety Standards for—*ASME B20.1*

Elevators & Escalators

   Electrical Equipment (2001)—*ASME A17.5*

   Inspector's Manual for—*ASME A17.2*

   Safety Code for, (2003)—*ASME A A17.1*

      (Includes Interpretation No.24)

Safety Code for Existing (2000)—*ANSI A17.3*

Handbook—*ANSI A17.1 HDBK*

Low-Lift & High-Lift Trucks, Safety Standards for—*ASME B56.1*

Personnel Hoists, Safety Requirements for (1990)—*ANSI A10.4*

Platform Lifts & Stairway Chairlifts, Safety Standards for (2002)—*ASTM A18.1*

Conveying Equipment

FACILITY SERVICES

Fire codes & standards

Canada, Fire Code, National—*NFCC*

Boiler & Combustion Systems Hazards Code—*ANSI/NFPA 85*

Building Construction & Safety Code—*ANSI/NFPA 5000*

Disaster/Emergency Management & Business Continuity Programs—*ANSI/NFPA 1600*

Fire Suppression

Electric Code, National (2005 NEC)—*NFPA 70; 70-LL*

 Handbook & NEC (2000)—*NFPA 70 SET; SET-LL*

 Installation of Sprinkler Systems, National—*NFPA 13*

 Handbook, Automatic Sprinkler Systems—*NFPA 13*

 One- & Two-Family Dwellings, Requirements for—*ANSI/NFPA 70A*

Explosive Materials Code—*ANSI/NFPA*

Fire Codes

 International (2000)—*ICC*

 International (2000)—*ICC/ICBO*

 National (2002)—*ANSI/NFPA*

  Master Index, with (11 Vols.)—*ANSI/NFPA*

 Uniform—*ANSI/NFPA 1*

Fire Marshall Code—Prevention & Control (Chap. 633)

Fire Standards—*ASTM 04.07*

Flammable & Combustible Liquids (Materials)

 Code—*ANSI/NFPA 30*

 Dipping & Coating Processes Using—*ANSI/NFPA 34*

 Spray Application Using—*ANSI/NFPA 33*

Fuel Gas Code, National—*ANSI/NFPA 54*

Inspection Code for Existing Dwellings, Electrical—*ANSI/NFPA 73*

Life Safety

 Alternative Approaches to—*ANSI/NFPA 101-4*

 Code, National (2006)—*NFPA 101*

  Handbook (2000)—*NFPA*

Lightning Protection Code (1989)—*NFPA78*

LP Gas

 Code—*ANSI/NFPA 58*

 Plant Code, Utility—*ANSI/NFPA 59*

Fire protection

Acetylene Cylinder Charging Plants—*ANSI/NFPA 51A*

Aerosol Products, Manufacture & Storage of—*ANSI/NFPA30B*

Cellulose Nitrate Film, Storage & Handling of—*ANSI/NFPA 40*

Combustible Particulate Solids, Prevention of Fire & Dust Explosions from Manufacturing, Processing & Handling of—*ANSI/NFPA 654*

Compressed Gas & Cryogenic Fluids in Portable & Stationary Containers & Tanks, Storage, Use & Handling of—*ANSI/NFPA 55*

Construction, Alteration & Demolition Operations, Safeguarding—*ANSI/NFPA 241*

Cooking Operations, Commercial, Ventilation Control & Fire Protection of—
ANSI/NFPA 96

Dampers

    Ceiling—*UL 555C*

    Fire—*UL 555*

    Smoke—*UL 555S*

Exhaust Systems for Air Conveying of Vapors, Gases, Mists & Noncombustible

    Particulate Solids—*ANSI/NFPA 91*

    Purged & Pressurized Enclosures for Electrical Equipment—*ANSI/NFPA 496*

Explosion

    Prevention System—*ANSI/NFPA 69*

    Suppression Systems—*FMRC 5700*

Fire Facilities, Engineering Design & Construction, Fire Protection—*MIL HDBK-1008*

Fire Protection—*ITU-T-L.22*

    Handbook—*NFPA FPH*

    Handbook of—*SFPE*

    Performance Based, Engineering Guide to—*NFPA/SFPE*

Fire Resistance Sound Control Design Manual

    Design Manual—*GA*

    Directory (2003, 4-Vol. Set)—*UL*

    Vol. 1—Beams, Floors, Roofs, Columns, Walls, Partitions

    Vol. 2—Joint Systems & Through-Penetration Firestop Systems, Curtain Walls, Circuit Protection, Duct Assemblies

    Vol. 3—Dampers, Fire Doors, Glazing Materials, Glass Blocks,

    Leakage Related Door Assemblies

    Vol. 4—Directory

Fire Risk Assessments, Guide for the Evaluation of—*ANSI/NFPA 551*

Fire Service Mains

    Their Appurtenances, Installation of—*ANSI/NFPA 24*

    Private, Installation of—*ANSI/NFPA 24*

    Water Control Valves, OS & Y & NRS Type Gate Valves—*FMRC 1120/1130*

Flammable & Combustible Liquids, Underground Leakage of—*ANSI/NFPA 329*

Gas & Vacuum Systems—*ANSI/NFPA 99C*

Hazardous Material Emergencies, Vapor-Protective Ensembles for—*ANSI/NFPA 1991*

Incinerators & Waste & Linen Handling Systems & Equipment—*ANSI/NFPA 82*

Laser Fire Protecting—*ANSI/NFPA-115*

Liquefied Natural Gas (LNG), Production, Storage & Handling of—*ANSI/NFPA 59A*

Materials Flammability Test Control, Clean Room—*FMRC 4910*

Fire extinguishing equipment & systems

Aerosol Fire Extinguishing Systems, Fixed—*ANSI/NFPA 2010*

Carbon Dioxide Extinguishing Systems—*NFPA 12*

Chemical

    Dry, Extinguishing Systems—*ANSI/NFPA 17*

    Fire Extinguishers—*ANSI/UL 299*

    Pre-Engineered, Extinguishing System Units—*ANSI/UL 1254*

    Wet, Extinguishing Systems—*ANSI/NFPA 17A*

Equipment Directory, Fire Protection—*UL 2001*

Extinguishing Agents, Fire, Chemical Specialties & End Use Product

    General Products—*ASTM 15.05*

Fire Extinguishers—*ANSI/UL 6*

    Carbon Dioxide—*ANSI/UL 154*

    Portable—*ANSI/NFPA 10*

    Rating & Fire Testing of—*ANSI/UL 711*

Fire Hose—*FMRC 2111*

    Appliances—*ANSI/NFPA 1965*

    Connections—*ANSI/NFPA 1963*

    Couplings & Nozzles, Inspection, Care & Use of—*ANSI/NFPA 1962*

    Service Testing of—*ANSI/NFPA 1962*

Foam

    Chemicals for Fire in Class A Fuels—*ANSI/NFPA 1150*

    Class A, Guide for the Use of, in Manual Structural Fire Fighting—*ANSI/NFPA 1145*

    Equipment & Liquid Concentrates—*ANSI/UL 162*

    Low-, Medium- & High-Expansion—*ANSI/NFPA 11*

    Water Sprinkler & Foam-Water Spray Systems, Installation of—*ANSI/NFPA 16*

Halon

    1211 & Halon 1302, Part 1: Specifications for—*ISO 7201-1*

    1211 Fire Extinguishing Systems—*ANSI/NFPA 12B*

    1301 Fire Extinguishing Systems—*NFPA 12A*

Halogen Agent Extinguishing System Units—*ANSI/UL 1058*

Halogenated

    Agent Fire Extinguishers—*ANSI/UL 1093*

    Hydro Carbons, Fire Extinguishing Media, Fire Protection

    Organic Solvents—*ASTM 15.05*

Laboratory Equipment—*ANSI/UL 1262*

Life Safety Rope & Equipment for Emergency Services—*ANSI/NFPA 1983*

Nozzles, Spray—*ANSI/NFPA 1964*

Portable Fire Extinguishers, Standard for—*NFPA 10*

Pumps

    Centrifugal Fire—*ANSI/NFPA 20*

    Stationary Pumps for Fire Protection, Installation of—*ANSI/NFPA 20*

Valves (< 2 in Nominal Size)

    Quick Opening—*FMRC 1140*

    Trim Water Pressure Relief—*FMRC 1359*

    Water Pressure Relief—*FMRC 1161*

Water

Spray Fixed Systems for Fire Protection—*NFPA 15*

Type-Fire Extinguishers, 2.1-Gallon. Stored-Pressure—*ANSI/UL 626*

Wetting Agents—*NFPA 18*

Hydrants

Fire Hydrants

Dry-Barrel—*AWWA C502*

Wet-Barrel, Fire—*AWWA C503*

Wet-Barrel Type, for Private Fire Service—*FMRC 1510*

Sprinkler systems

Automatic Sprinkler Systems—Fire Protection

Part 1: Requirements & Test Methods for—*ICO 6182-1*

Automatic Sprinkler Systems

    Handbook—*NFPA 13HB*

    Plastic Piping & Fittings for, Automatic Sprinkler Systems—*FMRC 1635*

    Standard & Handbook—*NFPA 13 SET*

Deluge Foam-Water Sprinkler & Spray Systems—*ANSI/NFPA 16*

Sprinkler Systems

    Inspection, Testing & Maintenance of—*NFPA 13A*

    Installation of—*NFPA 13*

        Dwellings, One- & Two-Family, & Manufactured Homes—*NFPA 13D*

        Handbook, Automatic Sprinkler Systems—*NFPA 13*

        Residential Occupancies up to & Including Four Stories in Height—*NFPA 13R*

Protective apparatus (personnel)

Breathing Apparatus for Fire & Emergency Services,

Open-Circuit Self-Contained—*ANSI/NFPA 1981*

    Selection, Care & Maintenance of—*ANSI/NFPA 1852*

Flash Fire, Protection of Industrial Personnel Against

Flame Resistant Garments for—*ANSI/NFPA 2112*

  Selection, Care, Use & Maintenance of—*ANSI/NFPA 2113*

Hazardous Materials Emergencies

  Liquid Splash-Protective Ensembles & Clothing for—*ANSI/NFPA 1991*

  Protective Ensemble for

  Proxity Fire Fighting—*ANSI/NFPA 1975*

Structural Fire Fighting—*ANSI/NFPA 1971*

  Selection, Care & Maintenance of—*ANSI/NFPA 1851*

Respiratory Protection

  Breathing Air Quality for Fire & Emergency Services—*ANSI/NFPA 1989*

  Training, Fire Service—*ANSI/NFPA 1404*

Gas & gas storage systems

Compressed Gases, Handbook of

Design & Operation of Liquefied Petroleum Gas (LPG) Storage Facilities,

  Fire Protection Considerations for the—*API PUBL 2510A*

Fossil Fuels,

  Coal & Coke—*ASTM 05.05*

  Gaseous Fuels—*ASTM 05.06*

Fuel Gas Code

  International (2000)—*ICC*

  International (2000)—*ICBO/ICC*

  National (2002)—*NFPA 54*

    Handbook (2002)—*NFPA 54*

  National—*NFPA 54/AGA*

    Handbook—*NFPA 54/AGA*

Gas Vaporizers, Gas-Air Mixers & Vaporizer-Mixers

  Liquefied Petroleum—*FMRC 7151, 7156 & 7157*

Oxygen Fire Safety—*ASTM 14.04*

  Laboratory Apparatus—General Methods for Instrumentation—*ASTM 15.05*

Tanks

Abandonment or Removal of Used Underground Service Station Tanks,
Recommended Practice for the—*604*

Large Aboveground Atmospheric, Storage

Plumbing Codes

  Canadian—*CSA*

  Handbook—*ICC*

  International—*ICC*

  National Standard—*NAPHCC*

Plumbing

Plumbing—*A112.18.1*

>Fixture—*ASME A17.2*

>Inspector's Manual—*ICC*

Plastic Sinks—*ANSI Z124.6*

Boilers

>Boiler & Pressure Vessel Code—*ASME*

>Heating Boilers, Sec. IV, Rules for Construction of—*ASME S00100 & ADDENDA*

>Heating Boilers, Sec. VI, Recommended Rules for the Care & Operation of,—*ASME S00040 & ADDENDA*

>Power Boilers, Sec. I, Rules for Construction of—*ASME S00010 & ADDENDA*

>Power Boilers, Sec. VII—Recommended Rules for the Care & Operation of—*ASME S00070 & ADDENDA*

Boiler Plant & Distribution System Optimization Manual

Care & Operation of Heating Boilers, Recommended Rules for—*ASME*

Care & Operation of Power Boilers, Recommended Rules for—*ASME*

Controls & Safety Devices for Automatically Fired Boilers; Interpretations—*ASME BPVC*

Heating, Boiler & Pressure Vessel Code, Sec. IV—Boilers—*ASME*

Non-Nuclear, Code Cases & Referenced Standards, Sec. I, II, V, VIII, X—*ASME BPVC*

Power, Boiler & Pressure Vessel Code, Sec. I—*ASME*

Pressure Vessels, Division 1—Boiler & Pressure Vessel Code, Sec. VIII—*ASME*

Pressure vessels

Pressure Vessel Code, Boiler &—*ASME*

Fiber-Reinforced Plastic Pressure Vessels, Sec. X—*ASME S00100 & ADDENDA*

Pressure Vessels, Secs. II, IID, VIII & Referenced Standards—*ASME*

Pressure Vessels, Sec. VIII, Div. 1—*ASME S00081 & ADDENDA*

>Alternative Rules, Division 2—*ASME S00082 & ADDENDA*

>Alternative Rules for Construction of High Pressure Vessels, Division 3—*ASME S00083 & ADDENDA*

Inspection of Pressure Vessels: Tower, Drums, Reactors, Heat Exchangers & Condensers—*API RP 572*

Maintenance Inspection, Rating, Repair & Alteration, Inspection Code Pressure Vessels—*API 510*

Pressure Vessels, Sec. VIII, Division 1—*ASME B00081*

Relief Devices

>Installation—*API 520 P2*

>Maximum Allowable Working Pressure (15 psig or greater); Refineries—*API*

Pressure—*ASME PTC 25*

Sizing & Selection—*API RP 520 P1*

Stainless Steel Plate, Sheet, and Strip for Pressure Vessels & General Applications, Chromium & Chromium-Nickel—*ASTM A240/A 240M*

Steel—Pressure Vessels—*ASTM 01.04*

Materials specifications

Construction of High Pressure Vessels, Alternative Rules, Division 3—*ASME S00083 & ADDENDA*

Materials Specifications, Sec. II

Ferrous Material, Part A:—*ASME S0002A & ADDENDA*

Nonferrous Material, Part B:—*ASME S0002B*

Properties, Part D:—*ASME S0002D & ADDENDA*

Nondestructive Examination, Sec. V—*ASME S00050 & ADDENDA*

Welding & Brazing Qualifications, Sec. IX—*ASME*

Welding Rods, Electrodes & Filler Metals, Part C:—*ASME S0002C & ADDENDA*

Mechanical

Bearings, Rolling Elements, Steel Products:—*ASTM 01.08*

Mechanical—*CSI SPECTEXT S15000*

Safety Standard for Mechanical Power Transmission Apparatus (2003)—*ASTM B13.1*

Transmission Apparatus, Mechanical Power, Safety Standard for (2000)—*ASME B15.1*

Refractories

Installation Quality Control Guidelines

Inspection & Testing Monolithic Refractory Linings & Materials—*API RP 936*

Refractories—*ASTM 15.01*

Refrigeration

Handbook, Refrigeration (2002, IP Ed.)—*ASHRAE*

Piping, Mechanical Refrigeration—*CSI SPECTEXT S15000*

Refrigeration & Air Conditioning (3rd Ed.)—*ARI*

Safety Code for Mechanical Refrigeration (1989/91)—*ASHRAE*

Safety Standard for Refrigeration Systems (2001)—*ASHRAE 15*

Valves

Air Valves, Air Release, Air/Vacuum & Combination—*AWWA C512*

Backflow-Prevention Assembly—*AWWA*

Double Check Valve—*C510*

Reduced-Pressure Principle—*C 511*

Ball Valves, 6 in (150 mm) through 48 in (1,200 mm)—*AWWA C507*

Butterfly Valves, Rubber-Seated—*AWWA C504*

Flanged Valves, Threaded & Welding End—*NSI B16.34*

Gate Valves—*AWWA*

    Metal-Seated, for Water Supply Service—*C500*

    Resilient-Seated, for Water Supply Service—*C509*

    Resilient-Seated, Reduced-Wall, for Water Supply Service—*C515*

Relief Valves—*FMRC*

    Pressure—

    Timm Water < 2 in Nominal Size—*1359*

    Water—*1361*

Slide Gates—*AWWA*

    Cast Iron—*C560*

    Composite, Fabricated—*C 563*

    Open-Channel, Fabricated Metal—*C513*

    Power-Actuating Devices for Valves &—*C540*

    Stainless Steel, Fabricated—*C561*

Quick Opening Valves < 2 in Nominal Size—*FMRC 1140*

Safety Relief Valves for Anhydrous Ammonia & Liquid Petroleum Gas—*UL 132*

Swing-Check Valves for Waterworks Service, 2 in (50 mm) through 24 in (600 mm)—*AWWA 508*

Protective Interior Coatings for Valves & Hydrants—*AWWA C550*

Valves, Dimensions of, Face-to-Face & End-to-End—*ASME B16.10*

Water hammer arresters

Water Hammer Arresters, Performance Requirements—*ASSE 1010*

Pipe/piping/fittings

Asbestos-cement

Asbestos-Cement—*AWWA*

Pressure Pipe Installation of—*C603*

Pressure Pipe 4 in (100 mm) through 16 in (400 mm) for

    Water Distribution Systems—*C400*

        Selection of—*C401*

Transmission Pipe 18 in (450 mm) through 42 in (1,050 mm) for

    Water Supply Service—*C402*

        Selection of—*C403*

Clay

Engineering Manual, Clay Pipe

Installation Handbook, Clay Pipe

Vitrified Clay Pipe—*ASTM 04.05*

Concrete

Concrete—*AWWA*

Cylinder Pipe, Prestressed, Design of—*C304*

Pressure Pipe

　Bar-Wrapped, Steel Cylinder Type—*C303*

　Prestressed, Steel Cylinder Type—*C301*

　Reinforced, Steel Cylinder Type—*C300*

　Reinforced, Noncylinder Type—*C302*

Installation Manual, Pipe

Pipe—*ASTM 04.05*

Ductile-iron & gray-iron

Ductile Iron Pipe—*AWWA*

　Cement-Mortar

　　Lining for, & Fittings for Water—*C 104/ANSI 21.3*

　　Lining of Water Pipelines in Place—4 in (100 mm) & Larger—*C602/ANSI*

　Centrifugally Cast, for Water or Other Liquids—*C 151/ANSI 21.51*

　Flanged, with Ductile-Iron or Gray-Iron Threaded Flanges—*C115/ANSI 21.15*

　Polyethylene Encasement for, Systems—*C 105/ANSI 21.5*

　Rubber-Gasket Joints for, Pressure Pipe & Fittings—*C111/ANSI 21.11*

　Thickness Design of—*C150/ANSI 21.50*

Ductile-Iron & Gray-Iron

　Protective Fusion-Bonded Epoxy Coatings for the Interior & Exterior Surface of, Fittings for Water Supply Service—*C116/ANSI 21.16*

　Fittings for Water—*C110-/ANSI 21.10*

　Water Mains & Their Appurtenances, Guide for Installation of—*C600*

Fiberglass

Pressure Pipe, Fiberglass—*AWWA 950*

Plastic

Plastic Pipe &

Building Products—*ASTM 08.04*

Fittings for Automatic Sprinkler Systems—*FMRC 1635*

Polyethylene Pressure Pipe

Aluminum-Polyethylene & Cross-Linked Polyethylene Composite, 1/2 in (12 mm) through 2 in (50m) for Water Service—*C903*

Fittings, 4 in (100 mm) through 63 in (1,575 mm) for Water Distribution & Transmission—*C906*

Tubing, 1/2 in (13mm) through 3 in (76 mm) for Water Service—*C901*

PVC Pressure Pipe &

Fabricated Fittings, 4 in (100 mm) through 12 in (300 mm) for Water Distribution—*AWWA C900*

Fabricated Fittings, 14 in (350 mm) through 48 in (1,200 mm) for Water Transmission & Distribution—*C905*

Fittings for Water, Underground Installation of—*C605*

Injection-Molded, 4 in (100mm) through 12 in (300 mm) for Water Distribution—*C907*

Molecularly Orientated, 4 in (100 mm) through 24 in, (600 mm)—*C909*

Sewer Pipe, Recommended Practice for the Installation of—*AWWA*

Underground Fire Protection Service—*FMRC 1612*

Water, 2 in through 12 in, Standard for—*C900*

PVC Self-Tapping Saddle Tees for Use on PVC Pipe—*C908*

Steel

Guide for Design & Installation—Steel Pipe—*AWWA M11*

Seamless & Welded Austenitic Pipe, Standards Specification for Stainless Steel—*ASTM 312/A 312M*

Tube & Pipe Systems, Austenitic Stainless Steel, in Sanitary (Hygienic) Applications Specification for Welding—*AWS D18.1*

Water Pipe

Dimensions for Fabricated Steel—*AWWA C651*

Standard for Steel—*AWWA C200*

Welded & Seamless Wrought Steel Pipe—*ASME B36.10M*

Pipe & pipe fittings

Buttwelding Fittings

Ends (2002)—*ASME B16.25*

Factory-Made Wrought Steel—*ASME B16.9*

Dimensions for Fabricated Steel Water Pipe—*AWWA C208*

Flanges & Flanged, Pipe—*ASME B16.98; NSI B16.5*

Forged, Socket-Welding & Threaded—*ASME B16.11*

Steel Piping, Tubing &—*ASTM 01.01*

Flared Copper Tubes, Fittings for, Cast Copper Alloy (1998)—*ASME B 16.28*

Forged Steel Fittings, Socket-Welding & Threaded (2001)—*ASME B16.11*

Grooved & Shouldered Joints—*C 606*

Hangers & Supports, Pipe, Selection & Application

Metallic Gaskets for Pipe Flanges: Ring Joint, Spiral-Wound & Jacketed (2003)—*ASME B16.20*

Nonmetallic Flat Gaskets for Pipe Flanges (1999)—*ASME B16.21*

Pipe Flanges & Flanged Fittings (2001)—*ASME B16.5*

Pipe Flanges & Flanged Fittings, Cast Copper Alloy (2001)
Class 150, 300, 400, 600, 900, 1500, 2500—*ASME B16.24*

Pipe Flanges & Flanged Fittings, Cast Iron (2003)—*ASME B16.1*

Pressure Relief Devices—*ASME PTC 25*

Solder Joint Drainage Fittings, Cast Copper Alloy (1998, DMV)—*ASME B16.23*

Solder Joint Pressure Fittings, Cast Copper Alloy (1999)—*ASME B16*

Solder Joint Drainage Fittings DWV, Wrought Copper & Wrought Copper Alloy—*ASME B16.34*

Solder Joint Pressure Fittings, Wrought Copper & Wrought Copper Alloy (2000)—*ASME 16.22*

Threaded Fittings

    Malleable Iron (2003)—*ASME B16.3*

    Cast Bronze, Class 125 & 250—*ANSI B16.15*

    Cast Bronze (1999)—*ASME B16.15*

    Cast Iron (2003)—*ASME B16.4*

Threaded Drainage Fittings, Cast Iron (2001)—*ASME B16.12*

Piping & tubing

Building Services Piping—*ASME B31.9*

Cathodic Protection of Piping Systems, Underground Petroleum Storage Tanks &

Chemical Plant & Petroleum Refinery Piping—*ASME/ANSI B31.3*

Gas Transmission & Distribution Piping Systems—*ASME/ANSI B31.8*

Insulation, Piping—*SPECTEX T, CSI S15000*

Piping Systems, Identification of, Scheme for—*ANSI A13.1*

Piping & Tubing—*ASTM 01.01*

Power Piping—With Interpretations—*ASME/ANSI B31.1*

Process Piping—*ANSI/ASME B31.3*

Refrigeration Piping—*SPECTEX T, CSI S15000*

Repair, Alteration & Re-Rating of In-Service Piping Systems, Piping Inspection Code—*API 570*

Steel Piping, Tubing & Fittings—*ASTM 01.01*

Pipelines

Coatings, Pipeline—*ASTM 06.02*

Hazardous Liquid Pipelines, Managing System—*API STD 1160*

Petroleum & Natural Gas Industries, Steel Pipe for Pipelines, Technical Delivery Conditions

    Part 1: Pipes of Requirement Class A—*ISO 3183-1*

    Part 2: Pipes of Requirement Class B—*ISO 3183-2*

Pipeline Safety Regulations (1990)—*USDOT*

Safety Regulations (Parts 190–199)—*CFR 49*

Welding of Pipelines & Related Facilities—*API STD 1140*

Heating, Ventilating & Air Conditioning

Air conditioning

A/C System Design Manual—Carrier Corp.

    Air Distribution: PT 2

    Load Estimating: PT 1

    Piping Design: PT 3

    Piping Design: PT 1-12

Air Cleaning Devices—*SMACNA 23 40*

    Electronic—*SMACNA 23 43*

Air Conditioners

    Room—*ANSI 1992*

    Room—*UL 484*

Air Conditioning & Ventilating Systems, Standards for the Installation of (2002)—*NFPA 90A*

Air-Cooling Equipment, Evaporative—*SMACNA 23 76*

Air Filtration

    Gas-Phase—*SMACNA 23 42*

    Particulate—*SMACNA 23 41*

Air Terminal Units, Outlets & Inlets—*SMACNA 23 36; SMACNA 23 37*

Boilers, Heating—*SMACNA 23 52*

    Feedwater Equipment—*SMACNA 23 53*

Central

    Heating Equipment—*SMACNA 23 50*

    Station, Indoor, Air-Handling Units—*SMACNA 23 73*

Chimneys

    Fireplaces, Vents & Solid Fuel-Burning Appliances—*ANSI/NFPA 211*

    Stacks, Breeches—*SMACNA 23 51*

Cooling

    Equipment, Heating &—*UL*

    Towers—*SMACNA 23 65*

Piping & Pumps—*SMACNA 23 20*

Plenums & Chases—*SMACNA 23 32*

Systems & Equipment, Handbook (I-P Ed.)—*ASHRAE*

Water Treatment—*SMACNA 23 25*

Oil Burning Equipment, Installation of—*ANSI/NFPA 31*

Ovens & Furnaces—*ANSI/NFPA 86*

Piping

Refrigerant—*SMACNA 23 23*

Piping & Pumps

Hydronic—*SMACNA 23 21*

Steam & Condensate—*SMACNA 23 22*

Radiant Heating Units—*SMACNA 23 83*

Room Air Conditioners—*UL 484*

Sheet Metal Manual, Architectural—*SMACNA*

Solar Energy Heating Equipment—*SMACNA 23 56*

Thermal Storage—*SMACNA 23 71*

Ventilation for Acceptable Indoor Air Quality

Ventilation Hoods—*SMACNA 23 38*

Warm Air Heating & Air Conditioning Systems, Installation of—*ANSI/NFPA 90B*

Water Chillers, Packaged—*SMACNA 23 64*

Air conveying

Air Conveying Materials, Exhaust Systems for—*NFPA 91*

Ventilation

Heating & Cooling Equipment—*UL*

Industrial Ventilation: A Manual of Recommended Practice—*ACGIH*

Ventilating Systems, Standards for Installation of Air Conditioning & (2002)—*NFPA 90A*

Ventilation

Acceptable Indoor Air Quality (2001)—*ASHRAE STD 62.1*

Includes Addendums: H, N, AE, X, AF, AD, Z, R, O, K, V, U, T, Y, & AA—*ASHRAE STD 62*

Low-Rise Buildings—*ASHRAE 62.2*

Directory—Covers National, Standard, and Uniform Codes; and Standards—*ASHRAE*

Moisture Control for Residential Roofing

Venting Principles—*SPC*

Vents, Chimneys, Fireplaces & (1988)—*NFPA 211*

Ducts

Duct Construction Standards, HVAC, Metal & Flexible—*SMACNA*

Fibrous Glass Duct, Construction Standards—*SMACNA*

Metal & Flexible Standards, HVAC—*SMACNA 1481*

Residential Duct Systems

Round Duct Construction Standards—*SMACNA 1520*

Gas/fuel

Gas Code, National Fuel—*NFPA 54*

Gas Code, Standard—*ICC*

Gas Transmission & Distribution Piping Systems—*B31.8*

Gases, Storage & Handling of Liquefied Petroleum—*NFPA 58*

Petroleum Gases, Storage & Handling of Liquefied—*NFPA 58*

Heating & cooling

Electrical—*CSI SPECTEXT S16000*

  Forced Air Furnaces

  Direct-Fired Furnaces

Furnace Explosions, Prevention of—*NFPA 85C*

Heating & Cooling Equipment—*UL*

Hydronic Heating Systems, Installation Guide for Residential—*IBRS*

Oil Burning Equipment, Installation of (1987)—*NFPA 31*

Single Burner Boiler-Furnaces, Explosions in Fuel Oil & Natural Gas-Fired, Prevention of—*NFPA 85A*

Refrigeration

Refrigerants, Designation & Safety Classification—*ASHRAE STD 34*

Refrigeration

  Air Conditioning—*ARI*

  HVAC Handbook (I-P Ed.)

  Systems, Safety Standard—*ASHRAE 15*

Mechanical systems

Fluid Systems & Components for General Use—*ISO ICS 23*

Mechanical Systems & Components for General Use—*ISO ICS 21*

Information Technology Equipment, Safety

Part 1: General Requirements—*IEC 60950-1*

Records, Protection of—*ANSI/NFPA 232*

Standards & specifications

  ANSI/IEEE Standards

  Bronze Book—*STD 739*

Integrated Automation

Electrical

Brown Book—*STD 399*

Buff Book—*STD 242*

Gold Book—*STD 493*

Gray Book—*STD 241*

Green Book—*STD 142*

Orange Book—*STD 446*

Red Book—*STD 141*

White Book—*STD 602*

Code, National Electrical Code—*NFPA 70; NFPA 70 HDBK*

Configuration Management, National Consensus Standard for—*EIA 649*

CSI Spectext—*S16000*

Electrical Requirements

Electrical Sensing & Measurement

Electric Controls & Relays

Electromagnetic Compatibility (EMC)

Part 6-2: Generic Standards Immunity for Industrial Environments, Part 6-2—*BS EN 50419*

Part 4-2: Testing & Measurement Techniques, Part 4-2—*IEC 61000-4-2*

Energy Standard for Buildings (2001, IP Ed.)—*ASHRAE 90.1*

Protection Provided by Enclosures, Degree of (IP Code)—*IEC 60529*

Static Electricity—*ANSI/NFPA 77*

Appliances & equipment

Battery Chargers, Electric—*UL 1236*

Explosion-Proof Electrical Equipment, General Requirements—*FMRC 3615*

Detection Instruments, Hydrogen Sulfide—*ANSI/IA S12.15*

Enclosures for Electrical Equipment—*ANSI/NEMA 250*

Equipment

Commercial, Electric Clothes

Drying—*UL 1240*

Washing—*UL 1206*

Coin-Operated, Electric Clothes

Washing—*ANSI/UL 1555*

Drying—*ANSI/UL 1556*

Laboratory—*ANSI/UL 1262*

Gas Detectors

Combustible—*FMRC 6310*

Performance Requirements for Combustible—*ANSI/ISA S12.13.1*

Household & Similar Electrical Appliances, Safety of

Part 1: General Requirements—*BS EN 60335-1*

Laboratory Use, Measurement, Control &, Electrical Equipment, Safety Requirements for

Part 1: General Requirements—*BS EN 61010-1*

Medical Electrical Equipment

Part 1: General Requirements for Safety—*UL 2601-1*

Safety Containers & Filling, Supply & Disposal Containers—*FMRC 6051*

Audio equipment

Amplifiers, Audio, Testing & Measurement Methods for—*EIA/CEA 490*

Cabling Standard, Multi-Room Audio—*CEA 2030*

Cabinets, Racks, Panels & Associated Equipment—*CEA 310*

Burglar alarms

Burglar Alarm Systems

Installation & Classification of Mercantile & Bank—*UL-681*

Police Station Connected—*UL-365*

Proprietary Alarms & Units—*UL-1067*

Central Station Service for Fire Alarms & Protective Equipment Supervision—*FMRC 3011*

Thermostats

Thermostats, Materials for, Electrical Heating & Resistance Contacts & Connectors—*ASTM 02.04*

Electrical equipment

Busway Rated 600 V, Handling, Installation, Operation & Maintenance of General Instructions for—*NEMA BU 1.1*

Enclosures for Electrical Equipment (1000 V Maximum)—*NEMA 250*

Maintenance, Electric Equipment—*ANSI/NFPA 70B*

Electronic equipment

General Guidelines for Electronic Equipment—*MIL HDBK-454*

Marking of Electrical & Electronic Equipment in Accordance with Article 11 (2) of Directive 201/96/EC (WEEE)—*BBBS EN 50419*

Protection of Electronic Computer/Data Processing Equipment—*NFPA 75*

Reliability Prediction of Electronic Equipment—*MIL HDBK-217*

Test, Measuring & Process Control Equipment, Electrical & Electronic—*FMRC 3610*

Hazardous locations

Energy Lockout/Tagout & Alternative Methods, Control of—*ANSI Z244.1*

Hazardous (Classified) Locations

Apparatus & Associated Apparatus, Intrinsically Safe, for Use in Class I, II & III, Div. 1—*ANSI/UL 913; FMRC 3610*

Circuit Breakers & Circuit-Breaker Enclosure, Electric, for Use in—*ANSI/UL 877*

Electrical Equipment for Use in

Class I, Div. 2—*ANSI/ISA S12.12*

Class I, Div. 2; Class II, Div. 2; Class III, Div. 1 & 2—*FMRC 3611*

Electrical Installations in—*NFPA*

Explosion-Proof & Dust-Ignition-Proof, for Use in—*ANSI/UL 1203*

General Requirements—*FMRC 3600*

Heaters, Electric, for Use in—*ANSI/UL 823*

Lighting

Fixtures, Electric, for Use in—*ANSI/UL 844*

Units, Portable, for Use in—*ANSI/UL 781*

Motors & Generators, Electric, for Use in—*ANSI/UL 674*

Lighting Units, Portable, for Use in—*ANSI/UL 781*

Nonincentive Electrical Equipment, Class I & II, Div. 2, Class III, Div. 1 & 2, for Use in—*FMCR 3611*

Outlet Boxes & Fittings, Electrical, for Use in—*ANSI/UL 886*

Purged & Pressurized Electrical Equipment for—*FMRC 3520*

Safe Apparatus & Associated Apparatus, Intrinsically, Class I, II & III, Div. 1 & 2, Zone 0 & 1, for Use in—*FMRC 3610*

Sewage Pumps for Use in—*ANSI 1207*

Switches for Use in—*ANSI/UL 894*

Valve, Electrically Operated, for Use in—*ANSI/UL 1002*

Insulation

Electrical

(I) D 69 – D 2484—*ASTM 10.01*

(II) D 2518 – Latest—*ASTM 10.02*

Insulating Liquids & Gases—*ASTM 10.03*

Lighting/illumination

Architectural Daylighting, Concepts & Practice of Commercial Lighting Systems, Indoor, Installing—*NECA/IESNA 500*

Electrical—*CSI SPECTEXT S16000*

Lighting Fixtures

Site Lighting

Emergency Lighting

Emergency Power Supply

Theatrical Lighting

Exterior Lighting Systems, Recommended Practice for Installing—*NECA/IESNA 501*

Fluorescent Lamp Ballast, High-Frequency—*ANSI C82.11*

Industrial Lighting, Practice for—*IESNA RP 7*

Lightning

Electrical Storms & Lightning Protection—*DOE M440.1-1*

Electronic Equipment & Facilities, Grounding, Bonding & Shielding for—*MIL STD 188-124*

Vol. I—Basic Theory

Vol. II—Applications

Lightning Protection

Electrical Systems—*CSI SPECTEXT 16000*

Department of Defense (Chapter 7)—*DDESB—6055*.9

Installation Requirements for, Systems—*UL 96A*

Practices & Procedures for Grounding, Bonding & Shielding—*FAA 6950.19P*

Requirements for Facilities—*FAA 019d*

Surge Protection Requirements, Grounding, Bonding, Shielding &—*NWS 30-4105*

Lightning Safety—*DOE/EH 0530*

Protection Against Ignitions Arising out of Static, Lightning & Stray Currents—*API 2003*

Machinery & equipment

Enclosures for Electrical Equipment—*250*

Industrial Machinery, Electrical Standard for (1991)—*NFPA79*

Machinery

Electrical Standard for Industrial (2002)—*NFPA 79*

Safety of, Electrical Equipment of

Part I: General Requirements—*ICE 60204-1*

Medical Electrical Equipment

Part 1-2: General Requirements for Safety

Collateral Standard Electromagnetic Compatibility Requirements & Test—*EICE 60601-1-2*

Protective Equipment, Electrical—*ASTM 10.03*

Measuring & control equipment/devices

Control

Devices, Controllers & Assemblies, Industrial—*ANSI/NEMA ICS 2*

Equipment, High-Voltage Industrial—*ANSI/UL 347*

Electric Industrial Control Equipment—*ANSI/UL 506*

Electrical & Electronic

  Measuring Equipment, Test &—*ANSI/ASA S82.01; ANSI/ASI S82.02*

  Process Measuring & Control—*ANSI/ISA S82.05*

Hazardous (Classified) Locations, Industrial Control Equipment for Use in—*ANSI/UL 698*

Radio-Noise Emissions from Low-Voltage Electrical & Electronic Equipment in the Range of 9 kHz to 40 kHz—*ANSI C63.4*

Time-Indicating & Recording Appliances, Electric—*ANSI/UL 863*

Power facilities & energy systems

Bussways Rated 600 Volts or Less, Instructions for Handling, Installation, Operation & Maintenance of—*NEMA BU 1.1*

Combustion Engines & Gas Turbine, Installation & Use of Stationary—*ANSI/NFPA 37*

Conductors, Electrical—*ASTM 02.03*

Control Equipment, Industrial—*UL 508*

Cooling Towers, Water—*NFPA 220*

Emergency & Standby Power

  Industrial/Commercial, Practice for

  IEEE Orange Book (1987)—*ANSI/IEEE STD 446*

  Systems—*NFPA 110*

Enclosures

  Degrees of Protection Provided by—*IEC 60529*

  Electrical Equipment, 1000 Volts Maximum—*NEMA 250*

  Hazardous Locations, for Use in Class II, Groups E, F, and G—*CSA C22.2 25*

  Industrial Controls & Systems—*NEMA III CS6*

  Specification of Protection by—*BS EN 60335-1*

Energy & Heat Transfer Engineering—*ISO ICS 27*

Explosion proof Electrical Equipment General Requirements—*FMRC 361.5*

Fuel Cell Power Systems, Installation of Stationary—*ANSI/NFPA 853*

Grounding

  Guide for Safety in AC Substation—*ANSI/IEEE 80*

  Industrial & Commercial Power Systems—IEEE Green Book—*ANSI/IEEE STD 142*

Installation & Inspection, Electrical (2002)—*ITP*

Low Voltage Differential Signaling (LVDS) Interface Circuits, Electrical Characteristics of—*TIA/EIA 644*

Low Voltage Electrical & Electronic Equipment in the Range of 9 kHz to 40 GHz, Methods of Measurement of Radio-Noise Emissions from—*ANSI C63.4*

NETA Technical Papers—*NETA*

Polymeric Materials—Use in Electrical Equipment Evaluation—*UL 746C*

Potentially Explosive Atmospheres, Electrical Apparatus for/with

    Flameproof Enclosures "D"—*BS EN 50014*

    Intrinsic Safety, General Requirements—*BS EN 50018*

    Intrinsic Safety "T"—*BS EN 50020*

    Protection "N"—*BS EN 50021*

Power Systems, Protection of Industrial & Commercial—IEEE Buff Book—*ANSI/IEEE STD 242*

Power Distribution for Industrial Plants, Practice for Electric—IEEE Red Book—*ANSI/IEEE STD 141*

Protective Equipment, Electrical—*ASTM 10.05*

Racks, Panels & Associated Equipment—*EIA 310*

Solar & Geothermal Energy—*ASTM 12.02*

Soldered Electrical & Electronic Assemblies, Requirements for—*JSTD-001*

Wire: Types ET (250 Volts), E (660 Volts) & EE (1,000 Volts), Electrical & Electronic

    PTFE (Polytetrafluoro-Ethylene)-Insulated High Temperature Hook-Up—*NEMA HP 3*

Wiring Devices—Dimensional Requirements—*NEMA WD6*

Construction

Construction & Maintenance Techniques, Electrical

Construction, General Information for Electrical—*UL*

Construction Materials Directory, Electrical—*UL*

General Information for, Electrical Construction—*UL*

Inspection

Inspection & Plan Exam Manual, Electrical (1990)—*SBCCI*

Inspections, Basic Checklist for Building Electrical

Meters & controls

Electricity Metering, Electric Meters for—*ANSI C12.1*

Safety

AC Substation Grounding, Guide for Safety in—*ANSI/IEEE 80*

Accident Prevention Tags for Temporary Hazards—*ANSI Z535.5*

Construction Workers, OSHA Safety & Health Standards Digest for Electrical—*OSHA 1926*

Design Safety Standards, Understanding Regulations of OHSA, Electrical

Employee Workplaces Electrical Safety, Requirements for (1968)—*NFPA 70E*

European Union's Low Voltage Directive Based on Electrical Safety:

    A Tool for Understanding the—*EN 60950*

Electrical Work Rules, Understanding Regulations on—*OSHA 1926*

Electronic Equipment for Use in Power Installations—*BS EN 50/78*

Intrinsically Safe Electrical Systems, Specifications for—*BS 5501 P9*

Safety

   Color Code—*ANSI Z35*

   Signs, Environmental & Facility—*ANSI Z35.2*

   Symbols, Criteria for (1991)—*ANSI Z535.3*

Substation Grounding, Guide for Safety in AC—*ANSI/IEEE 80*

Workplace, Electrical Safety in the—*ANSI/NFPA*

Testing

Acceptance Testing Specifications—*NETA*

Electromagnetic Compatibility (EMC)

   Part 2: Testing & Measurement Techniques—*IEC 61000*

Electronic & Electrical Components Parts, Test Method—*MIL STD-202*

Electrostatic Discharge Immunity Test

Consolidated Edition, A1 & A2 Incorporated—*IEC 61000*

Maintenance Testing Specifications—*NETA*

Standard for Electronic and Electrical Component Parts, Test Method—*MIL STD 202*

Testing Specifications, Maintenance—*NETA*

Cables

Cable Insulation Manual—*BICSI*

Cables of Ruggedized Design for Burial Installations as Single Conductors or Assemblies of Single Conductors, Standard for 600-Volt Rated—*ICEA S-81-570*

Concentric Neutral Cables, Standard for 5,000-46,000-Volt Rated—*ICEA S-94-649*

Construction, Installation & Protection of Cables & Other Elements Outside Plant, (Series L)—*ITU-T L.32*

Industrial Electric Cable, Standard for Aerospace &—*NEMA WC 27500*

Nonshielded Power Cable, 2,000 Volts or Less—*NEMA WC 70*

Protection Device for Through-Cable Penetrations of Fire Sector Partitions (Series L)—*UTC-TL.32*

Polyethylene Covered Conductors, Weather Resistant—*ICECA S-70-547*

Power Cable Assemblies, Neutral Supported with Weather Resistant Extruded Insulation, Rated 600 Volts—*ICEA S-76-474*

Tests for Electrical & Optical Fiber Cables, Vertical-Tray Fire-Propagation & Smoke Release—*UL 1685*

Utility Shielded Power Cables 5,000-46,000 Volts—*ICEA S-97-682*

Connnectors/couplings/conductors

Circular, Miniature, High Density, Quick Disconnect (Bayonet, Threaded & Breech Couplings;

Environment Resistant, Removable Crimp & Hermetic Solder Contacts;

General Specifications for Connectors—*MIL-DTL-38999*

Electrical Conductors—*ASTM 02.03*

Electric Connectors

Connectors to Use between Aluminum-to-Aluminum or Aluminum-to-Copper Conductors—*ANSI C119.4*

Sealed Insulated Underground Connector Systems, Rated 600 Volts—*ANSI C119.1*

Controls

Industrial Control Equipment—*UL 508*

Control, Thermocouple Extension & Instrument Cables, Standard for—*NEMA WC57*

Duct/conduit/tubing

Duct for Underground Installations, PVC-Plastic Utilities—*NEMA TC 6 & 8*

Fittings for

PVC Plastic Utilities Duct for Underground Installation—*NEMA TC 9*

Use with Rigid PVC Conduit & Tubing—*NEMA TC 3*

Electrical insulation

Electrical Insulation

I: D 69 2484—*ASTM 10.01*

II: D 2518—*ASTM 10.02*

Liquid Gases; Electrical Protective Equipment, Electrical Insulating—*ASTM 10.03*

Motors & generators

Generators & Receivers for Use in Balanced Digital Multipoint Systems—*TIA 485*

Motors & Generators—*NEMA MGI; NEMA MGI SET*

Safety Standards & Guide for Selection, Installation & Use of—*NEMA MG2*

Squirrel Cage, Sever-Duty Totally Enclosed Fan-Cooled (ZTEDC)

Induction Motors—Up to & Including 370 kW (500 nhp)—Standard for the Petroleum & Chemical Industry—*IEEE 841*

Communication Systems, Installation, Maintenance & Use of Public Fire Service— *NFPA 1221*

Communications

Telecommunications

Audio & Video Engineering—*ISO ICS 33*

Facilities, Fire Protection of—*ANSI/NFPA 76*

Electronic Safety & Security

Electronics (Laser Equipment and the like)—*ISO ICS 31*

Signaling systems
Signaling & Nurse Call Equipment, Hospital—*UL 1069*

Signaling Systems—*NFPA 72*

Appliances for Protective, Installation, Maintenance & Use of—*NFPA72G*

Central Station Service, Installation, Maintenance & Use of (1989)—*NFPA71*

Testing Procedures for Local, Auxiliary, Remote Station & Proprietary Protective (1988)—*NFPA72H*

Security
Correctional Facilities, Detention &—*ASTM 15.08*

Fencing

Security & Fire Alarm Systems, Design & Application of

Security Systems—*ASTM 15.08*

Equipment — *ASTM 15.08*

Homeland Security Applications—*ASTM 1508*

Solar Heating for Swimming Pools (1982)

Solar Water & Pool Heating Manual—Vols. I & II (1985)

SITE & INFRASTRUCTURE

Earthwork

Excavation
Grading Code, Standard—*ICC*

Handbook, Standard,—*OSHA*

Dredging

Mining & Minerals—*ISO ICS 73*

Soil & Rock

I: D420 – D5611 (201)—*ASTM 04.08*

II: D5714 – Latest (169)—*ASTM 04.09*

Blasting/explosives
Blaster's Handbook

Explosives & Rock Blasting

Earthquake/siesmic protection
Safety Devices, Earthquake Activated—*FMRC 7431*

Siesmic Restraint Manual: Guidelines for Mechanical Systems (1998)—*SMACNA*

Geosynthetics

Geosynthetics (111)—*ASTM 04.13*

Geotextiles—*ASTM 04.08*

Surveying

Image Technology—*ISO ICS 37*

Surveying Instructions, Manual of—Government Manual for Public Land Surveys (1973)

Underground

Underground Utiltities, Technology &—*ASTM 04.12*

Landscape Architectural Standards for

Sitework—*CSI SPECTEXT—S02000*

Distribution Piping Systems, Gas Transmission &—*B31.8*

Underground

    Construction Work, Construction Contract Procedures—Part C: General- *DIN 18312*

    Utilities, Technology & Property Management Systems (169)—*ASTM*

Utility Accommodation Guide—Safe Operation of Highway Facilities, Above Ground & Underground

Exterior Improvements

Utilities

Roads/highways/tunnels/bridges

Aerial Tramways, Aerial Lifts & Tows, Safety Requirements—*ANSI B77.1*

Bridge Welding Code—*AASHTO/AWS D1.5M/D1.5*

Highway

    Bridges, Standards Specifications for—*AASHTO HB-17*

    Signs, Luminaiers & Traffic Signals, Standard Specifications for Structural Support for—*AASHTO LTS-4*

Materials & Methods of Sampling & Testing, Standard Specifications for Transpiration

    The Materials Handbook—*AASHTO HM-22*

Road & Bridge Construction

    Standard Specifications for

Road Construction: Set & Slab Pavements & Surrounds

    Construction Contract Procedures—*DIN 18318*

Segmented Concrete Bridges, Guide Specifications for Design & Construction of—*AASHTO—GSCB*

Road Tunnels, Bridges & Other Limited Access Highways—*ANSI/NFPA 502*

Utility Accommodation Guide—Safe Operation of Highway Facilities, Above Ground & Underground

Transportation

Paving/pavement

Aluminum Highway Bridges, Guide Specifications for

Asphalt

Guide Specifications for Polymer Modified—*AASHTO/ARTBA V-TF 31-1*

Paving Manual—*MS 8*

ASTM Standards—*AST- 04.03*

Aggregates

Quality Assurance

Road & Paving Materials

Test Methods, Precision for Construction Materials

Barrier Hardware, Guide to Standardized—*AASHO/AGC/ARTBA V-BRH-2*

Bearing Design & Detailing Guidelines, Steel Bridges—*AASHTO VSBB-1*

Bridges

Aluminum Highway, Guide Specifications—*AASHTO V-GSAHB-1-M*

Condition Evaluation of, Manual for—*AASHTO V-MCEB-2-M*

Fabrication, Highway, with HPS70W Steel, Guide Specifications for—*AASHTO V-HBF-2*

Highway, Standard Specifications for—*AASHTO V-HB-17*

Segmental Concrete, Design & Construction, Guide Specifications for—*AASHTO V-GSCB-M*

Load Resistance Factor Rating of Highway (LRFRF)

Condition Evaluation &—*AASHTO VLRFR-1-M*

Design Specifications, with Customary

US Units—*AASSHTO-LRFDUS-3-M*

SI Units—*AASHTO-LRFDSI-3-M*

Movable Highway

Design Specifications, LFRD—*AASHTO V-LRGDMOV-1-11*

Standard Specifications for (Some AREA Standards & Specifications) -*AASHTO V-MHB-5*

Pedestrian, Guide Specifications for—*AASHTO V-GSDPB-1*

Segmental Highway, Standard Specifications—*ASSHTO V-GSCB-M*

Steel Girder Highway, Horizontally Curved, Guide Specifications for- *AASHTO V-GHC-4* (With Design Examples for I-Girder & Box-Girder Bridges)

Temporary Works, Guide Design Specifications for—*AASHTO V-GSBTW-1*

Truss, Strength Design of, Guide Specifications for—*AASHTO SDTB-1*

Cathodic Protection of, Guide Specifications for—*AASHTO/AGC/ARTBA*

Part 1: Concrete Bridge Decks—*V-TF 29-1*

Part 2: Concrete Overlay of Pavements & Bridge Decks—*V-TF 30-1*

Coatings Systems with Inorganic Zinc-Rich Primer, Guide Specifications—*AASHTO SBCS-1*

Concrete—*AASHTO/AGC/ARTBA*

    Fiber Reinforced, Use & State-of-the Practice of—*V-TF 36-1*

    Polymer Concrete Bridge Deck Overlay, Guide Specifications—*V-TF 34*-1

Corrosion Protection of Components in Bridges—*AASHTO/AGC/ARTBA V-TF 32.1*

Drainage

    Pipe Specifications for Waterways, Airports, Railroads, Transit & Highways, Cross-Reference for—*AASHTO/AGC/ARTBA VTF 22-1*

    Products, Guide to Standardized Highway—*AASHTO/AGC/ARTBA V-GSHDP-1*

Highway Construction, Guide Specifications for—*AASHTO V-GSH-8*

    Manual for—*AASHTO V-CM-4*

Highways & Streets, Policy on Geometric Design of—*AASHTO*

Lighting Pole Hardware, Guide to Standardized Highway—*AASHTO/AGC/ARTBA V-LPH-1*

Maintenance, Asphalt in Pavement—*MS 16*

Materials

    Road & Paving: Vehicle-Pavement Systems—*ASTM 04.03*

    Transportation, & Methods of Sampling, Standard Specifications for—*AASHTO—U-HM-25-m*

Pavement Structures

    Guide for Design of—*AASHTO GDPS 4*

    Supplement Guide—*AASHTO GDPS 4S*

    Vehicle-Pavement Systems (256)—*ASTM 04.03*

Paving Materials, Road—*ASTM 04.03*

Precision Test Methods

Quality Assurance

Repair of Highway Bridges, Guide Specifications of Shotcrete— *AASHTO/AGC/ARTBA V-T 37-1*

Roadside Design Guide—*AASHTO RSDG 3*

Seismic Isolation, Guide Specifications for—*AASHTO V-GSID-2-M*

Sign Support Hardware, Guide to Small—*AASHO/AGC/ARTBA V-GSSSH-1*

Signs, Luminaires & Traffic Signals, Structural Supports for,

    Standard Specifications for—*AASHTO V-LTS-1-12*

Soil

    Improvement Techniques, In Situ—*AASHO/AGC/ARTBA V-TF 27-1*

    Modifications, Using Polozanic Stabilized Mixture (Base Course of Subbase) & Fly Ash for In-Place Subgrade, Guide Specifications for—*AASHTO/AGC/ARTBA V-TF 28-1*

Sound Barriers, Structural Design, Guide Specifications for—*AASHTO-V-GSSB-1-M*

Surface Treatment

Construction Techniques—*ES 2*

Specifications—*ES 11*

Welding Code, Bridge—*AASHTO/AWS-D1.5M/D1.5*

Wood Decks, Stress-Laminated, Guide Specifications for the Design of—*AASHTO V-SLWD-1*

Public works
Inspector's Manual, Public Works

Specifications, Standard, for Public Works Construction (2000)—*GREENBOOK*

Waterway & Marine Construction

Marine construction
Marine Structures, Shipbuilding &—*ISO ICS 47*

PROCESS EQUIPMENT

Pollution Control Equipment

Environmental
Air Quality, Building—A guide for Building Owners & Facilities Managers—*EPA/NISF*

API Health, Environment & Sciences Department Publications—*API HESD*

Atmospheric Analysis;

Occupational Health & Safety; Protective Clothing (208)—*ASTM 11.03*

Water & Environmental Technology—*ASTM 11.03*

Auditing, Guidelines for Environmental

Audit Procedures, Part 1: Auditing of Environmental Management Systems—*ISO 14011*

General Principles—*ISO 14010*

Qualification Criteria for Environmental Auditors—*ISO 14012*

Auditing, Guidelines for Quality or Environment Management Systems (or both)—*ASTM 11.05*

Auditing, Guidelines for

Environmental Audit Procedures

Part 1: Auditing of Environmental Management Systems—*ISO 14011*

General Principles—*ISO 14010*

Qualification Criteria for Environmental Auditors—*ISO 14012*

Quality or Environment Management Systems (or both)—*ASTM 11.05*

Biological Effects & Environmental Fate: Water & Environmental Technology (122)—*ASTM 11.05*

Biotechnology: Water & Environmental Technology—*ASTM 11.05*

Controlled Environment, Clean Rooms & Associated—*ISO 146.44*

Environment, Protection of (1980)—*CFR 40-700-789*

Environmental

Aspects & Impacts, Identifying—*ASQ H1009*

Assessment for Commercial Real Estate—*40 CFR PART 312*

Control, Health, Safety & (1989)

Labels

Declarations, Type III—*ISO TR 14025*

General Principles—*ISO 14200*

Principles & Procedures, Type I—*ISO 14024*

Self Declared, Environmental Claims, Type II—*ISO 14021*

Sites & Organizations, Environmental Management—*ISO 14015*

Water & Environmental Technology—*ASNI 11.04*

Exploration & Production Operations, Waste Management in, Environmental Guidance Document—*API ES*

Hazardous Substances & Oil Spill Responses, Water & Environment Technology—*ASTM 11.04*

Health Protection, Safety (Excludes ISO 14000)—*ISO ICS 13*

Identifying, Environmental Aspects & Impacts—*ASQ H1009*

ISO

Certification, 14001—*ASQ P601*

Compendium, 14000—*BS EN ISO 14004*

Handbook, 14000—*ASQ*

Life Cycle Assessment, Environmental Management

Goal & Scope Definition & Inventory Analysis—*ISO 14041*

Examples of Application of—*ISO 14041-14049*

Life Cycle Impact Assessment—*ISO 14043*

Principles & Framework—*ISO 14041*

Management, Environmental—*ISO 14000 SERIES*

Management, Systems, Environmental—*ISO 14000*

Compendium—*ISO 14000 A COMPENDIUM; BS EN ISO 14004*

General Guidelines on Principles, Systems, and Supporting Techniques—*ISO 14004*

Requirements with Guidance for Use—*ISO 14001*

International Standards for Quality Management—*ISO 9000*

Vocabulary—*ISO 14050*

Management Systems, Environmental

    Specification with Guidelines for Use—*ISO 14001*

    Specification with Guidance for Use—*ASQ T65*

Mechanical Environmental Tests—*AECTP—400*

Mold: A Growing Concern—*ASPREI*

Oil Spill Responses: Water & Environmental Technology—*ASTM 11.04*

Performance Evaluation

    Guidelines, Environmental—*ISO 14031*

Risk Management, International Environmental:

    ISO 14000 & Systems Approach—*ISO RISK MANAGEMENT*

Safety & Health Fact Sheets—*ASW SHF*

Waste Management in Exploration & Production Operations, Guidance Document—*API ES*

Water & Environmental Technology—*ASTM 11*

    Occupational Health & Safety—*ASTM 11.03*

    Pesticides—*ASTM 11.05*

    Water I (133)—*ASTM 11.01*

    Water II (183)—*ASTM 11.02*

Welding on Health, Effects of—*AWS EWH SET*

Environmental management

Environmental, Management—Series—*ISO 14000*

    Compendium—*SIO 14000 A COMPENDIUM*

    International Standards for Quality Management—*ISO 9000*

    Performance Evaluation: Examples of—*ISO TR 130032*

    Vocabulary—*ISO 14050*

Environmental Management Systems

    General Guidelines on Principles, Systems, and Supporting Techniques—*ISO 14004*

    Specification with Guidelines for Use—*ISO 14001*

    Specification with Guidance for Use—*ASQ T65*

Life Cycle Assessment,

    Goal & Scope Definition & Inventory Analysis—*ISO 14041*

    Examples of Application of—*ISO 14041 to ISO 14049*

    Life Cycle Impact Assessment—*ISO 14043*

    Principles & Framework—*ISO 14041*

Occupational Health & Safety, Water & Environmental Technology—*ASTM 11.03*

Performance Evaluation

    Examples of Environmental, Environmental Management—*ISO TR 130032*

    Guidelines, Environmental—*ISO 14031*

Pesticides: Environmental Assessment;

Hazardous Substances & Oil Spill Responses (174)—*ASTM 11.05*

Petroleum Storage Tanks

Guidelines & Procedures for Entering & Cleaning—*API RP 2016*

Safe Entry & Cleaning—*API STD 2015*

Protection of Environment—*40 CFR*

Risk Management, International Environmental:

ISO 14 Systems Approach—*ISO 14000 RISK MANAGEMENT*

Threshold Limit Values for Chemical Substances & Physical Agents (2000)

TLCs & BEIs—*ACGIH BIOLOGICAL EXPOSURE*

Training, Criteria for Accepted Practices in Safety, Health & Environmental—*ASSE/ANSI Z490.1*

Waste Management (125)

Water & Environmental Technology—*ASTM 11.04*

Asbestos

Abatement on Asbestos Projects, Guidelines for Conducting the AHERA TEM Clearance Test to Determine Completion of

Airborne Asbestos Following an Abatement Action, Measuring

Asbestos Abatement Projects, Standard Practice for Visual Inspection of

Exposure Assessment in Buildings: Inspection Manual, Asbestos—*EPA*

Managing Asbestos in Place: A Building Owner's Guide to Operations & Maintenance Programs for Asbestos-Containing Materials (1990)—*EPA 20T-2003*

Simplified Sampling Scheme for Friable Surfaces, Asbestos in Buildings

Visual Inspection of Asbestos Abatement Projects, Standard Practice for (1990)

Waste Management Guidance: Generation, Transport & Disposal, Asbestos (1985)

Workplace Exposure to Asbestos: Review & Recommendations (1981)

Chemical resistant materials

Chemical-Resistant Nonmetallic Materials—*ASTM 04.05*

Vitrified Clay

Concrete

Fiber Cement Products

Masonry

Mortars

Drinking water Treatment Chemicals, Health Effects—*NSF 60*

Hazardous Industrial Chemicals, Material Safety Data Sheets—*ANSI Z400.1*

Threshold Limit Values for Chemical Substances & Physical Agents (2000)—*ACGIH*

Hazardous materials/toxic waste

Chemical Hazards, Pocket Guide to (1990)—*NIOSH*

Emergency Handling of Hazardous Materials & Surface Transportation

Hazardous Substances & Oil Spill Responses (174)—*ASTM 11.05*

    Water & Environment Technology—*ASTM 11.04*

Leakage of Flammable & Combustible Liquids, Underground—*NFPA329*

Spill Cleanup Manual, Underground—*API 1628*

Pesticides

Water & Environmental Technology—Pesticides—*ASTM 11.05*

Protective clothing

Water & Environmental Technology, Protective Clothing—*ASTM 11.03*

Tanks

Fiberglass-Reinforced Plastic Tanks, Thermosetting—*AWWA D120*

Prestressed Concrete Water Tanks,

    Circumferential, with—*AWWA D115*

    Wire & Strand-Wound, Circular—*AWWA D110*

Water-Storage—*AWWA*

    Cathodic Protection for the Interior of Steel Water Tanks,

        Automatically Controlled, Impressed-Current—*D104*

    Coating Steel, Tanks—*D102*

    Factory-Coated Bolted Steel Tanks for—*D103*

    Portable, Flexible-Membrane-Lining & Floating-Cover Materials—*D130*

    Welded Steel Tanks, for—*D100*

Water treatment

Coagulation—*AWWA*

Chloride

    Diallyldimethylammonium, Poly—*451*

    Liquid Ferric—*B407*

    Liquid Polyaluminum—*B408*

Polyacrylamide—*B453*

Sulfate

    Aluminum—Liquid, Ground, or Lumps—*B403*

    Ferric—*B406*

    Ferrous—*B402*

Sodium

    Aluminate—*B405*

    Silicate, Liquid—*B 404*

Facilities Disinfection—*AWWA*

    Water Mains, Disinfecting of—*C651*

    Water-Storage Facilities, Disinfection of—*C662*

    Water Treatment Plant, Disinfection of—*C663*

    Wells, Disinfection of—*C654*

Filtration—*AWWA*

    Filter

        Material, Granular—*B100*

        Media, Precoat—*B101*

    Manganese Greensand for Filters—*B102*

Scale & Erosion Control—*AWWA*

    Calcium Chloride—*B550*

    Carbon Dioxide—*B510*

    Diosodium Phosphate, Anhydrous—*B505*

    Monosodium Phosphate, Anhydrous—*B504*

    Polyamines, EPI-DMA—*B452*

    Potassium Hydroxide—*B511*

    Sodium Dioxide—*B512*

    Sodium Hydroxide (Caustic Soda)—*B501*

    Sodium Tripolyphosphate—*B503*

Softening—*AWWA*

    Chloride, Sodium—*B200*

    Quicklime & Hydrated Lime—*B202*

    Soda Ash—*B201*

Disinfection—Chemicals—*AWWA*

    Ammonium Sulfate—*B302*

    Chlorine, Liquid—*B301*

    Hypochlorites—*B300*

    Sodium Chlorite—*B303*

Taste & Odor Control—*AWWA*

    Activated Carbon

        Granular—*B604*

            Reactivation of—*B605*

        Powdered—*B600*

    Copper Sulfate—*B602*

    Permanganates—*B603*

    Sodium Metabisulfite—*B601*

Prophylaxis—*AWWA*

Fluorosilicic Acid—*B703*

Sodium Fluoride—*B701*

Sodium Fluorosilicate—*B702*

Waste management

Incinerators, Waste & Linen Handling Systems (1990)—*NFPA 82*

Water

Disinfecting Water Mains, Standard for

Water

Mains & Their Appurtenances, Standard for Installation of Ductile Iron—*AWWA C-600*

Softeners, Voluntary Industry Standards for Household, Commercial & Portable Exchange

Tanks for Private Fire Protection (1987)—*NFPA 22*

Wells—*AWWA A100*

Wastewater/sewer systems

Modern Sewage Design—*AISI*

Private Sewage Disposal Code, International (2000)—*ICC*

Wastewater Treatment Plants, Design of Municipal (2 Vols.)

4

Project Specifications

The American Institute of Architects (AIA) classifies project specifications as an integral part of the bid documents for awarding a legal construction contract with the bid document including the agreement between the owner and the constructor, general conditions, drawings, and specifications. The information contained in project specifications should be stated one time only, never repeated in any of the other documents; it should be entered in the most logical location to simplify its retrieval and substantially reduce the possibility of conflicts and discrepancies.

Specifications provide a written description of the project in an orderly and logical manner. They should not overlap or duplicate the information contained in the drawings; rather they should expand or clarify drawing notes, establish the scope of work, spell out the responsibilities of the constructor (contractor), and describe:

Type and quality of materials, equipment, and fixtures

Quality of workmanship

Methods of fabrication, installation, and erection

Test and code requirements

Gages of manufacturer's equipment

Allowances and unit prices

Alternatives and options

CSI/CSC MASTERFORMAT 2004

The masterformat, published jointly by the Construction Specifications Institute (CSI) and Construction Specifications Canada (CSC), provides a uniform list of section titles under 50 respective division headings to permit specifiers total flexibility in organizing a project's specifications.

FACILITY CONSTRUCTION

02 EXISTING CONDITIONS

4100 Demolition—Building, site works & selective demolition; abandonment of existing utilities

4200 Structure Moving—Preparation & relocation of structures & directly associated activities

6500 Underground Storage Tank Removal—Removal of fuel contents & disposal of contaminated soil

8400 Polychlorinated Biphenyl (PCB) Remediation—PCBs; other toxic substances regulated under TSCA

03 CONCRETE

0130.65 Resurfacing & Rehabilitation of Concrete—Materials for patching, repairing, leveling & topping

0130.75 Concrete Repair—Repair of concrete & patching or repair of damaged or deteriorated concrete

0511   Concrete Color Additive

0521   Integral Waterproofing of Concrete—Waterproofing admixture; treatment of concrete joints

0531   Adhesive Anchors—Ultrabond epoxy bonding adhesive for rebars and threaded pipe

1000   Concrete Forming & Accessories—Materials to form & maintain cast-in-place concrete until stripping

1116.13   Concrete Form Liners—Plastic & elastomeric architectural form liners

2000   Concrete Reinforcing—Reinforcing steel & required supports for cast-in-place concrete

3000   Cast-in-Place Concrete -In-situ concrete for structural building frame, slabs on grade, and other applications

3513   High-Tolerance Concrete Floor Finishing—Special coatings, sealers & hardeners; concrete slabs & toppings

3523   Exposed Aggregate Concrete Finishing—Materials & techniques for exposed architectural finish & cleaning

3533   Stamped Concrete Finishing—Concrete stamping system

3713   Shotcrete—Concrete pneumatically-applied; reinforcement & surface finishing

3800   Post-Tensioned Concrete—Post-tensioning of cast-in-place concrete structural framing members

3900   Concrete Curing—Procedures & materials for curing horizontal & vertical concrete surfaces

3931   Cutting, Sealing & Hardening Concrete Floors—Ashford Formula, chemically reactive densifier

4100   Precast Structural Concrete—Plant precast & prestressed concrete framing members

4113   Precast Concrete Hollow Core Planks—Plant precast prestressed concrete roof & floor planks, cored

4500   Precast Architectural Concrete—Plant cast architecturally finished concrete wall panels

4713   Tilt-Up Concrete—Site cast concrete wall panels; with supports, anchors, to bearing devices

4900   Glass-Fiber Reinforced Concrete—Plant cast, architecturally finished glass fiber-reinforced concrete wall units

5216   Lightweight Insulating Concrete—Portland cement concrete fill used mainly to achieve sloped roof decks

5400   Cast Underlayment—Liquid applied, gypsum or cemetitious base, installed over interior subfloors

5417   Cementitious Underlayment—Latex modified cement-based, self-leveling

04 MASONRY

0100   Maintenance of Masonry—Cleaners, restoration treatments, strippers & water repellents

0100   Maintenance of Masonry—Water, steam, or chemical cleaning & blasting, repointing & coatings

0511   Masonry Mortaring & Grouting—Mortar & grout for all masonry work

0519.14   Seismic-Rated Masonry Reinforcement—Seismic-rated systems

2000   Unit Masonry—Most ordinary uses of masonry, including walls or partitions

2001   Masonry Veneer—Unit masonry for non-load-bearing exterior veneer walls

2002   Single-Wythe Unit Masonry—Load-bearing or non-load-bearing single wythe masonry walls or partitions

2300   Glass Unit Masonry—Plain & decorative designs, reinforcement, joints & accessories

2316   Glass Unit Masonry Floors—IBP grid systems; IBP glass block grid system

2319   Glass Unit Masonry Skylights—IBP grid systems; IBP glass block grid system

2500   Unit Masonry Panels—Shop fabricated masonry panels of face brick veneer on steel framing

2714   Thin Brick Veneer Masonry—Thin brick units

2723   Cavity Wall Unit Masonry—Concrete masonry, brick & clay tile units; reinforcement & accessories

2731   Reinforced Unit Masonry—Engineered, steel-reinforced, structural & load-bearing masonry

4200   Exterior Stone Cladding—Thin stone veneer for exterior & interior walls, attached to structural steel

4301   StoneMasonry Veneer—Natural stone, set in mortar, for veneer on exterior & interior walls

7200   Cast Stone Masonry—Cast stone for exterior & interior use

05 METALS

1200   Structural Steel Framing—Structural steel framing, anchor bolts, base plates, accessories

2100   Steel Joist Framing—Structural steel open web joists & joist girders for roof and floor framing

3100   Steel Decking—Structural metal deck for floor & roof applications; SDI specification

4000   Cold-Formed Metal Framing—Steel studs, slotted channels, joists, purlins; axially loaded & wind-loaded

4400   Cold-Formed Metal Trusses—Factory-built light gage cold-formed steel floor & roof trusses

5000   Metal Fabrication—Shop-fabricated metal items of steel or aluminum

5100   Metal Stairs—Shop-fabricated steel stairs with various types of treads & landings

5134   Aluminum Ladders—Fixed & folding aluminum wall ladders & ship's ladders

5135   Exit Ladder Devices—Emergency egress & equipment access ladders

5213   Pipe & Tube Railings—Pipe & tube railing system; aluminum or steel; custom fabricated

5305   Metal Gratings & Floor Plates—Metal bar gratings & floor plates, pedestrian or light vehicular

7000   Decorative Metal—Grilles & louvers; security grills & doors; railings

7113   Fabricated Metal Spiral Stairs—Production of custom-manufactured spiral stairs; varying materials & finishes

7300   Decorative Metal Railings—Aluminum, stainless steel; picket, glazed & pipe

7311   Decorative Metal Pipe Railings—Ornamental aluminum pipe component

7313   Glazed Decorative Metal Railings—Structural glass railings & clamped glass assemblies

7316   Wire Rope Decorative Metal Railings—Guardrails with stainless steel cable or rod infill

7511   Ornamental Metal Mesh Panels—Architectural metal mesh for ornamental metal fabrication

06 WOOD, PLASTICS, COMPOSITES

0584   Pre-finished Wood Panels—Panels prefinished with NOVA ultraviolet-cured flatline

0587   High-Pressure Decorative Laminates

1000   Rough Carpentry—Wood framing & sheathing, rough wood blocking & curbing

1054   Wood Blocking & Curbing—Rough wood blocking & curbing for miscellaneous locations

1324   Heavy Timber Framing—Structural wood framing consisting of components with 5 inches at the minimum

1325   Heavy Timber Trusses—Heavy timber truss framing, bolted metal connector plates & split ring

1500   Wood Decking—Structural wood decking of softwood lumber, plywood, or glued laminated wood

1514   Wood-Polymer Composite Decking—Wood-polymer composite deck planks

1733   Wood I-Joists—I-shaped, with wood flanges glued to OSB or plywood web

1736   Metal-Web Wood Joists—Structural joists of wood chords with tubular metal web truss web & steel

1753   Shop-Fabricated Wood Trusses—Shop-fabricated wood trusses with wood or steel plate connectors

1800   Glued-Laminated Construction—Shop-fabricated glued-laminated structural wood beams, purlins & arches

2000	Finish Carpentry—Interior & exterior finished carpentry & woodwork items
2500	Prefinished Paneling—Modules & plank; decorative interior wall panels
2517	Slotted Display Paneling—Decorative wall panels for merchandising display
4000	Architectural Woodwork—Custom woodwork, doors, windows, louvers & trim
4100	Architectural Wood Casework—Special fabricated custom design casework of wood or particle board
4144	Cabinet Locks—Door, drawer & metal cabinet locks
4216	Wood Veneer Paneling—Architectural quality, custom, shop-fabricated wood veneer paneling
4441	Architectural Wood Columns—Architectural wood columns, caps & bases
4442	Porch Posts & Railings—Porch posts & porch railings
6100	Simulated Stone Fabrication—Gel-coated cast plastic cultured marble
6105	Solid Plastic Vanity Counters—High-density polyethylene & polypropylene
6113	Cultured Marble Fabricators—Factory-molded synthetic marble lavatories, countertops, tubs, and sinks
8101	Architectural Polymer Composite Columns—Architectural polymer composite columns, caps & bases
8102	Polyurethane Balustrades—Balustrades
8200	Glass Fiber Reinforced Plastic—Custom-sized & shaped fiber-reinforced epoxy or polyester resin
8200	Glass Fiber Reinforced Plastic—Standard & custom items
8205	Fiberglass Reinforced Plastic Panels—Decorative fiberglass-reinforced polyester sanitary wall surfacing

07 THERMAL INSULATION & WATERPROOFING

WATERPROOFING/DAMPROOFING

0150.19	Preparation for Reroofing—Removal of existing horizontal roof covering in preparation roof replacement
1113	Bituminous Dampproofing—Hot & cold applied asphalt & hot applied coal tar bitumen dampproofing
1200	Built-Up Bituminous Waterproofing—Hot or cold applied asphalt or hot applied coal tar bitumen waterproofing
1300	Sheet Waterproofing—Numerous types of sheet membrane waterproofing
1355	PVC Sheet Deck Membrane—PVC membrane for exterior horizontal surface
1400	Fluid-Applied Waterproofing—Rubberized asphalt, synthetic liquid rubber & cold applied elastometric material
1513	Lead Waterproofing—Sheet lead waterproofing for concealed instillation, protection band
1613	Polymer Modified Cement Waterproofing—Portland cement-based coating; positive or negative side; potable water

1616 Crystalline Waterproofing—Positive/negative side cementitious type that seals by forming crystals in

1619 Metal Oxide Waterproofing—Coatings applied to interior side of concrete floors & walls below grade

1713 Betonies Panel Waterproofing—Panel waterproofing for below grade vertical & horizontal surfaces

1800 Traffic Coatings—Fluid-applied electrometric waterproofing for traffic surfaces

1900 Water Repellents—Transparent water repellents for masonry & other porous surfaces

THERMAL INSULATION

2100 Thermal Insulation—Rigid or semi-rigid boards of various types, plus bats & blankets

2117 Pre-Engineered Building Insulation—Thermal design simple saver system; roof & wall insulation; vapor barrier

2119 Foamed-in-Place Insulation—Foam insulation installed on site by spray, frothing, or pouring

2121 Sprayed Foam Insulation for Building Envelope—Sprayed polyurethane foam for building envelope

2122 Sprayed Foam Insulation for Cold Storage Facilities—Sprayed polyurethane foam insulation for coolers

2123 Loose Fill Insulation—Pour grade vermiculite or perlite granular insulation

2126 Blown Insulation—Glass fiber or cellulose fiber insulation, manually or pneumatically placed

2129 Sprayed Insulation—Sprayed glass fiber or treated cellulose thermal & acoustic insulation

2133 Reflective Insulation/Radiant Barrier—Reflective insulation/radiant barrier material

EXTERIOR INSULATION—ROOFING

2133 Reflective Insulation/Radiant Barrier—Reflective foil & radiant barriers

2217 Polyisocyanurate Roof Board Insulation—Polyisocyanurate board, composite board, and related products

2400 Exterior Insulation & Finish Systems—PB (thin) & PM (thick) EIFS; insulation, finish & reinforcing

2500 Weather Barriers—Materials used to prevent air & water vapor passage through building

2501 Weather Resistant Membranes

2502 Sheathing Membrane—Typar housewrap

2600 Vapor Retarders—Reinforced, laminated; roof deck, wall, under concrete slab

EXTERIOR INSULATION—SIDING

4213   Metal Wall Panels—Prefinsihed, formed metal wall panels, liner panels & insulation for field erection

4214   Insulated Metal Wall Panels—Inner & outer metal skins & insulation core; prefinished

4244   Aluminum-Composite Wall Panels—Standard & fire rated metal wall panels

4244   Aluminum-Composite Wall Panels—Custom exterior cladding

4414   Aggregate-Faced Architectural Building Panels—Aggregate coated fiberglass reinforced resin panels

4457   Composite Architectural Building Panels—Fiberglass reinforced composite panels for exterior use

4616   Aluminum Siding—Aluminum siding, soft systems & trim

4623   Wood Siding—Wood board & panel siding, including flat & beveled boards & plywood

4626   Hardboard Siding—Panel & lap siding, simulated shakes, soffit panels, trim

4631   Oriented Strand Board Siding—Preservative-treated OSB panel/lap siding

4633   Plastic Siding—Vinyl siding, soffit & trim; simulated shingles & shakes

4644   Wood-Fiber Cement Siding—Fiber cement siding, soffit, trim & accessories

ROOFING SYSTEMS

3113   Asphalt Shingles—Mineral granule surfaced asphalt composition shingles

3116   Metal Shingles—Aluminum, galvanized steel; copper; for steep roofs; underlayment & flashings

3126   Slate Shingles—Natural slate roofing shingles, including underlayments & flashings

3129   Wood Shingles & Shakes—Cedar & redwood shingles & shakes for installation on sloped wood decks

3213   Clay Roof Tiles—Clay tile roofing for steep roofs, including underlayment & accessories

3216   Concrete Roof Tiles—Concrete tile roofing for steep roofs, including underlayment & accessories

4113   Metal Roof Panels—Factory-fabricated steel & aluminum panel roofing systems, structural &

5100   Built-Up Bituminous Roofing—Multi-ply felt roofing with asphalt or coal tar bitumen

5200   Modified Bituminous Membrane Roofing—SBS & APP membranes, in both conventional & protected applications

5201   Rubberized Asphalt Roofing—Single-ply rubberized asphalt bitumen sheet roofing in a protected membrane

5300   Elastomeric Membrane Roofing—Single-ply roofing of EPDM, PVC, neoprene, etc., including protected membrane

5414   Mechanical Att. Single-Ply Ethylene Propylene Roofing—Stevens EP, insulation & accessories

5700   Coated Foamed Roofing—Sprayed polyurethane foam insulation with sprayed protective overcoat

5700   Coated Foamed Roofing—Coated polyurethane foam systems for new and remedial roofing

6100   Sheet Metal Roofing—Break formed sheets; flat, standing, battened seam; prefinihsed or unfinished

ROOFING APPURTENANCES

6200   Sheet Metal Flashing & Trim—Flashing & trim associated with roofing & waterproofing membranes

6500   Flexible Flashing—Laminated copper & synthetic through-wall

7100   Roof Specialties—Copings & fascias, flexible flashings, snow guards, vents & similar items

7123   Manufactured Gutters & Downspouts—Metal & plastic rainwater gutters & downspouts for low rise construction

7234   Roof Hatches & Smoke Vents—Hatches & vents with integral support curb or for use with site built wood

7253   Snow Guards

7601   Roof Pavers & Ballast Materials—Square decorative pavers & pedestals; interlocking ballast pavers

FIREPROOFING

8100   Applied Fireproofing—Cementitious & mineral fiber fireproofing, spray applied

8123   Intumescent Mastic Fireproofing—Thin-film paint-like fire-resistive coating for exposed structural steel

8205   Board & Barrier Fireproofing—Calcium silicate, mineral fiber, ceramic fiber boards, flexible blanket

8414   Firestopping—Products for closing openings in fire-rated walls, partitions & floors

8474   Partition-Head Fireproofing—Metal track system for fire-resistive gypsum partitions

JOINT SEALERS

9005   Joint Sealers—Gummable & pourable slants, compressible foam sealers & gaskets

9005   Joint Sealers—Foam sealers, joint fillers & cold temperature sealers

9100   Preformed Joint Seals—Precompressed, self-expanding polyurethane foam sealers

9513   Expansion Joint Covers Assemblies—Proprietary products for interior floor, wall, ceiling expansion or control joints

08 OPENINGS—DOORS & WINDOWS

DOORS

1113   Hollow Metal Doors & Frames—Steel doors, frames & transom panels

1113   Hollow Metal Doors & Frames—Hollow-steel; fire-rated, non-rated, sound-rated; flush & stile & rail

1115   Bullet-Resistant Steel Doors & Frames

1116   Aluminum Doors & Frames—Flush & tubular aluminum doors & frames, primarily for interior use

1119   Stainless-Steel Doors & Frames

1213   Hollow Metal Frame—Hollow steel frames for use without steel doors; fire-rated, nonrated, sound proof

1216   Aluminum Frames—Steel & aluminum, adjustable throat design

1416   Flush Wood Doors—Wood veneer, plastic laminate, hardboard; fire rated, acoustical, lead-lined

1433   Stile & Rail Wood Doors—Non-rated; wood panel or glazed; stock & custom

1613   Fiberglass Doors—Heavy duty FRP, for abuse & chemical resistance; fire-rated; FRP & metal

3100   Access Doors & Panels—Metal access door & frame units for walls, ceilings & floors

3200   Sliding Glass Doors—Light commercial quality; wood, PVC, or extruded aluminum

3201   Lift-Sliding & Sliding-Folding Glass Doors—Wood, aluminum, PVC; lift-slide, lift-tilt-slide, sliding-folding

3214   ICU/CCU Sliding Doors—Hospital sliding doors

3314   Overhead Coiling Wood Counter Doors—Wood-slat-type counter doors; operators

3323   Overhead Coiling Doors—Industrial & commercial quality; steel stainless steel & aluminum

3326   Overhead Coiling Grilles—Aluminum, steel, stainless steel, bronze, manual & electric

3436   Darkroom Doors—ABS & Steel revolving light-proof doors; pop-out, hinged

3458   Records vault Doors—Fire resistant or burglary-resistant doors for use at records vaults & file storerooms

3513.13   Accordion Folding Doors—Acoustic & non-acoustic types; vinyl coated fabric; overhead track

3513.13   Accordion Folding Doors—Acoustical, non-acoustical, security doors, room dividers

3513.23   Folding Fire Doors—Horizontal sliding, accordion folding automatic-closing; up to 180 minute UL rating

3613   Sectional Doors—Wood, steel, aluminum overhead sectional floors; manual & electric; glazing

3613   Sectional Doors—Coplay sectional overhead doors, insulated & non-insulated

3815   Double-Acting Traffic Doors—Self-closing swing doors for personnel, carts, forklifts; bumpers, plates

3918   Watertight Doors & Flood Barriers

3923   Hurricane Resistant Doors—Small & large-missile-impact rated; French & sliding

3953   Blast-Resistant Doors—Doors, frames & hardware

4229   Automatic Entrances—Packaged sliding/swinging doors; electric, hydraulic, pneumatic operators

4229.13 Folding Automatic Entrances—Automatic folding door packages

4229.23 Sliding Automatic Entrances—Aluminum & all-glass sliding door packages; operators; actuators

4229.33 Swinging Automatic Entrances—Swinging door packages, operators, actuators & safeties

4233   Revolving Door Entrances—Aluminum, stainless steel, bronze; manual & motor assisted

4236   Balanced Door Entrances—Aluminum, stainless steel, bronze, all-glass, hollow

4313   Aluminum-Framed Storefronts—Aluminum-framed, glazed; one-story application; doors, windows

HARDWARE

7100   Door hardware—Door hardware, thresholds & gasketing

7101   Architectural Hungers—Butt hinges, special hinges, etc. for commercial projects

7102   Continuous Geared Hinges

7103   Sliding & Folding Door Hardware—Hardware for wood & glass doors, pocket, sliding & folding

7103   Sliding Door Hardware—Bi-fold, by-pass & pocket door hardware

7104   Door Locks—High security multipoint locks, solid brass trim & related appurtenances

7109   Door Trim—Architectural door trim push/pulls, kickplates, stops, etc.

7111   Thresholds & Weather Stripping—Thresholds, weather-stripping & astragale

7114   Low-Energy Door Operators—Automatic door operators & activators

7415   Fire Door Operators—Automatic door operators & activators

7311   Electrical Locking Controls—Electromagnetic locks, electric strikes, switches

7500   Window Hardware—Sliding-bi-folding, tilt turn, side-hinged, horizontal pivoting

WINDOWS

0505   Glass Venetian Blinds—Aluminum, Factory installed between glass; aluminum & wood

4326   All-Glass Storefronts—All-glass entrances, swinging, balanced, sliding types

4413   Glazed Aluminum Curtain Walls Aluminum glazed wall system for multi-story application; operable

5113   Aluminum Windows—Extruded aluminum; fixed or operable sash; glass & glazing hardware

5123   Steel Windows—Hot-rolled steel, commercial; formed steel, light commercial/ residential

5171   Custom Storm Windows—Custom aluminum storm windows

5200   Wood Windows—High quality, stock residential & commercial quality, wood windows

5313   Vinyl Interior Windows—High & low, quality residential & commercial quality PVC windows

5501   Hurricane Resistant Windows—Small & large-missile-impact rated windows

5654   Security & Detention Windows—Forced entry & ballistic resistance; with/without bars; with glazing

6200   Unit Skylights—Skylights with a plastic dome & aluminum perimeter frame

6223   Tubular Skylights—Residential & commercial reflective tube skylight

6300   Metal-Framed Skylights—Site-assembled aluminum skylight system, glass & plastic glazing

GLAZING

8000   Glazing—Glass & plastic glazing, using various glazing methods

8300   Mirrors—Glass & plastic mirrors; various attachments & glazing methods

8412   Cellular Plastic Glazing—Polycarbonate structured sheets & glazing systems

8713   Solar Control Films—V-Kool film with high performance plus high

8717   Safety & Security Glazing Films—Transparent plastic film for new/existing glazing: for safety glazing & blast proof

9100   Louvers—Operable, fixed, acoustical, vertical blade; with frame; blank-off panels

9200   Louvered Equipment Enclosures—Aluminum screens for concealing equipment, usually on rooftop

09 FINISHES, SEALANTS & ADHESIVES

FIBERGLASS

0515   Bullet-Resistant Fiberglass Panels—UL-listed bullet-resistant architectural panels

GYPSUM/PLASTER

2116   Gypsum Board Assemblies—Gypsum wallboard & other gypsum panel types, wall & ceiling framing

2216   Non-Structural Metal Framing—For interior partitions, ceilings; exterior non-wind-load resisting, non-load-bearing

2236.23 Metal Lath—For gypsum & Portland cement plaster; furring, ceiling framing

2300 Gypsum Plastering—Gypsum plaster interior finish: gypsum lath; trim accessories

2400 Portland Cement Plastering—Interior & exterior finish; stucco

2441 Exposed Aggregate Pool Finish

2613 Gypsum Veneer Plastering—Interior, maximum 1/4-in. thick; gypsum veneer base; trim accessories

2713 Glass-Fiber-Reinforced Plaster Fabrications—Standard & custom items

TILE/TILING

3000 Tiling—Floor & wall tile; generic accessory materials

3000 Ceramic, quarry & paver tile for floor, wall, base & stair tread

3001 Clay Tile & Stair Treads

3002 Slate Tile—Natural slate flooring, including setting materials

3005 The Setting Materials & Accessories—Setting & grouting products

3005 Tile Setting Materials & Methods—Mortars, grouts, underlayments, water-proofing, crack control

3005 Tile Setting Materials & Accessories—Mortars & grouts for ceramic tile, stone, porcelain, and the like

CEILINGS

5100 Acoustical Ceilings—Suspension system; metal grid, mineral fiber, metal-faced glass fiber panels

5114 Fabric-Faced Acoustical Ceilings—Fabric-faced, fiberglass suspended acoustical ceilings

5153 Direct-Applied Acoustical Ceilings—Mineral Fiber acoustic tile ceiling finish

5416 Luminous Ceilings—Suspension system, metal grid, translucent ceiling panels, painting ceiling

5423 Linear Metal Ceilings—Suspended, pre-finished, steel & aluminum ceiling & soffit systems

5800 Integrated Ceiling Assemblies—Suspension system, metal grid, acoustic panels, integral light fixtures, diffusers

FLOORING

6223 Bamboo Flooring—Solid & engineered bamboo plank flooring

6313 Brick Flooring—Industrial, decorative fired clay & shale brick; mortar set; interior

6340 Stone Flooring—Interior thin stone; mortar set or thin set; bases, thresholds, treads, and risers

6423   Wood Parquet Floors—Hardwood strip. Plank & parquet flooring, glued to substrate

6429   Wood Strip & Plank Flooring—Hardwood strip & plank, flooring nailed to the substrate, resilient cushion

6434   Engineered Wood Plank Flooring—Solid wood & engineered wood plank flooring

6500   Resilient Flooring—Vinyl, vinyl composition, rubber, composites; sheet, tile, base, stair treads & risers

6537   Static Control Flooring—ESD vinyl floor tile & liquid applied epoxy flooring

6566   Resilient Athletic Flooring—Fluid-applied polyurethane; rubber/vinyl sheet; interlocking, nonadhered

6613   Portland Cement Terrazzo Flooring—Cementations, ground & rustic; monolithic, sand cushion & bonded

6617   Resilient Terrazzo Tile—Marble & granite terrazzo tile

6623   Resinous Matrix Terrazzo Flooring—Interior, thin, bonded epoxy, polyacrylate/ Portland cement, or polyester

6700   Fluid-Applied Flooring—Fluid-applied flooring of any type, except ground plastic matrix terrazzo

6714   Resilient Urethane Flooring—Resilient, fluid-applied, polyurethane elastomeric, self-leveling flooring

6717   Concrete Floor Coatings—Epoxy & epoxy/urethane; coatings, aggregate-filled, thick mortars

6717   Floor Coatings—Epoxy & methyl methacrylate (acrylic); colored quartz

6800   Carpeting—Broadloom carpet; stretched-in & direct-blued; carpet cushion; trim

6813   Tile Carpeting—Carpet tile (modules); fully adhered or loose laid; matching roll carpet

6900   Access Flooring—Elevated, modular panels; support system; carpet, resilient, plastic laminate

WALLS

7200   Wall Coverings—Vinyl-coated fabric wall covering

7219   Textile Wall Coverings—Xorel & Xorel two fabrics for wall covering & upholstery

7744   Rustic Wall Terrazzo—Spray- and trowel-applied; epoxy, cementitious, or other synthetic matrix

8311   Acoustical Wall Systems—Fabric-covered walls, on-site instillation, minimal fabric seams & concealed seams

8400   Acoustic Room Components—Fabric-covered panels; back-mounted to walls or ceilings or as ceiling-hung

8411   Metal-Faced Acoustical Panels—Acoustic panels; steel, aluminum; wall, ceiling

8412   Acoustical Panels, Baffles, Diffusers, Reflectors—Wall panels, ceiling products, sound diffusers & reflectors

PAINTS/COATINGS

9000   Painting & Coating—Paints, stains, varnishes, urethanes & epoxy coatings

9000   Painting & Coating—Interior & exterior paints, stains & decorative coatings

9000   Painting & Coating—Paints, stains, varnishes, urethanes, epoxies & intumescent

9000   Painting & Coating—Paints, stains; on ordinary building surfaces, mechanical, electrical work

9000   Painting & Coating—Paints & stains for building surfaces, mechanical

9010   Exterior Painting & Staining—Paints & stains for common exterior substrates

9020   Interior Painting & Staining—Interior paints & stains

9200   Painting & Coating—Interior & exterior paints, stains & decorative coatings

9300   Staining & Transparent Finishing—Stains, transparent finishes & maintenance products

9300   Staining & Transparent Finishing—Wood stains, protective coatings & repair products

9600   High-Performance Coatings—Fluid-applied coatings for durability, chemical resistance, corrosion resistance

9600   High-Performance Coatings—Interior & exterior coatings for severe & moderate exposure

9600   High-Performance Coatings

9600   High-Performance Coatings—Epoxy/urethane, acrylic/epoxy, alkalyd, aggregate-filled

9726   Cementitious Coatings—Spray deck textured coatings

10 SPECIALTIES

1101   Visual Display Boards—Chalkboards, markerboards, tackboards, aluminum & wood frames

124   Tackable Wall Systems—Fabric-covered walls, on-site installation, minimal fabric seams

1424   Plastic Signage—Door & wall signs; individual characters; no frames

1425   Door & Room Signs

2113.13   Metal Toilet Compartments—Baked enamel, porcelain enamel, stainless steel; floor-, wall-, ceiling-mounted

2113.16   Plastic-Laminate-Clad Toilet Compartments—High-pressure laminate veneered; floor-, wall-, ceiling-mounted

2113.19   Plastic Toilet Compartments—No veneer; floor-, wall-, ceiling-mounted; urinal compartments

2123   Cubicles—Curtains & overhead track; light-duty

2213   Wire Mesh Partitions—Steel, stainless steel, aluminum, woven or expanded metal; doors, hardware

2214 Wire Mesh Partitions & Railings—Partitions, industrial barriers, mezzanine railings

2216 Folding Gates—Folding, pantographic action steel gates

2219 Demountable Partitions—Reusable, modular components; door frames, insulation, wall covering

2226.13 Accordion Folding Partitions—Acoustic & non-acoustic type; manual & electric; overhead track

2226.33 Folding Panel Partitions—Folding panel; sliding panel, acoustical or fire-rated; manual or motorized

2601 Wall & Corner Guards—Corner guards, bumper rails, corridor hand rails; PVC, stainless steel, wood

2613 Corner Guards

2617 Handrails

2618 Wall Guards

2624 High-Impact Wall Covering—Acrylic/PVC alloy wall covering panels & trim

2800 Toilet, Bath & Laundry Accessories—Toilet room, shower & tub, residential bath & utility room accessories

2813 Toilet Accessories

2814 Electric Hand Dryers

3100 Manufactured Fireplaces—Steel cabinet; fireplace; chimney; optional doors, screens & accessories

3101 Gas-Burning Fireplaces & Stoves—Wood-burning & gas fireplaces & stoves

4400 Fire Protection Specialties—Extinguishers; cabinets; mounting hardware; fire blankets

5100 Lockers—Steel wardrobe lockers, benches, locks

5113 Wire Mesh Storage Lockers

5127 Polyethylene Lockers—High-density polyethylene lockers; locker benches

5523 Mail Boxes—Indoor & outdoor mail boxes

5523 Mail Boxes—Multiple mail boxes; interior & exterior

5591 Mail Chutes—Repair of existing mail chutes only

5613 Metal Storage Shelving—Four post, cass-type, cantilever style; freestanding or fixed

5617 Wall Mounted Standards & Shelving—Residential & commercial; wood, glass, laminate

5623 Wine Storage Shelving—Coated wire closet shelving; laminate shelves

5626 Mobile Storage Shelving—Electronic, mechanically operated & manual

7113 Exterior Sun Control Devices—Rolling sunscreen & blackout/room darkening shades; exterior & interior

7113.13 Exterior Shutters—Louvered, accordion-folding, roll-up, removable storm panels

7113.19   Rolling Exterior Shutters—Roller shutters, rolling shutters of aluminum & PVC

7121   Coiling Insect Screens—Vinyl-covered woven fiberglass mesh; motorized or manual

7300   Protective Covers—Pre-engineered walkway covers

7313   Awnings—Fixed awnings; standard or custom shale; aluminum or steel pipe or tube

7424   Prefabricated Steeple & Cupola—Prefabricated aluminum steeples & cupolas

7500   Flagpoles—Steel, aluminum, stainless steel, bronze, fiberglass; manual & electric

8113   Bird Control Devices—Stainless steel needles strips for bird control

11 EQUIPMENT

1200   Parking Control Equipment—Gates; vehicle detection; ticket, card, coin, or remote controlled access

1234   Vehicle Gates & Operators—swing-up arm gates, operators for overhead, swinging

1313   Loading Dock Bumpers—Rubber, molded or laminate, reinforced; steel frame and joiners, anchor

1316   Loading Dock Seals & Shelters

1319.13   Loading Dock Levelers—Mechanical vehicle safety restrains

3100   Residential Appliances—Residential kitchen & laundry appliances

4000   Foodservice Equipment—General specification requirements

4001   Custom-Fabricated Foodservice Equipment—Fixed stainless steel furniture & sinks

5213   Projection Screens—Front & rear projection screens; wall, ceiling & frame mounted

5300   Laboratory Equipment—General specification requirements

5313   Laboratory Fume Hoods—Bypass fume hoods in casework-compatible styles

5314   Self-Contained Filtered Laboratory Enclosures

5335   Laboratory Glassware Washer/Dryers

5353   Biological Safety Cabinets

6614   Swimsuit Water Extractors

6623   Gymnasium Equipment—Indoor basketball goals; wall-mounted exercise equipment; movable equipment

6813   Playground Equipment—Outdoor play structures for schools & parks

8227   Waste Compactors—Packaged commercial waste compactors; not shredders or pulping machines

12 FURNISHINGS

2113   Horizontal Louver Blinds—Steel, aluminum, or wood; with lifting cord and cord or wand tilting slats

2216   Drapery Track & Accessories—Formed steel or extruded aluminum; manual or electrically operated

2413   Roller Window Shades—Motorized & manual window coverings and black-out systems

3100   Manufactured Metal Casework—Factory-fabricated, commercial or institutional quality; countertops

3530   Residential Casework—Factory-fabricated modular particleboard; plastic laminate, wood veneer

3600   Countertops—Plastic laminate, solid surfacing, laminated wood, tile, stone, stainless steel

4813   Entrance Floor Mats & Frames—Surface & recessed; carpet, vinyl link, rubber link, and cocoa types

4816   Entrance Floor Grilles—Entrance grates & mats

5191   Mailroom Furniture—Mail receiving, sorting, distribution components

6100   Fixed Audience Seating—Upholstered & non upholstered interior seating, one-piece & with folding seats

6613   Telescoping Bleachers—Wood, molded plastic, or extruded aluminum seats

13 SPECIAL CONSTRUCTION

1100   Swimming Pools—Shotcrete, or modular aluminum, or fiberglass; accessories

1713   Hot Tubs—Shop-fabricated site-assembled or site-constructed; decking; equipment

2126   Cold Storage Rooms—Modular, prefabricated insulated wall/ceiling panels; floor; doors

2426   Saunas—Shop-fabricated site-assembled or site-constructed; room enclosure

2426   Steam Baths—Shop-fabricated site-assembled or site-constructed; wood finish; equipment

2600   Fabricated Rooms—Wall systems and equipment, for interior use

3100   Fabric Structures—Fabric structures supported by rigid structures & cables; design-build

3413.16 Solariums—Patio enclosures; glazed aluminum framed, curved & straight eaves

3416   Grandstands & Bleachers—Pre-engineered aluminum, permanent & temporary

3419   Metal Building Systems—Standard packaged steel; buildings; frame, metal panels, installation, doors

3421   Site & Street Shelters—Metal roofed gazebos, shelters, kiosks, toilet systems

4905   X-Ray Radiation Protection—Medical diagnostic only; sheet lead; doors, windows, film transfer cabinets

4941 RFI/EM Shielding—Custom, architecturally integrated RFI & electromagnetic shielding

4942 Modular RF/EM Shielded Rooms—Modular rooms for radio frequency interference & electromagnetic

14 CONVEYING EQUIPMENT

ELEVATORS, ESCALATORS & DUMBWAITERS

1100 Manual Dumbwaiters—Hand-operated dumbwaiters

1200 Electric Dumbwaiters—Electric; drum or traction drive; standard manufactured units

2010 Passenger Elevators—Geared & gearless electric traction; conventional hydraulic & holeless

2020 Freight Elevators—Electric & Hydraulic freight elevators; standard manufactured units

2030 Residential Elevators—Residential electric drum & hydraulic

2705 Custom Elevator Cabs & Hoistway Doors

2817 Passenger Elevator Control Systems

2819 Elevator Equipment

3100 Escalators—Standard packaged escalators; glass & solid balustrades; 30 degree incline

9100 Facility Chutes—Gravity chutes for waste, linen & recyclables

SCAFFOLDS/SCAFFOLDING

8400 Powered Scaffolding

8400 Powered Scaffolding—Davits, platforms, safety anchors & other equipment

FACILITY SERVICES

21 FIRE SUPPRESSION

0500 Common Work Results for Fire Suppression—Pipe materials, fittings & valves for liquid fire protection

0513 Common Motor Requirements for Fire Suppression—Electric motors & accessories for fire suppression

0530 Retrofit-Sprinkler Piping Cover System

0548 Vibration & Seismic Controls for Fire Suppression—Inertia bases & vibration isolators for equipment

0553 Identification for Fire Suppression Piping & Equipment—Nameplates, labels; piping identification

0719 Fire Suppression Piping Insulation—Thermal insulation; jackets; accessories

1200 Fire-Suppression Standpipes—Wet or dry standpipes; fire hose cabinets & hose

1300   Fire-Suppression Sprinkler Systems—Automatic systems

2200   Clean-Agent Fire Extinguishing System—Detection, controls & flame extinguishing agent storage/distribution

3000   Fire Pumps—Electric motor & diesel engine drivers; electric jockey pumps

22 PLUMBING

0513   Common Motor Requirements for Pluming Equipment—Electric motors & accessories

0516   Expansion Fittings & Loops for Plumbing Piping—Fittings & practices to compensate for thermal expansion

0519   Meters & Gages for Plumbing Piping—Fixed measuring devices showing local indication of condition

0524   Thermostatic Water Mixing Valves—Water temperature controls

0531   Non-Penetrating, Port, Rooftop Supports & Walkways

0531   Non-Penetrating Rooftop Hangers & Supports—Pipe hangers, conduit hangers & struts, duct/equipment

0548   Vibration & Seismic Controls for Plumbing Piping—Inertia bases, vibration isolators, seismic restraints for Rotary/reciprocating equipment

0553   Identification for Pluming Piping & Equipment—Field-installed name plates, labels; piping identification

0554   Piping & Valve Identification—Markers, stencils, valve tags & valve chart

0716   Plumbing Equipment Insulation—Thermal insulation; jackets; accessories

0171   Piping Safety Covers—Piping safety covers & under sink enclosures for lavatories

0179   Plumbing Piping Insulation—Thermal insulation; jackets; accessories

1005   Plumbing Piping—Soil, waste, vent, domestic water, storm water & natural gas piping

1006   Plumbing Piping Specialties—Roof & floor drains; cleanouts; hose bibs; hydrants, backflow prevention

1500   General-Service Compressed Air Systems—Non-medical; pipe & pipe fittings; compressors; equipment

3000   Plumbing Equipment—water heaters; heat exchangers; storage tanks; pumps for plumbing systems

4000   Plumbing Fixtures—Representative examples of plumbing fixtures & trim

4120   Prefabricated Tubs & Showers—Fiberglass tubs & showers; acrylic & gel coat finishes

4205   Restroom Plumbing Fixtures—Toilets, urinals, lavatories & faucets

4205   Restroom Toilets, Urinals & Faucets—Pressure assist toilets, urinals, flush valves, faucets

4233   Restroom Lavatories—Soiled surface lavatory systems

4300   Healthcare Plumbing Fixtures—Fixtures especially designed for medical & psychiatric facilities

5100 Swimming Pool Plumbing Systems—Piping & equipment normally installed by a single installer

6005 Medical Air, Gas & Vacuum Systems—Most common medial gas systems & components; specialized outlets

23 HEATING, VENTILATING & AIR CONDITIONING

0513 Common Motor Requirements for HVAC Equipment—Electric motors & accessories for HVAC systems

0516 Expansion Fittings & Loops of HVAC/Piping—Fittings & practices to compensate for thermal expansion

0519 Meters & Gages for HVAC Piping—Fixed measuring devices showing local indication of conditions

0548 Vibrating/Seismic Controls for HVAC Piping & Equipment—Inertia bases & vibration indicators for rotary & reciprocating equipment

0553 Identification for HVAC Piping & Equipment—Field-installed nameplates, labels; piping identification

0593 Testing, Adjusting & Balancing for HVAC—Air & water systems testing, adjusting & balancing

0713 Duct Insulation—Thermal & acoustic insulation; jackets; for ducts & air handling devices

0716 HVAC Equipment Insulation—Thermal insulation; jackets; accessories

0719 HVAC Piping Insulation—Thermal insulation; jackets; accessories

0913 Instrumentation & Control Devices for HVAC—Devices normally found in pneumatic, digital & electric control systems

0914 Thermostats—Digital, multistage/heat pump commercial thermostats

0923 Direct-Digital Control System for HVAC—Components & software for a direct digital HVAC control system

0943 Pneumatic Control System for HVAC—All types of devices normally; complete pneumatic control system

0993 Sequence of Operations for HVAC Controls—Used for the description of overall operation, coordinating all HVAC operations

1113 Facility Fuel-oil Piping—Tanks, piping, fittings, pumps & valves

2113 Hydronic Piping—Heating, glycol, chilled water, condenser water & engine exhaust piping

2113-39 Ground-Loop Heat-Pump Piping—Polyethylene piping for water/other solutions; copper (refrigerant) piping

25 INTEGRATED AUTOMATION

26 ELECTRICAL

0501 Minor Electrical Demolition—Removal & abandonment of wiring, conduit & equipment

0513 Low-Voltage Electric Power Conductors & Cables—Wire & cable with insalivations rated 600 V & less

0520   Undercarpet Cables—Flat conductor cable & fittings for power, communication & data circuits

0521   Manufactured Wiring Assemblies—Prefabricated flexible wiring assemblies for branch circuit distribution

0526   Grounding & Bonding for Electrical Systems—Basic materials & methods; for electrical systems, building structures

0529   Hangers & Supports for Electrical Systems—Straps, clamps, steel channel & fastening hardware for supporting

0534   Conduit—Metal & nonmetallic electrical conduit & tubing

0535   Surface Raceways—Metal & nonmetal raceways, multi-outlet assemblies, wireways & wall

0535.11   Surface Metallic Raceways—Surface metallic raceways system

0535.12   Surface Nonmetallic Raceways—Raceways for voice, data, video, branch circuit & other low voltage equipment

0535.12   Surface Nonmetallic Raceways—Surface-mounted nonmetallic raceway systems

0536   Cable Trays for Electrical Systems—Metal & fiberglass cable trays

0537   Boxes—Wall & ceiling outlet boxes, floor boxes, pull & junction boxes

0540   Underfloor Ducts—Underfloor duct, fittings & accessories; installation of wire and cable

0553   Identification for Electrical Systems—Field-installed nameplates, labels, etc. for equipment, components & wiring

0573   Overcurrent Protective Device Coordination Study—Performance requirements & short circuit & coordination study

0914   Electrical Power Monitoring—Instrument transformer, switches, relays, transducers & meters

0915   Peak Load Controllers—Standalone controllers that sense power demand; for alarm or load shedding

0916   Electric Controls & Relays—Switches, pushbuttons, relays, timers, counters, control power transformers

0917   Programmable Controllers—Controllers & programming accessories

0918   Remote Control Switching Devices—Low voltage control of 120 v & 277 v lighting & general purpose branch

0919   Enclosed Contactors—For feeders & branch circuits for lighting, heating & general purpose

SUBSTATIONS, TRANSFORMERS & SWITCHGEAR

1116   Secondary Unit Substations—Secondary unit substations; primary voltage to 34.5 kV; low-voltage

1200   Medium-Voltage Transformers—Liquid-filled; dry-type; primary 2 kV to 34.5 kV; secondary 600 V

1300 Medium-Voltage Switchgear—Switchgear rated 2 kV to 15 kV; air-magnetic & vacuum interrupter circuit

1321 Air Interrupter Switches—Air-brake type interrupter switches for medium-voltage applications, 34.5 kV

1322 Medium-Voltage Oil Switches—For applications at 34.5 kV and less

1839 Medium-Voltage Motor Controllers—NEMA Class E2 controllers, rated 6.6 kV or less; fused

2101 Overhead Line Materials—Enclosed for lighting & power loads' primary/secondary voltage 600 V

2200 Low-Voltage Transformers—Enclosed circuit breaker & fusible switch types; for service & distribution

2413 Switchboards -Enclosed circuit breaker & fusible switch types; for service & distribution

2416 Panelboards—Fusible switch & circuit breaker types; switches & breakers; load centers

2419 Motor-Control Centers—Enclosures; automatic controllers for AC introduction motor; disconnects

2501 Feeder & Plug-in Busway—Rated 150 amperes to 5,000 amperes. 600 volts and less

2600 Power Distribution Units—Unit power conditioning equipment for electronic data processing installation

2701 Electrical Service Entrance—Incoming 600 volts or less, equipment & metering

ACCESSORIES

2716 Electrical Cabinets & Enclosures—Metal cabinets & enclosures for terminal blocks & electrical devices

2717 Equipment Wiring—Connections for mechanical, architectural & other equipment

2723 Indoor Service Poles—Freestanding indoor utility columns for power, telephone & data outlets

2726 Wiring Devices—Receptacles, wall switches, dimmers, telephone jacks & access floor boxes

2813 Fuses—Fuses for use in low voltage power distribution circuits

2817 Enclosed Circuit Breakers—Molded case circuit breakers; trip units; current limiters; enclosures

2818 Enclosed Switches—For use as disconnects in service & distribution systems rated 600 volts and less

2913 Enclosed Controllers—Manual & automatic controllers for AC induction motors

2923 Variable-Frequency Motor Controllers—Three-phase motor controllers of the pulse-width-modulated design

POWER GENERATION

3213 Engine generators—Complete generator set for emergency & standby power

3229 Rotary Converters—AC to DC converters, AC frequency changers & single-to three-phase

3233 Rotary Uninterruptible Power Units—Converters & frequency changers with energy storage: for computers, etc.

3305 Battery Emergency Power Supply—Small battery & inverter power supply (generally under 10 kVA)

3353 Static Uninterruptible Power Supply—Larger than 10 kVA, but under 300 kVA

3613 Capacitors—Unit capacitors, assemblies, automatically-switched capacitors; 600 volts and less

3800 Transfer Switches—Automatic & manual transfer & bypass isolation switches; 600 volts & less

PROTECTIVE DEVICES

4113 Lightning Protection for Structures—UL-listed or LPI-certified, or both; air terminals, conductors, grounding

4200 Cathodic Protection—Passive, underground corrosion protection using sacrificial anodes

LIGHTING

5100 Interior Lighting—Luiminaires, emergency lighting units, exit signs, and luminaire accessories

5537 Obstruction & Landing Lights—FAA-required building marking; helicopter port landing lights

5561 Theatrical Lights—Lighting fixtures; dimming & control equipment & accessories

5600 Exterior Lighting—Luminaires, poles & accessories

27 COMMUNICATIONS

1005 Structured Cabling for Voice/Data-Inside-Plant—Copper/fiber optic; outlets, patch panels, & service entrance

5117 Public Address Systems—Speakers, amplifiers, players, cable; for paging, announcements, & background

5124 Video Surveillance—Closed circuit television equipment & accessories for security monitoring

5132 Television Systems—Annunciator & intercom equipment; call stations; master stations

5314 Clock Systems—Systems for announcing & recording time intervals

28 ELECTRONIC SAFETY & SECURITY

1300 Access Control—Devices & electronic systems for controlling access to buildings

1600 Intrusion Detection—Detectors & alarm devices & systems to detect intrusion

2300   Video Surveillance—Closed circuit television equipment & accessories for security monitoring

3100   Fire Detection & Alarm—Addressable & conventional; NFPA 72; design & installation

3105   Fire Alarm System Equipment—Fire alarm control panels, sensors, stations & related equipment

SITE & INFRASTRUCTURE

31 EARTHWORK

0916.21   Pile Load Tests—Pile Load testing requirements for one or more of the piling sections

1000   Site Clearing—Vegetation clearing & protection; removal of existing debris & trash

2200   Grading—Topsoil removal, rough & finish grading, topsoil placement & grading

2316   Excavation—Basic excavating for foundations, slab-on-grade, & building utilities

2316.13   Trenching—Excavating, bedding & backfilling for site utilities

2316.26   Rock Removal—Mechanical or explosive removal of subsurface rock during excavation

2323   Fill—Basic filling & backfilling for foundations, slabs-on-grade & utilities

3116   Termite Control—Chemical treatment to control subterranean termites and other insects

3213.16   Cement Soil Stabilization—Treatment of subsoil with cement for physical stability prior to construction

3213.19   Lime Soil Stabilization—Treatment of subsoil with lime for physical stability prior to construction

3700   Riprap—Loose stone or bagged aggregate for soil stabilization & slope protection

6213.19   Precast Concrete Piles—Driven prestressed concrete piles, with or without steel points, connecting

6213.26   Pressure Injected Footings—Concrete footings, compacted in place to form an expanded bulbous base

6216.13   Sheet Steel Piles—Permanent earth retaining structures; caissons, quaywalls & retaining walls

6216.16   Steel H-Piles—Driven H-section steel piles, with protective coatings

6219   Timber Piles—Driven wood friction piles, with or without preservative treatment

6223.13   Concrete-Filled Steel Piles—Concrete-filled steel pipe piles, with or without conical tip, & bearing type

6316 Auger Cast Grout Piles—Made by injecting concrete grout through hollow auger shaft while

6329 Drilled Concrete Piers & Shafts—End bearing & friction type cast-in-place concrete piers in bored shafts

32 EXTERIOR IMPROVEMENTS

0116.74 In-Place Hot Reused Asphalt Paving—Milling or heating & removing, remixing & replacing existing asphalt

0120 Preparation for Resurfacing Concrete Pavements—Preparation of existing concrete pavements for new asphalt or concrete

0190 Operation & Maintenance of Planting—Turf, shrubs, trees, ground cover; during establishment period or longer

1123 Aggregate Base Courses—Aggregate base course for placement under asphalt or concrete pavements

1216 Asphalt Paving—Bituminous concrete for roads, parking areas, or sidewalks

1313 Concrete Paving—Concrete roads, parking areas, sidewalks, median barriers, & integral curbs

1413 Precast Concrete Unit Painting—Various types of concrete pavers for exterior dry installation on sand bed

1416 Brick Unit Paving—Clay brick pavers, primarily for exterior use, with various setting methods

1423 Asphalt Unit Paving—Manufactured asphalt block & plank pavers; asphalt adhesive bed

1440 Stone Paving—Marble, granite, or slate pavers for exterior installation on sand bed or mortar

1443 Porous Unit Paving—Plastic rings for gravel fill

1713 Parking Bumpers—Precast concrete & wood; also curbs; on asphalt & concrete pavements

1729.13 Painted Pavement Markings—Lines & symbols for parking lots, roadways, curbs

1731 Steel Guardrail—Formed steel guardrail on steel or timber posts; for vehicle barriers

1816.13 Playground Protective Surfacing—For the ground under outdoor play structures for schools & parks

3113 Chain Link Fences & Gates—Fences, manually operated gates; exterior post foundation

3223 Segmented Retaining Walls—Modula concrete units; geotextile soil reinforcement

3226 Metal Crib Retaining Walls—Earth-filled wire mesh facing

8423 Underground Sprinklers—Pipe underground system; piping, sprinkler heads, valves & controls

9291 Seeding—Seeding of lawns; can cover re-seeding

9223   Sodding—Sod for lawns, including installation & maintenance until acceptance

9300   Plants—Trees, bushes, vines & ground covers; topsoil & soil preparation

33 UTILITIES

0513   Manholes & Structures—Precast, cast-in-place, FRP & masonry shaft construction & covers

1116   Site Water Utility Distribution Piping—Pipe materials, fittings & valves for systems between building &

1300   Disinfecting of Water Utility Distribution—Disinfection of domestic site water services, utility supply & water wells

1613   Aboveground Water Utility Storage Tanks—Elevated & surface-mounted; steel, concrete; for domestic & fire water

2100   Water Supply Wells—Drilling a water well, casing & grouting, pump & accessories

3111   Site Sanitary Utility Sewerage Piping—Gravity sanitary drain piping from building to sewer

3600   Utility Sewer Tanks—Septic tank, distribution box & filter drainage field system

4111   Site Storm Utility Drainage Piping—Gravity storm drainage from building & from paved & landscaped areas

4213   Pipe Culverts—Corrugated steel & concrete pipe culvert & accessories

4600   Subdrainage—Weep tile drainage system, including filter aggregate & filter fabric

4613   Combination Foundation Drainage, Radon Venting—Perimeter drainage, radon evacuation, & footing

4924   Underground Storm Water Retention Chamber—Load-bearing plastic structure

5111   Site Natural-Gas Distribution—Pipe materials, fittings & valves for natural propane gas systems

7116.33   Wood Electrical Utility Poles—Wood poles & accessories for overhead site wire services

7119   Electrical Underground Ducts & Manholes—Concrete-encased conduit & duct; concrete manholes

7900   Site Grounding—Grounding grids, loops & other site-related grounding systems

PROCESS EQUIPMENT

40 PROCESS INTEGRATION

0100   Operation & Maintenance of Process Integration

1000   Gas & Vapor Process Piping

1100   Steam Process Piping

1400   Fuel Gas Process Piping

1500	Combustion System
1700	Welding & Cutting Gases Piping
1800	Vacuum Systems Process Piping
2000	Liquids Process Piping
2100	Liquid Fuel Process Piping
2300	Water Processing
2400	Specialty Liquid Chemical Piping
3000	Solid & Mixed Materials Piping & Chutes
3200	Bulk Materials Piping & Chutes
3300	Bulk Materials Valves
3400	Pneumatic Conveying Lines
4000	Process Piping & Equipment Protection
4100	Process Piping & Equipment Heat Tracing
4200	Process Piping & Equipment Insulation
4600	Process Corrosion Protection
4700	Refractories
4090	Instrumentation & Control for Process Systems
4091	Primary Process Measurement Devices
4092	Primary Control Devices
4093	Analog Controllers/Recorders
4094	Digital Process Controller
4095	Process Control Hardware
4096	Process Control Software
4097	Process Control Auxiliary Devices

41 MATERIAL PROCESSING & HANDLING EQUIPMENT

0100	Operation & Maintenance of Material Processing &Handling Equipment
0800	Commissioning of Material Processing & Handling Equipment
1000	Bulk Material Processing Equipment
1100	Bulk Material Sizing Equipment
1200	Bulk Material Conveying Equipment
1300	Bulk Material Feeders
1400	Batching Equipment
2000	Piece Material Handling Equipment
2100	Conveyors
2200	Cranes & Hoists
2300	Lifting Devices
2400	Special Material Handling Equipment
3000	Manufacturing Equipment

3100   Manufacture Lines & Equipment

4000   Containers Processing & Sealing

4132   Forming Equipment

4133   Machining Equipment

4134   Finishing Equipment

4135   Dies & Molds

4136   Assembly & Testing Equipment

5000   Material Storage

5100   Automatic Material Storage

5200   Bulk Material Storage

5300   Storage Equipment & Systems

6000   Mobile Plant Equipment

6100   Mobile Earth Moving Equipment

6400   Rail Vehicles

6500   Mobile Support Equipment

6600   Miscellaneous Mobile Equipment

6700   Plant Maintenance Equipment

44 POLLUTION CONTROL EQUIPMENT

0100   Operation & Maintenance of Pollution Control Equipment

1000   Air Pollution Control Equipment

2000   Noise Pollution Control Equipment

4000   Water Treatment Equipment

5000   Solid Waste Control

48 ELECTRICAL POWER GENERATION

0100   Operation & Maintenance for Electric Power Generation

0800   Commissioning of Electric Power Generation

1000   Instrumentation & Control for Electric Power Generation

1100   Fossil Fuel Plant Electric Power Generation Equipment

1200   Nuclear Fuel Plant Electric Power Generation Equipment

1300   Hydroelectric Plant Electric power Generating Equipment

1400   Solar Energy Electric Power Generation Equipment

1500   Wind Energy Electric Power Generation Equipment

1600   Electrochemical Electric Power Generating Equipment

1700   Fuel Cell Power Generation Equipment

1900   Electric Power Control Equipment

7000   Electric Power Generation Testing

7100   Electric Power Generation Test Equipment

5

Government Regulations

FEDERAL ACTS & LAWS

Asbestos Hazard Emergency Response Act—1986
Public Law 99-519
100 Stat. 643-42 USC 2647

Asbestos

Endangered Species Act Amendments—1982
Public Law 97-424
96 Stat. 1412-1415
16 USC 1533, 1536

Endangered Species

Endangered Species Act—1978
Public Law 95-632
Stat. 3751-16 USC 1531

Endangered Species Act—1973; Amendments—1976
Public Law 94-359
90 Stat. 911
16 USC 1533 (f) (2) (B) (ii)

Endangered Species Act—1973
Public Law 93-203
87 Stat. 355
29 USC 773; 29 USC 780

Energy Policy & Conservation Act—1990
Public Law 101-383

Energy Conservation

National Appliance Energy Conservation Act—1987
Public Law 100-12

Emergency Conservation Act—1979
Public Law 96-102
93 Stat. 757
42 USC 8511, 8512, 8521

National Energy Conservation Policy Act—1978
Public Law 95-619
92 Stat 3206-41 USC 8201

Department of Energy Organization Act—1977
Public Law 95-91
91 Stat. 565-42 USC 7101

Federal Energy Administration Authorization Act—1977
Public Law 95-70
91 Stat. 275-15 USC 7101

Energy Conservation & Production Act—1976
Public Law 94-385
90 Stat. 1125-42 USC 6891

Energy Policy

Energy Policy & Conservation Act—1990
Public Law 101-383

Department of Energy Act—1977
Civilian Applications
Public Law 95-238-92 Stat. 47

Federal Energy Administration Act—1974
Public Law 93-275
88 Stat. 101-15 USC 766

Environmental Protection

Compensation & Liability Act—1980
(Comprehensive Environmental Response)
Public Law 96-510
94 Stat. 2785-42 USC 9608

Fasteners

Industrial Fasteners Act—1990
Public Law 101-592

Fire Protection/ Prevention

Hotel & Motel Fire Safety Act—1990
Public Law 101-391

Federal Fire Prevention & Control Act—1974
Public Law 93-498
88 Stat. 1548-15 USC 22218

Hazardous & Solid Wastes

The Hazardous & Solid Waste Amendments—1984
Public Law 98-616
98 Stat. 3232; Stat. 3251
42 USC 6924; 42 USC 6921

Solid Waste Disposal Act—1980
Public Law 96-482
94 Stat. 2336-16 USC 6921

Solid Waste Disposal—1970
84 Stat. 1232-42 USC 1051

Historic Preservation

Historic Sites, Buildings & Antiquities Act—1985
Public Law 96-344
94 Stat. 1133-16 USC 461

National Historic Preservation Act Amendments—1980
Public Law 96-515
94 Stat. 2988-42 USC 470a

Historic Sites & National Monuments—1974

Public Law 93-477

88 Stat. 1420

16 USC 495g-2

Housing & Urban Development Reform Act (HUD)—1989 **Housing**

Public Law 101-235 (1989)

Emergency Housing Act—1975

Public Law 94-50

89 Stat. 249-12 USC 2701

Housing & Community Development Act—1974

Public Law 93-383

88 Stat. 663, 703, 711

42 USC 1437f, 5406, 5414

Noise Control—1977 **Noise Control**

86 Stat. 1234

42 USC 4903

Environmental Pesticide Act—1973 **Pesticides**

86 Stat. 973

7 USC 136s

Water Quality Act—1987 **Pollution**

Public Law 100-4 **Control**

101 Stat. 40; 101 Stat. 47

33 USC 1314; 33 USC 1319

Clean Air Act Amendments—1977

Public Law 95-95

91 Stat. 685

42 USC 7401

Clean Water Act—1977

Public Law 96-217

91 Stat. 1566

22 USC 1251

Air Pollution—1970

84 Stat. 1679, 1696, 1699, 1702

42 USC 1857c-3, 1857f-6c, 1857f-6e

Safety & Health Standards—1970 **Safety & Health**

84 Stat. 1594, 1596, 1597

19 USC 655 (1970)

Transportation

Federal Public Transportation Act—1982
Public Law 97-424
96 Stat. 2153
49 USC 1612

Water Resources

Coastal Barriers Improvement Act—1990
Public Law 101-591

Water Resources Development Act—1988
Public Law 100-675

Water Resources Development Act—1986
Public Law 99-662
100 Stat. 4087; 100 Stat. 4101
100 Stat. 4104; 100 Stat. 4204
33 USC 2214; 33 USC 2233
33 USC 2236; 33 USC 579a

Safe Drinking Water Act Amendments—1986
Public Law 99-339
100 Stat. 643, 646
42 USC 300g-1

Water Resources Development & Preservation Act—1974
Public Law 92-251
88 Stat. 43
16 USC 460ee

Flood Disaster Protection Act—1973
Public Law 92-203
87 Stat. 975
42 USC 4104

CONSTRUCTION CRITERIA BASE

National Institute of Building Sciences (NIBS)
Washington, DC
Publishes:
Four-disc system containing the complete specifications of all US government agencies.

Disc A

Army Corps of Engineers (COE)
    Civil Works Guide Specifications
    Construction Guide Specifications
Department of Energy (DOE)
    General Design Criteria Manual

Department of Veterans Affairs (VA)
    Master Specifications
Federal Aviation Administration (FAA)
    Construction Specifications
General Services Administration (GSA)
    Master Specifications
National Aeronautics & Space Administration (NASA)
    Detailed Specifications
    KSC-Local Master Specifications
    ARC-Local Master Specifications
National Institute of Health (NIH)
    Specifications
Naval Facilities Engineering Command (NAVFAC)
    Guide Specifications
    Regional Guide Specifications
Single Master Reference
    NAVFAC, COE, NASA
Water & Power Resources Service (WPRS)
    (Formerly Bureau of Reclamation)
    Standard Specifications
SPECSINTACT
Architectural & Transportation Barriers
    Access Board (ATBCB)
    Uniform Federal Accessibility Standards
    Minimum Guidelines/Requirements for
    Accessible Design (Part 1190)
    Americans with Disabilities Act-1990
BCMC-Proposed Model Code for People with
Physical Disabilities
Department of Energy (DOE)
    Energy Performance Standards (Title 10, Part 435)
    Envelope Compliance Program & User Manual
Environmental Protection Agency (EPA)
    Asbestos Standards (Title 40, Part 763)
    Hazardous Waste Management Regulations
    (Title 40, Parts 260, 261, 263, 264 & 266)
Federal Acquisition Regulations Systems (FARS)
    Federal Acquisition Regulations for:

Disc B

Department of the Army

Department of the Navy

Department of the Air Force

Department of Defense

Department of Veterans Affairs

General Services Administration

National Aeronautics & Space Administration

Occupational Safety & Health Administration (OSHA)

Occupational Safety & Health Standards

Occupational Safety & Health Regulations for:

Construction

Longshoring

Marine Terminals

Shipyard Employment

Referenced Fed/Mil Specifications

Referenced Private Industry Standards (150 Organizations)

Building/Mechanical/Plumbing/Fire Prevention Codes

Disc C

Army Corps of Engineers (COE)

M-CAES Cost Estimating System

CADD Symbols

CADD Manuals

MIL-HDBK-1021

Airfield Rigid Pavement Design Software

Naval Facilities Command (NAVFAC)

CADD Symbols

Cost Engineering System

Value Engineering System

Disc D

Air Force-*USAF*

Manuals

Procedures

Regulations

Technical Letters

Corps of Engineers (USCOE)

Architectural & Engineering Instructions

Engineering Manuals

Engineering Regulations

Engineering Technical Letters

Department of Defense (DOE)
    MIL HDBK-1190-Series Facility
    Planning & Design Guide
General Services Administration (GSA)
    Design Manual: Facility Standards for the
        Public Building Service
Military Criteria Indices
Naval Facilities Engineering Command (NAVFAC)
    Design Manuals
    Design Policy Letters
    MIL-BUL-34 Engineering & Design Criteria
    MIL-BUL-35 Matrix of Guide Specifications
    MIL Standard 1691 Series
    Cost Engineering System
    MIL Standard 1691 Schedule for Medical/Dental Facilities
National Institute of Building Sciences (NIBS)
    Directory of Online Construction Databases
    Wood Protection Guidelines
National Institute of Standards & Technology (NIST)
    Standards Associations Listing

DOCUMENT DISTRIBUTORS

Library of Congress (LOC)
Codes & Standards Section
101 Independence Avenue
Washington, DC 20540
Tel: (202) 707-5655
Contact: Jim Scala, Staff Specialist
National Technical Information Service/DOC (NTIS)
5285 Port Royal Road
Springfield, VA 22161
Tel: (703) 605-6515
Fax: (703) 605-6742
Web: *www. ntis.gov*
Contact: Office of Product Management

Standardization Document Order Desk (LOC)

(Replaced Naval Publications & Forms Center)

Building 4, Section D

700 Robins Avenue

Philadelphia, PA 19111-5094

Tel: (215) 697-2667

Web: *www.loc.gov*

Contact: George Caldwell

US Government Printing Office (GPO)

732 N Capitol Street NW

Washington, DC 20401

Tel: (202) 572-0000

Web: *www.gpo.gov*

Contact: Superintendent of Documents

RESEARCH & DEVELOPMENT

Hundreds of US government agencies, as well as a vast network of engineering and scientific organizations maintained or supported by the federal government, engage in research and development (R&D) generating a vast amount of information on engineering, design, and construction—standards; materials, and technology.

Acoustics

Acoustic Characteristics Facility (NRL)

Acoustic Anechoic Chamber (NIST)

    Acoustic Reverberation Chamber

Wind System Vibration & Noise Testing (DOE)

    Solar Energy Research Institute (SERI)

Airports

Federal Aviation Administration (FAA/DOT)

    Research, Engineering & Development

Arid Regions

Laboratory of Biomedical & Environmental Sciences Arid Regions Research (DOE)

Asbestos

Asbestos Technical Assistance Program (EPA)

Atmospheric Sciences

Atmospheric Sciences Division (NSF)

    Directorate for Geosciences

Barrier-Free Design

Architectural & Transportation Barriers (Access Board ATBCB)

Clearinghouse on the Handicapped (HEW)

Housing Technology Information Service (HUD)

Rehabilitation Research & Development Center (VA)

Bridges

Bridge Administration (USGS)

Bridge Test Hanger (COE)

    Belvoir Research & Development Engineering Unit

Building & Fire Research Laboratory (NIST)   **Building**
- Structures Division   **Technology**
  Earthquake Engineering
  Structural Evaluation
- Building Environment Division
  Computer Integrated Construction
  Indoor Air Quality & Ventilation
  Lighting
  Mechanical Systems & Controls
  Thermal Machinery
- Building Materials Division
  Construction Materials Reference
  Inorganic Building Materials
  Organic Building Materials
Center for Building Technology (NIST)
- Calibrated Hot Box Facility
- Center for Fire Research
- Fire Research Facilities
Large Environmental Chamber (NIST)
National Institute of Building Sciences (NIBS)
Public Buildings (GSA)
- Design & Construction
- Information Management Services
- Public Building Services
  Information Systems
  Real Property Development (Design)
  Real Property Resources Management Service
Materials Science & Engineering Laboratory (NIST)   **Ceramics**
  Ceramics Division
Metals & Ceramics Information Center
  Battelle-Columbus Laboratories
Chemical & Thermal Systems Division (NSF)   **Chemicals**
  Directorate for Engineering
Coastal Engineering Information Analysis Center (CEAIC)   **Coastal**
  US Army, Fort Belvoir
Coastal Engineering Information Analysis Center (CEAIC)
Coastal Engineering Research Center (CERC)
  US Army Waterways Experiment Station
Naval Coastal Systems Center (NCSC)

Cold Regions

Arctic Research Commission (ARC)

Cold Regions Science & Technology (CRST)
   Information Analysis Center

Cold Regions Research & Engineering Laboratory (CRREL)
   US Army Corps of Engineers

Institute of Polar Studies
   Ohio State University

Polar Programs Division (NSF)
   Directorate for Geosciences

Combustion Technology

Combustion Research Facility

US Department of Energy (DOE)

Sandia National Laboratory

Computers

Computer & Information Science & Engineering

National Science Foundation (NSF)

Directorate

- Computers & Computer Research Division
- Information, Robotics & Intelligent Systems Division
- Networking & Communications Research & Infrastructure Division

Institute for Computer Sciences & Technology

National Institute of Standards & Technology (NIST)

Concrete

Concrete Technology Information Analysis Center (CTIAC)

Army Waterways Experiment Station

Polymer-Concrete Development Laboratory

US Department of Energy (DOE)

Conservation

National Soil Erosion Research Laboratory (USDA)

Soil Conservation Service (SCS/USDA)

Soil & Water Conservation Research Unit (USDA)

Construction Materials

Building Materials Division

National Institute of Standards & Technology (NIST)

- Construction Materials Reference
- Inorganic Building Materials
- Organic Building Materials

Metallurgy Division-Corrosion

Materials Science & Engineering Laboratory

National Institute of Standards & Technology (NIST)

Construction Technology

Construction Engineering Research Laboratory (CERL)

US Army Corps of Engineers

Office of Technology Services

National Institute of Standards & Technology (NIST)

National Institute of Corrections Information Center

US Department of Justice

US Army Corps of Engineers

- Board of Contract Appeals

- Board of Engineers for Rivers & Harbors

- Facilities Engineering Support Agency

Aquifer Properties Test Facilities

US Department of Energy (DOE)

Center for Computational Seismology

US Department of Energy (DOE)

Center for Water Quality Systems

US Environmental Protection Agency (EPA)

Earth Resources Observation Systems (EROS)
   Data Center

US Geological Survey (USGS)

Earth Science Division

National Science Foundation (NSF)

Directorate for Geosciences

Earth Science Information Network

US Geological Survey (USGS)

Geographic Information Retrieval & Analysis

Great Lakes Environmental Research Laboratory

US National Oceanic & Atmospheric Administration (NOAA)

Center for Building Technology

National Institute of Standards & Technology (NIST)

Center for Computational Seismology

US Department of Energy (DOE)

Lawrence Berkeley Laboratory

University of California

Earthquake Engineering Research Center

National Information Service for Earthquake Engineering (NISEE)

National Earthquake Information Service

US Geological Survey (USGS)

National Geophysical Data Center

National Oceanic & Atmospheric Administration (NOAA)

Soil Mechanics Information Analysis Center

US Army Engineer Waterways Experiment Station

Tri-Directional Test Facility

National Institute of Standards & Technology

Correctional Facilities Corps of Engineers

Earth Sciences

Earthquakes

Ecology	Delaware River Basin Commission
	Susquehanna River Basin Commission
Electrical/ Electronics	Electrical & Communications Systems (ECS)
	Electronics & Electrical Engineering Laboratory (EEEL)
	• Electrical Reference Standards
	• Electricity Division
	Reliability Analysis Center (USAF)
	Thermophysical & Electronic Properties Information Analysis Center
	Purdue University
Emergencies/ Disasters	Disaster Assistance
	US Small Business Administration (SBA)
	Federal Emergency Management Agency (FEMA)
	• Office of National Preparedness Program
	• Office of State & Local Programs & Support
Energy	Buildings Energy Use
	US Department of Energy (DOE)
	Pacific Northwest Laboratory
	Conservation & Energy Inquiry & Referral Center
	US Department of Energy (DOE)
	Conservation & Renewable Energy Inquiry & Referral Service
	US Department of Energy (DOE)
	Energy Information Administration
	US Department of Energy (DOE)
	National Energy Information Center
	Energy Technology Engineering Center
	US Department of Energy (DOE)
	Environmental & Energy Study Conference
	US Congress
	Federal Energy Regulatory Commission
	US Department of Energy (DOE)
	Geothermal Test Facility
	US Department of Energy (DOE)
	Heat Engine Research
	US Department of Energy (DOE)
	Morgantown Energy Technology Center
	Heat Pump Laboratory
	US Department of Energy (DOE)
	Brookhaven National Laboratory

Department of Applied Sciences
Institute for Energy Analysis
US Department of Energy (DOE)
Oak Ridge Associated Universities
Mechanical Engineering Unit
US Department of Energy (DOE)
Idaho National Laboratory
National Appropriate Technology Assistance Service
US Department of Energy (DOE)
National Energy Information Center
US Department of Energy (DOE)
Energy Information Administration
National Energy Software Center
US Department of Energy (DOE)
Argonne National Laboratory
National Renewable Energy Laboratory
US Department of Energy (DOE)
Office of Environment & Energy
US Department of Housing & Urban Development (HUD)
Office of Nuclear Energy
US Department of Energy (DOE)
Solar Energy Research Institute (SERI)
US Department of Energy
SERI Daylighting Laboratory
National Engineering Laboratory (NEL)
Environmental Data & Information Service
National Oceanographic & Atmospheric Administration (NOAA)
National Oceanographic Data Center
Environmental Restoration & Waste Management
US Department of Energy (DOE)
Environmental Science Information Center
National Oceanic & Atmospheric Administration (NOAA)
Environmental Data & Information Service
Infrared Information & Analysis Center
Environmental Research Institute of Michigan (ERIM)
National Environmental Data Referral Service
US National Oceanic & Atmospheric Administration (NOAA)
National Environmental Satellite, Data &

**Engineering
Technology
Environmental**

Information Service

National Geophysical Data Center

US National Oceanic & Atmospheric Administration (NOAA)

National Institute of Environmental Health Sciences

US Department of Health & Human Resources (HUD)

Fire Protection/ Prevention

Building & Fire Research Laboratory

National Institute of Standards & Technology (NIST)

Calibrated Hot Box Facility (NIST)

National Institute of Standards & Technology (NIST)

- Center for Fire Research
- Fire Research Facilities

Departments

Defense

Air Force

- Engineering & Service Center (Civil Engineering)

Army

- Chief of Corps of Engineers

Navy

- Naval Facilities Engineering Command
- Naval Publications & Forms Center

Interior (DOI)

- Water & Power Resources Services (WPRS)

(Formerly Bureau of Reclamation)

Justice (DOJ)

Labor (DOL)

State (DOS)

Transportation

- Federal Highway Administration

    US Coast Guard

    Bridge Administration

    Deepwater Ports

    Marine Environmental Response

- Federal Aviation Administration

    Research Engineering & Development

- Federal Railroad Administration

    Research & Development

    Transportation Test Center

- Urban Mass Transit Administration

    Transit Research Center

- Research & Special Programs Administration
    Office of Hazardous Materials
    Office of Pipeline Safety
    Transportation Systems Center

Natural Hazards Research Information Center (FEMA)   **Hazards**

Office of Hazardous Materials (DOT)
    Research & Special Programs Administration

House Component & Equipment Field Test Facility (DOE)   **Housing**
    Oak Ridge National Laboratory

Housing & Technology Information Service (HUD)

Large Environmental Chamber

National Institute of Standards & Technology (NIST)

Rural Housing Research Unit

US Department of Agriculture (USDA)

Test House

US Department of Energy (DOE)

Brookhaven National Laboratory

Hydraulic Engineering Information Analysis Center   **Hydraulics**

US Army Engineer Waterways Experiment Station

Hydrologic Research Laboratory   **Hydrology**

US National Oceanic & Atmospheric Administration (NOAA)

Agricultural Stabilization & Conservation Service (ASCS)   **Maps &**

Army Corps of Engineers (COE)   **Mapping**

Bureau of Land Management (BLM)

Defense Mapping Agency

Federal Highway Administration (FHA)

Federal Power Administration (FPA)

International Boundary Commission (IBC)

Library of Congress

Mississippi River Commission

National Aeronautics & Space Administration (NASA)

National Ocean Survey (NOS)

National Oceanic & Atmospheric Administration (NOAA)

- Office of Charting & Geodetic Services

Soil Conservation Service

Tennessee Valley Authority (TVA)

US Geological Survey (USGS)

US Forest Service (USFS)

US Geological Survey (USGS)
- Map & Chart Information System
- National Cartographic Information Center
- Office of Geographic & Cartographic Research

Water & Power Resources Service
(Formerly Bureau of Reclamation)

Materials Science

Metals & Ceramics Information Center
US Department of Defense
Battelle-Columbus Laboratories
National Measurement Laboratory
National Institute of Standards & Technology (NIST)
Thermophysical & Electronics Properties
   Information Analysis Center
Purdue University

Nondestructive Testing

Nondestructive Testing Information Analysis Center
US Department of Defense (DOD)
Southwest Research Institute (SRI)

Nuclear Technology

National Nuclear Data Center
US Department of Energy
Brookhaven National Laboratory
Nuclear Safety Information Center
US Department of Energy
Oak Ridge National Laboratory
Radiation Shielding Information Center
US Department of Energy &
Nuclear Regulatory Commission
Oak Ridge National Laboratory

Pavements

Pavements & Soil Trafficability
   Information Analysis Center
US Army Engineer Waterways Experiment Station

Plastics

Plastics Technical Evaluation Center
US Army Armament Research & Development Command

Plumbing

Plumbing Research Laboratory
National Institute of Standards & Technology (NIST)

Shock & Vibration

Shock & Vibration Information Center (NRL)
Shock Wave Data Center
   Lawrence Livermore National Laboratory

Data & Analysis Center for Software (USAF) **Software**
   Systems Command

Rome Air Force Development Center

- Reliability Analysis Center

Soil Mechanics Information Analysis Center **Soil Mechanics**

US Army Engineer Waterways Experiment Station

National Institute of Standards & Technology (NIST) **Standards**

- Information Resources & Services

- Office of Technology Services

- Standards & Practices—National Engineering Laboratory

Structures Laboratory (COE) **Structures**
   Waterways Experiment Station

Tri-Directional Test Facility

National Institute of Standards & Technology (NIST)

National Technical Information Service (NTIS) **Technical Publications**

Thermodynamics Research Center **Thermody-namics**
   Texas A & M University

Oak Ridge National Laboratory **Toxic Hazards**

- Carbon Dioxide Information Center

- Chemical Effects information Center

- Hazardous Materials Information Center

- Toxicology Data Bank

- Toxicology Information Response Center

- National Library of Medicine's Toxicology Information Program

National Center for Groundwater Research **Water & Wastewater**

US Environmental Protection Agency (EPA)

National Water Data Exchange

US Geological Survey (USGS)

US Water Conservation Laboratory

US Department of Agriculture—USDA

USDA Sedimentation Laboratory

US Department of Agriculture (USDA)

Water Data Storage & Retrieval System

US Geological Survey (USGS)

Water Quality & Watershed Research Laboratory

US Department of Agriculture (USDA)

National Weather Service (NWS) **Weather/Climate**

Forest Products Laboratory (USDA) **Wood & Lumber**

Education (DoEd)

Energy (DOE)

- Conservation & Renewable Energy
- Energy Information Administration
- Environmental Restoration & Waste Management

Health & Human Services (HHS)

- National Institute of Environmental Health Services

Housing & Urban Development (HUD)

- Government National Mortgage Association

Appendix A   Reference Publications

AIR CONDITIONING

System Design Manual—Carrier Corporation
  PT 1: Load Estimating
  PT 2: Air Distribution
  PT 3: Piping Design
  PT 1-12: Piping Design

BOILERS

Boiler Control Systems, Lindsley

BUILDING CODES

ASTM Standards I Building Codes—ASTM
Building Construction & Safety Code—NFPA
On-site Guide to Building Codes, William David Smith & Laura Holland Smith
  Commercial & Residential
    Interior
    Exterior

CATHODIC PROTECTION

Cathodic Protection of Underground Petroleum Storage Tanks & Piping Systems

CEMENT/CONCRETE

Cementitious Grouts & Grouting
Concrete Masonry Handbook for Architects, Engineers & Builders

ELECTRICITY

National Electrical Code Handbook (NEC)—NFPA

HVAC

Duct Construction Standards: Metal & Flexible—SMACNA
Seismic Restraint Manual: Guidelines for Mechanical Systems—SMACNA

MAINTENANCE

Maintenance of Buildings, Preventive (1991)

Maintenance Testing Specifications (1989)—NETA

MOISTURE CONTROL

Moisture Control for Residential Roofing, Ventilation &

OSHA

Construction Safety & Health Compliance, OSHA 1926

Electrical Construction Workers, OSHA Safety & Health Standards Digest for Enforcement for Consulting Engineers, Realities of OSHA—ACEC

Federal OSHA, 29 CFD, 1926 OSHA—OSHA

Hazard Communication Standard: How to Comply With the OSHA— Complete Guide to Compliance with OSHA Worker Right Regulations—OSHA

Plant Safety, OSHA Compliance Manual—OSHA

Plant Safety Regulations & Index, OSHA Guide—OSHA

PIPE/PIPING

Building Services Piping—ASME

Cathodic Protection of Underground Petroleum Storage Tanks & Piping Systems

Clay Pipe Engineering Manual

Clay Pipe Installation Handbook

Concrete Pipe Installation Manual

Ductile Iron Pipe, Guide for Installation of

Pipe Hangers & Supports, Selection & Application

Pipeline Safety Regulations—USDOT

Polyvinyl Chloride (PVC) Pressure Pipe, Standard for—AWWA

Power Piping—With Interpretations

PVC Sewer Pipe, Recommended Practice for the Installation of

PLUMBING

Inspectors' Manual, Plumbing (1988)—SBCCI

PUBLIC WORKS

Public Works Construction, Standard Specifications for

PUMPS

Pumps, Centrifugal Fire—NFPA

QUALITY

Quality in the Constructed Project—ASCE

ROOFING

Asphalt Roofing Manual, Residential
Roofing, Ventilation & Moisture Control, Residential
Roof Decks, Design Manual for Composite, Form &—SDI
Roof Insulated Steel Deck—Loss Prevention Data
Roofing Manual, Residential Asphalt

SAFETY & HEALTH

AC Substation Grounding, Guide for, Safety in—ANSI/IEEE
Construction Safety, OSHA (Code of Federal Regulations)—OSHA
Construction Safety Manual, Dave Heberle
Conveyors & Related Equipment, Safety Standard for
Electrical Construction Workers, Safety & Health Standards Digest for—OSHA
Employee Workplaces, Electrical, Safety Requirements for—NFPA
Engineering & Management, System, Safety
Environmental Control, Safety, Health &
Industrial Safety,—OSHA- (Code of Federal Regulations)—OSHA
Manual of Accident Prevention for Construction AGC
Personnel Hoists, Safety Requirements for—ANSI
Pipeline, Safety Regulations—USDOT
Plant Safety, OSHA Compliance Manual—OSHA29
Plant Safety Regulations & Index, OSHA Guide—OSHA
Welding & Cutting, Safety in—ANSI

SECURITY

Security & Fire Alarm Systems, Design & Application of
Security Planning & Design, Joseph A. Dmkin—AIA

SERVICE STATIONS

Service Station Tanks, Recommended Practice for the Abandonment or
Removal of Used Underground

SEWERS & SEWAGE

Sewer Design, Modern—AISI
Sewer Pipe, Recommended Practice for the Installation of PVC Sewer Pipe
Sewers, Design & Construction of Sanitary & Storm

SHEET METAL

Architectural Sheet Metal Manual—SMACNA

SIGNALING SYSTEMS

Signaling & Nurse Call Equipment, Hospital—UL

Signaling System with Central Station Service, Installation, Maintenance & Use of—NFPA

Signaling Systems—NFPA

Signaling Systems, Central Station—NFPA

Signaling Systems, Installation, Maintenance & Use of
Notification Appliances for Protective—NFPA

Signaling Systems, Testing Procedures for Local, Auxiliary, Remote Station & Proprietary Protective—NFPA

SOLAR HEATING

Solar Heating for Swimming Pools

Solar Water & Pool Heating Manual

SPECIFICATIONS

STEEL

Load & Resistance Factor Design (Manual of Steel Construction)—AISC

STORAGE TANKS

Cathodic Protection of Underground Storage Tanks & Piping Systems

Combustible Liquids, Underground Leakage of Flammable &—NFPA

Storage Tanks & Piping Systems, Cathodic Protection of Underground—NFPA

Storage Tanks, Cleaning Petroleum—API

Storage Systems, Installation of Underground Petroleum—API

Underground Tanks for Flammable & Combustible Liquids, Steel—UL

SURVEYING

Surveying Instructions, Manual of—Government Manual for Public Land Surveys

TANKS

Abandonment or Removal of Used Underground Service Station Tanks, Recommended Practice for the—API

Flammable & Combustible Liquids, Steel Underground Tanks for—UL

Petroleum Storage Tanks, Cleaning—API

Underground Tanks, Installation Instructions for—STI

TESTING

Acceptance Testing Specifications—NETA

Surface Burning Building Materials, Test Methods—NFPA

Testing Specifications, Maintenance—NETA

VAPOR REMOVAL

Vapor Removal from Cooking Equipment—NFPA

VENTILATION

Ventilation & Moisture Control for Residential Roofing

Ventilation Directory—ASHRAE Standards

Ventilation for Acceptable Indoor Air Quality—ASHRAE

Venting Principles—SPC

Vents, Chimneys, Fireplaces &—NFPA

WASTE MANAGEMENT

Incinerators, Waste & Linen Handling Systems—NFPA

WATER/WASTEWATER

Disinfecting Water Mains, Standard for

Water Mains & Their Appurtenances, Standard for Installation of Ductile Iron—AWWA

Water Softeners, Voluntary Industry Standards for Household, Commercial & Portable Exchange

Water Tanks for Private Fire Protection—NFPA

Wastewater Treatment Plants, Design of Municipal

WELDING & BRAZING

Welding & Cutting, Safety in—ANSI

Welding Code for Aluminum, Structural

Welding Code for Sheet Steel, Standard

Welding Code for Steel, Structural

Welding Code-Reinforcing Steel, Structural

WELDING INSPECTION

Welding Inspection

Welds, Guide for Visual Inspection of

WOOD

Engineered Wood Handbook—APA

Timber Construction Details, Heavy

Timber Construction Manual—AITC

Wood Construction, National Design Specification for

Wood Engineering Handbook—Forest Products Laboratory

Wood Structural Design Data—APA

Wood Trusses, Design Specifications for Metal Plate Connected

Appendix B   Standards Writing Bodies

American National Standards Institute (ANSI)

1819 L Street NW #600

Washington, DC 20036

Tel: (202) 293-8020

Fax: (202) 293-9287

Web: *www.ansi.org*

Robert W. North, Chairman

11 West 42nd Street–13th Floor

New York, NY 10036

Tel: (212) 642-4900

Fax: (212) 398-0023

Web: *www.ansi.org*

S. Joe Bhatia, President/CEO

Does not develop standards.

Coordinates development of voluntary national standards in the United States by qualified technical and professional societies, trade associations & other groups.

Approves standards as American National Standards.

Manages & coordinates US participation in nongovernmental international standards developing organizations;

Maintains interface with government at all levels on standards-related matters.

American Society for Testing & Materials (ASTM) International

100 Barr Harbor Drive

P.O. Box C700

West Conshohocken, PA 19428-2959

Tel: (610) 832-9500

Fax: (610) 832-9500

Web: *www.astm.org*

James A. Thomas, President

Develops standards on characteristics & performance of materials, products, systems, & services, including classifications, guides, practices, specifications, terminology, and test methods.

Standards cover iron, steel & nonferrous metals; construction; paints & related coatings; textiles; plastics; rubber; electrical insulation; water & environmental technology; nuclear, solar & geothermal energy; general methods & instrumentation; and other materials, products, and methodologies.

International Coalition for Procurement Standards (ICPS)

Works through other organizations to develop standards, specifications, and test methods that do not exist currently.

Clinical & Laboratory Standards Institute (CLSI)

(Formerly: National Committee for Clinical Laboratory for Standards)

940 W. Valley Road #1400

Wayne, PA 19087-1898

Tel: (610) 688-0100

Fax: (610) 688-0700

Web: *www.clsi.org*

Glen Fine, Executive Vice President

Develops voluntary consensus standards for clinical laboratory procedures and practices for health care testing.

Construction Specifications Institute (CSI)

99 Canal Center Plaza #300

Alexandria, VA 22314-1791

Tel: (703) 684-0300

Fax: (703) 684-0465

Web: *www.csi.org*

Karl F. Borgstrom, Executive Director

Develops standards for the language and format of construction specifications; as well as format, organization, and coordination of the contents of the Project Manual for a construction project.

Develops SPEC-DATA II, an information retrieval system & an automated computerized system for specification text manipulation, adaptable to all types of master specification programs.

Publishes:

Manual of Practice providing techniques, procedures, and formats for the preparation and organization of construction documents

MASTERFORMAT that provides a uniform system for filing product information and other technical data

SPECTEXT, a 440 section library of master guide specifications for construction projects prepared in accordance with CSI recommended practices

SPECTEXT II, for smaller, less complex projects

Factory Mutual Research Corporation (FMRC)

1151 Boston-Providence Turnpike

Norwood, MA 02062

Tel: (781) 255-4000

Fax: (401) 464-6097

Web: *www.fmglobal.com*

Steven Zenofski, Assistant Vice President

Conducts research into property protection to understand the hazards that threaten client facilities and to reduce the probability and impact of potential loss, covering:

- Fire protection systems, including sprinklers and water-mist technologies
- Fire measurements for performance evaluation
- Natural hazard modeling and loss aggregation
- Cleanroom materials, research for flammability, smoke production, and corrosion
- Industrial risk assessment programs for engineering and underwriting
- Fitness-for-service evaluations
- System and equipment reliability
- Large-scale tests with real world conditions, using advanced instrumentations
- Small- and intermediate-scale tests simulating real-world conditions
- Small-scale measurements for use in sophisticated computer models

Maintains research laboratories for:

- Electrical Equipment
- Fire Technology
- Hydraulics
- Natural Hazards

Publishes:

Guidelines to help clients reduce the chances of property loss due to fire, weather conditions, and the failure of electrical and mechanical equipment

International Code Council (ICC)

5203 Leesburg Pike #600

Falls Church, VA 22041

Tel: (703) 931-4533

Fax: (703) 379-1546

Web: *www.iccsafe.org*

James Lee Witt, CEO

Developed the International Building Codes (IBC)—absorbing the three existing Model Codes in 2003:

Building Officials and Code Administrators International;

International Conference of Building Officials;

Southern Building Code Congress International.

National Conference of States on Building Codes & Standards (NCSBCS)

505 Huntmar Park Drive #210

Herndon, VA 22070

Tel: (703) 437-0100

Fax: (703) 481-3596

Web: *www.ncsbcs.org*

Robert M. Unthank, President

Works through other organizations to develop, update & maintain building codes & standards.

Is responsible for ANSI A225.1 Standard on Manufactured Housing Installations (Manufactured Home Sites, Communities, Setups).

Publishes:

Handbook of Building Codes

International (NCSL)

(National Conference of Standards Laboratories)

2995 Wilderness Place #107

Boulder, CO 80301-5404

Tel: (303) 440-3339

Fax: (303) 440-3384

Web: *www.ncsl.org*

Craig Gulka, Business Manager

Develops standards of practice for laboratories concerned with the measurement of physical quantities and the calibration of standards and instruments.

National Information Standards Organization (NISO)

4733 Bethesda Avenue #300

Bethesda, MD 20814

Tel: (301) 654-2512

Fax: (301) 654-1721

Web: *www.niso.org*

Patricia Stevens, Interim Executive Director

Develops, maintains, and publishes technical standards to manage information, including retrieval, storage, and preservation.

Designated by ANSI to represent US interests to the International Organization for Standardization's (ISO) technical committee 46 on information and documentation.

Standards Engineering Society (SES)

13340 SW 96th Avenue

Miami, FL 33176

Tel: (305) 971-4798

Fax: (305) 971-4799

Web: www.ses-standards.org

Dr. H. Glenn Ziegenfuss, Executive Director

Promotes standardization, knowledge & use of national & international standards.

Underwriters Laboratories Inc. (UL)

333 Pfingsten Road

Northbrook, IL 60062-2096

Tel: (847) 272-8800

Fax: (847) 272-8129

Web: www.ul.com/global

Develops standards and maintains laboratories and testing facilities to evaluate the safety of products.

Publishes:

Over 1,300 electrical, fire, and mechanical safety evaluation standards

Directories of products evaluated & passing the requirements of UL Standards

American National Standards Institute (ANSI)

11 West 42nd Street–13th Floor

New York, NY 10036

Tel: (212) 642-4900

Fax: (212) 398-0023

Web: *www.ansi.org*

S. Joe Bhatia, President/CEO

Document Center (DC)

1504 Industrial Way # 9

Belmont, CA 94002

Tel: (415) 591-7600

Fax: (415) 591-7617

Web: *www.document.center.com*

Claudia Bach, President

Document Automation & Production Services (DAPS)

Building 4, Section D

700 Robins Avenue

Philadelphia, PA 19111-5094

Tel:(215) 697-6396

Web: *www.assist.daps.dla.mil*

Contact: Order Desk

Document Engineering Company (DEC)

15210 Stagg Street

Van Nuys, CA 91405

Tel: (213) 873-5566

Fax: (818) 782-2374

Web: *www.doc.eng*

Eric Molinari, President

Global Engineering Documents (GED)

Information Handling Services, Div.

805 McGraw Avenue

PO Box 19539

Irvine, CA 92713-9539

Tel: (714) 261-1455

Fax: (877) 413-5184

Web: *www.global.ihs.com*

Bill Braley, General Manager

Information Handling Services (IHS)

15 Inverness Way East

Englewood, CO 80150

Tel: (303) 792-2181

Fax: (303) 792-2192

Web: *www.ihs.com*

Jay Jordan, President

Library of Congress (LOC)

101 Independence Avenue-SE

Washington, DC 20540

Tel: (202) 707-5655

Web: *www.loc.gov*

Contact: Jim Scala, Staff Specialist

National Technical Information Service (NTIS)

US Department of Commerce

5285 Port Royal Road

Springfield, VA 22161

Tel: (703) 487 605-6515

Fax: (703) 605-6742

Web: *www.ntis.gov*

Contact: Office of Product Management

Standardization Document Order Desk

Building 4, Section D

700 Robins Avenue

Philadelphia, PA 19111-5094

Web: *www.loc.gov*

Contact: George Caldwaell

US Government Printing Office (USGPO)

132 N Capitol Street

Washington, DC 20402

Tel: (202) 275-3054

Web: *www.gpo.gov*

Contact: Superintendent of Documents

Appendix D   Keyword Index

CODES & STANDARDS WRITING ORGANIZATIONS

American Institute of Architects (AIA)

Codes & Standards Committee

American National Standards Institute (ANSI)

Construction Specifications Institute (CSI)

Glazing Industry Code Committee (GICC)

International Association of Plumbing & Mechanical Officials (IAMPO)

International Coalition for Procurement Standards (ICPS)

International Code Council (ICC)

Manufactured Standardization Society of the Valve & Fittings Industry (MSSVFI)

National Conference of States on Building Codes & Standards (NCSBCS)

National Engineering Laboratory—Standards & Practices (NIST)

National Institute of Standards & Technology (NIST)

National Institute of Building Sciences (NIBS)

National Committee for Clinical Laboratories Standards (NCCLS)

Office of Technology Services (OTS)

Standards Engineering Society (SES)

Uniform Boiler & Pressure Vessel Laws Society (UBPVLS)

A
ABSORBENTS
Polyacrylate Absorbents, Institute for (IPA)

ACCESSIBILITY
Accessible design, minimum guideline requirements (ATBCB)

Accessibility standards, uniform federal (ATBCB)

Americans with Disabilities Act documents (ATBCB)

ACOUSTICS
Acoustic Characteristics Facility—Naval Research Laboratory (NRL)

Acoustic Anechoic Chamber (NIST)

Acoustic Reverberation Chamber (NIST)

Acoustical Society of America (ASA)

American Institute of Physics (AIP)

Noise Control Engineers, Institute of (INCE)

Noise Testing, Wind System Vibration &

Solar Energy Research Institute (SERI/DOE)

ADHESIVES

Adhesive & Sealant Council (ASC)

AGGREGATES

Slag Association, National (NSA)

Stone, Sand & Gravel Association, National (NSSGA)

Perlite Institute (PI)

AIR BALANCE/DIFFUSION/MOVEMENT

Air Balance Council, Associated (AABC)

Air Diffusion Council (ADC)

Air Movement & Control Association (AMCA)

AIR CONDITIONING

Air Conditioning & Refrigeration Institute (ACRI)

Air Conditioning Contractors of America (ACCA)

Air Conditioning Engineers, American Society of Heating, Refrigerating & (ASHRAE)

Air Conditioning Contractors' National Associations, Sheet Metal & (SMACNA)

American Society of Mechanical Engineers (ASME)

AIRBORNE CONTAMINANTS

Airborne contaminants (ACGH)

Indoor air quality information (EIA)

Methods for the microbiological examination of ambient air (ACGH)

Threshold limit values for airborne contaminants (ACGH)

AIRPORTS

Research Engineering & Development (FAA/DOT)

ALARMS

Burglar & Fire Alarm Association, National (NBFAA)

Central Station Alarm Association (CSAA)

Fire and burglar alarm systems and services (FMRC)

Industrial warning devices (ISEA)

ARCHITECTS/ENGINEERS/CONSTRUCTORS

Architects, American Institute of (AIA)

Association for Community Design

Code & Standards Committee

Architectural Engineering Institute (AEI/ASCE)

Automotive Engineers, Society of (SAE)

Builders & Contractors, Associated (ABC)

Building Design, American Institute of (AIBD)

Civil Engineers, American Society of (ASCE)

Consulting Engineers Council, American (ACEC)

Electrical & Electronics Engineers, Institute of (IEEE)

Energy Engineers, Association of (AEE)

General Contractors, Associated (AGC)

Industrial Engineers, Institute of (IIE)

Interior Designers, American Society of (ASID)

Mechanical Contractors Association of America (MCAA)

Rehabilitation Engineering Society of North America (RESNA)

Specialty Contractors, Associated (ASC)

ARID REGIONS

Arid Regions Research—Laboratory of Biomedical & Environmental Sciences (DOE)

ASBESTOS

Asbestos Cement Pipe Producers Association (ACPPA)

Asbestos Information Association/North America (AIA/NA)

Asbestos information & management (EIA)

Asbestos Technical Assistance Program (EPA)

Health and safety aspects of asbestos and its use (AIA/NA)

ASPHALT

Asphalt Emulsion Manufacturers Association (AEMA)

Asphalt Institute (AI)

Asphalt Pavement Association, National (NAPA)

Asphalt Paving Technologies, Association of (AAPT)

Asphalt Roofing Manufacturers Association (ARMA)

International Grinding & Grooving Association (IGGA)

ATMOSPHERIC SCIENCES

Atmospheric Sciences Division (ASD/NSF)

AUTOMATION

Automated Storage & Retrieval Systems (ASRS)

Instrumentation, Systems & Automation (ISA)

B

BALLASTS/FLUORESCENT LAMPS

Certified Ballast Manufacturers Association (CBMA)

BARCODES & MAGNETIC STRIPES

Bar code symbols & some aspects of magnetic stripe media (AIM/USA)

    Stripe media immunity to magnetic damage (AIM/USA)

BARRIER-FREE DESIGN

Architectural & Transportation Barriers Compliance Board (ATBCB)

Clearinghouse on the Handicapped (DOEd)

Housing Technology Information Service (HUD)

Rehabilitation Research & Development Center (RRDC/VA)

BOILERS/PRESSURE VESSELS

Boiler & Pressure Vessel Inspectors, National Board of (NBBPVI)

Boiler & Pressure Vessel Laws Society, Uniform (UBPVLS)

Boiler Manufacturers Association, American (ABMA)

Boiler combustion safeguards (FMRC)

Mechanical Engineers, American Society of (ASME)

Pressure Vessel Manufacturers Association (PVMA)

Tubular Exchanger Manufacturers Association (TEMA)

BRICKS

Brick Industry Association (BIA)

International Masonry Institute (IMI)

BRIDGES

Bridge Administration (USCG)

Bridge Test Hanger (COE)

BUILDING MAINTENANCE

Building Office Management Association (BOMA)

BUILDINGS

Frame Builders Association, National (NFBA)

Home Builders, National Association of (NAHB)

Institute of Building Sciences, National (NIBS)

Manufactured Housing Institute (MHI)

Metal Buildings Manufacturers Association (MBMA)

Remodeling Industry, National Association of the (NARI)

Theatre Technology, United States Institute for (USITT)

BUILDING TECHNOLOGY

Building & Fire Research Laboratory (NIST)

Structures Division

    Earthquake Engineering

    Structural Evaluation

Building Environment Division

    Computer Integrated Construction

    Indoor Air Quality & Ventilation

    Lighting

    Mechanical Systems & Controls

    Thermal Machinery

Building Materials Division

    Construction Materials Reference

    Inorganic Building Materials

    Organic Building Materials

Center for Building Technology (NIST)

    Calibrated Hot Box Facility

    Center for Fire Research

    Fire Research Facilities

Large Environmental Chamber (NIST)

National Institute of Building Sciences (NIBS)

Public Buildings Design & Construction (GSA)

Public Building Services (GSA)

    Information Systems

    Real Property Development (Design)

    Real Property Resources Management Service

C

CERAMICS/TILES

American Ceramic Society (ACS)

Ceramic Tile Institute of America (CTIOA)

Ceramics Division

    Materials Science & Engineering Laboratory (NIST)

    Metals & Ceramics Information Center (NIST)

Materials & Methods Standardization Association (MMSA)

Technical Ceramics Manufacturers Association (TCMA)

Tile Council of America (TCA)

CHAIN

National Association of Chain Manufacturers (NACM)

CHEMICALS

American Chemistry Council (ACC)

Chemical Engineers, American Institute of (AIChE)

Chemical & Thermal Systems Division (NSF)

Materials Technology Institute of the Chemical Processing Industries (MTICPI)

CHLORINE

Safe manufacturing, transportation & use of chlorine, caustic soda (CI)

Guidelines & recommended practices for handling chlorine, caustic soda & caustic potash (CI)

CLAY/CLAY PRODUCTS

Brick Industry Association (BIA)

Clay Pipe Institutes, National (NCPI)

CLEANING EQUIPMENT

Cleaning Equipment Trade Association (CETA)

COASTAL SYSTEMS

Coastal Engineering Information Analysis Center (CEIAC)

Coastal Engineering Research Center (CERC)

Coastal Systems Center, Naval (NCSC)

COLD REGIONS

Arctic Research Commission (ARC)

Cold Regions Science & Technology Information Analysis Center (COE)

Cold Regions Research & Engineering Laboratory (CRREL)

    Institute of Polar Studies

Polar Programs Division (NSF)

COLLEGES & UNIVERSITIES

American Higher Education Facilities Association (AHEFA)

COMBUSTION TECHNOLOGY

Combustion Institute, The (CI)

Combustion Research Facility (DOE)

COMPUTERS

Computer & Information Science & Engineering (NSF)

    Computers & Computer Research Division

    Information, Robotics & Intelligent Systems Division

    Networking & Communications Research & Infrastructure Division

Institute for Computer Sciences & Technology (NIST)

CONCRETE/CEMENT

American Concrete Pipe Association (ACPA)

Asbestos Cement Pipe Producers Association (ACPPA)

Concrete Contractors, American Society of (ASCC)

Concrete Institute, American (ACI)

Concrete Masonry Association, National (NCMA)

Concrete Pavement Association, American (ACPA)

Concrete Pipe Association (CPA)

Concrete Plant Manufacturers Bureau (CPMB)

Concrete Pressure Pipe Association, American (ACPPA)

Concrete Pumping Association, American (ACPA)

Concrete Reinforcing Steel Institute (CRSI)

Concrete Sawing & Drilling Association (CSDA)

Concrete Technology Information Analysis Center (CTIAC)

Expanded Shale Clay & Slate Institute (ESCSI)

Gunite/Shotcrete Contractors Association (GSCA)

Grooving & Grinding Association, International (IGGA)

Lime Association, National (NLA)

Masonry & Concrete Saw Manufacturers Institute (MCSMI)

Quartz Producers Council, National (NQPC)

Polymer-Concrete Development Laboratory (DOE)

Portland Cement Association (PCA)

Post-Tensioning Institute (PTI) Precast Association, Architectural (APA)

Precast/Prestressed Concrete Institute (PCI)

Ready Mixed Concrete Association, National (NRMCA)

Reinforced Concrete Research Council (RCRC)

Tilt-Up Concrete Association (TUCA)

Truck Mixer Manufacturers Bureau (TMMB)

Wire Reinforcement Institute (WRI)

CONSERVATION/SOIL & WATER

Soil & Water Conservation Research Unit (USDA)

Soil Conservation Service (SCS)

Soil Erosion Research Laboratory, National (USDA)

CONSERVATION/HISTORIC & ARTISTIC

American Institute for Conservation of Historic & Artistic Works (AICHAW)

CONSTRUCTION MATERIALS

Building Materials Division (NIST)

   Construction Materials Reference

Inorganic Building Materials

Organic Building Materials

Metallurgy Division (NIST)

Corrosion

Materials Science & Engineering Laboratory

CONSTRUCTION TECHNOLOGY

Construction Engineering Research Laboratory (CERL)

Office of Technology Services (OTS)

COOLING TOWERS

Cooling Tower Institute (CTI)

COOLING SYSTEMS

Hydronics Institute (HI)

Plumbing-Heating-Cooling Contractors National Association (PHCCNA)

CORDAGE & ROPE

Hard fiber, synthetic rope, and twines (CI)

CORPS OF ENGINEERS

US Army Corps of Engineers (COE)

Board of Contract Appeals

Board of Engineers for Rivers & Harbors

Facilities Engineering Support Agency

CORRECTIONAL FACILITIES

National Institute of Corrections Information Center (DOJ)

CORROSION

Lightning Protection Institute (LPI)

Metals from the standpoint of durability under weathering & possible damage from corrosion, physical impact, or reaction with dissimilar metals

CRANES/HOISTS

Crane Manufacturers Association of America (CMAA)

D

DEMOLITION

Demolition Contractors, National Association of (NADC)

Explosives, Institute of Makers of (IME)

DESALINATION

International Desalination Association (IDA)

DRAFTING

American Design Drafting Association (ADDA)

DRILLING & BORING

Test boring and core drilling (TBA)

Drilled shafts, design & construction of caissons & foundations (ADS/AIFD)

DOORS/WINDOWS

Architectural Manufacturers Association, American (AAMA)

Door Association, International (IDA)

Door & Access Systems Manufacturers Association International (DASMAI)

Door & Hardware Institute (DHI)

Insulated Steel Door Institute (ISDI)

Sash & Door Jobbers Association, National (NSDJA)

Steel Door Institute (SDI)

Steel Window Institute (SWI)

Window & Door Manufacturers Association (WDMA)

DRILLS/DRILLING

Concrete Sawing & Drilling Association (CSDA)

Foundation Drilling, The International Association of (ADSC/IAFD)

Horizontal Earth Boring Equipment Manufacturers (HEBEM)

E

EARTH SCIENCES

Aquifer Properties Test Facilities (DOE)

Earth Resources Observation Systems (USGS)

    Data Center

    Earth Science Division (NSF)

Earth Science Information Network (USGS)

Geographic Information Retrieval & Analysis

EARTHQUAKES

Center for Building Technology (NIST)

Seismology, Center for Computational (DOE)

Earthquake Engineering (NIST)

Earthquake Engineering Research Institute (EERI)

Earthquake Engineering Research Center, National (NISEE)

Earthquake Information Service, National (USGS)

Geophysical Data Center, National (NOAA)

Seismology Society of America (SSA)

Soil Mechanics Information Analysis Center (COE)

Tri-Directional Test Facility (NIST)

Vibration Institute (VI)

ECOLOGY

Delaware River Basin Commission (DRBC)

Susquehanna River Basin Commission (SRBC)

EDUCATIONAL FACILITIES

Educational Facility Planners International, Council of (CEFPI)

ELECTRICAL/ELECTRONICS

Electrical equipment (FMRC)

Electrical installations (NFPA)

Electronics & Electrical Engineering Laboratory (NIST)

Electrical & Communications Systems

Electrical Reference Standards

Electricity Division

High voltage underground cable design used by utilities (AEIC)

Reliability Analysis Center (USAF)

Thermophysical & Electronic Properties Information Analysis Center

ELECTRICAL EQUIPMENT/MACHINERY

Electrical Contractors Association, National (NECA)

Electrical Manufacturers Association, National (NEMA)

Underwriters Laboratories (UL)

ELEVATORS/ESCALATORS

Mechanical Engineers, American Society of (ASME)

Elevator Contractors, National Association of (NAEC)

ENGINEERING TECHNOLOGY

National Engineering Laboratory (NIST)

EMERGENCIES/DISASTERS

Disaster Assistance (SBA)

Emergency Management Agency, Federal (FEMA)

Office of National Preparedness Program

Office of State & Local Programs & Support

ENERGY

Buildings Energy Use (DOE)

Conservation & Energy Inquiry & Referral Center

Conservation & Renewable Energy Inquiry & Referral Service

Energy Information Administration (DOE)

Energy Information Center, National

Energy Software Center, National (DOE)
Energy Technology Engineering Center (DOE)
 Energy Analysis, Institute for
 Heat Engine Research
 Heat Pump Laboratory
 Technology Assistance Service, National Appropriate (DOE)
Federal Energy Regulatory Commission (DOE)
Renewable Energy Laboratory, National (DOE)
Office of Environment & Energy (HUD)
Office of Nuclear Energy (DOE)
Solar Energy Research Institute (SERI)
 SERI Daylighting Laboratory

ENVIRONMENTAL

Environmental Balancing Bureau, National (NEBB)
Environmental Business Association (EBA)
Environmental Data & Information Service (NOAA)
 Environmental Science Information Center
 Infrared Information & Analysis Center
 Environmental Data Referral Service, National
 Environmental Satellite, Data & Information Service, National
 Geophysical Data Center, National
Environmental Health Association, National (NEHA)
 Environmental health & protection of personnel in controlling environmental hazard
Environmental Health Sciences, National Institute of (HUD)
Environmental Information Association (EIA)
 Environmental site assessment information
 Lead-based paint information (EIA)
 Radon gas information (EIA)
 Underground storage tanks information (EIA)
Environmental Research Laboratory, Great Lakes (NOAA)
Environmental Restoration & Waste Management (DOE)
Environmental Sciences, Institute of (IES)
 Environmental standards, specifications & recommended practices; simulation, testing, contamination control techniques; and design criteria for equipment operation (IES)
Impact Assessment, International Association for (IAIA)
Occupational & Environmental Health, Society for (SOEH)
Technical Association of the Pulp & Paper Industry (TAPPI)
Water Environment Federation (WEF)

EROSION CONTROL

International Erosion Control Association (IECA)

ESTIMATING/COST CONTROL

Cost Engineering, Association for the Advancement of (AACE)

Value Engineers, Society of American (SAVE)

EXPANSION JOINTS

Expansion Joint Manufacturers Association (EJMA)

EXPLOSIVES

Demolition Contractors, National Association of (NADC)

Explosives, Institute of Makers of (IME)

F

FACILITIES DEVELOPMENT/MANAGEMENT

Building Owners & Managers Association (BOMA)

Development Research Council, International (IDRC)

Facility Management Association, International (IFMA)

Higher Education Facilities Officers, Association of (AHEFO)

Industrial & Office Properties, National Association of (NAIOP)

FABRICS/MATERIALS—STRUCTURES

Industrial Fabrics Association International (IFAI)

FASTENERS

Industrial Fasteners Institute (IFI)

Tubular Rivet & Machine Institute (TRMI)

FENCING

Chain Link Fence Manufacturers Institute (CLFMI)

International Fencing Institute of America (IFIA)

FIBERGLASS

Fiberglass Tank & Pipe Institute (FTPI)

FIRE PROTECTION/PREVENTION

Burglar & Fire Alarm Association, National (NBFAA)

Central Station Alarm Association (CSAA)

Electrical installations, flammable liquids, gases, life safety & marine environments (NFPA)

Fire Equipment Manufacturers & Services Association (FEMSA)

Fire & Emergency Manufacturers & Services Association (FEMSA)

Fire Protection Association, National (NFPA)

Fire Protection Engineers, Society of (SFPE)

Fire protection equipment, flammable liquid equipment, fuel &
  combustion control (FMRC)

Fire Retardant Chemicals Association (FRCA)

Fire Research Laboratory, Building & (NIST)

  Calibrated Hot Box Facility

  Center for Fire Research

  Fire Research Facilities

Fire Sprinkler Association, American (AFPA)

Fire Sprinkler Association, National (NFSA)

Fire Suppression System Association (FSSA)

FIRST AID

Industrial first aid (ISEA)

FLOORING/FLOOR COVERINGS

Maple Flooring Manufacturers Association (MFMA)

Oak Flooring Manufacturers Association, National (NOFMA)

Resilient Floor Covering Institute (RFCI)

Steel Deck Institute (SDI)

Wood Flooring Association, National (NWFA)

FLUID CONTROLS

Fluid Controls Institute (FCI)

Fluid Sealing Association (FSA)

FOOD EQUIPMENT

Food Equipment Service Association, Commercial (CFESA)

Food Equipment Manufacturers Association (FEMA)

FOUNDATIONS

Deep Foundations Institute (DFI)

Foundation Drilling, The International Association of (ADSC/IAFD)

Geosciences, The Association of Engineering Firms Practicing in (ASFE)

FURNITURE/FURNISHINGS/APPLIANCES

Home Appliance Manufacturers, Association of (AHAM)

Business & Institutional Furniture Manufacturers Association (BIFMA)

Carpet & Rug Institute (CRI)

Underwriters Laboratories (UL)

G
GALVANIZING

Galvanizers Association, American (AGA)

GASES

Flammable gases & liquids (NFPA)

Gas Association, American (AGA)

Compressed Air & Gas Institute (CAGI)

Compressed Gas Association (CGA)

Gas Appliance Manufacturers Association (GAMA)

Propane Gas Association, National (NPGA)

GEOLOGY/GEOSCIENCE

Engineering Geologists, Association of (AEG)

Geosciences, The Association of Engineering Firms Practicing in (ASFE)

GEOTHERMAL

Geothermal Test Facility (DOE)

GLASS/GLAZING

Glass Association of North America (GANA)

   Glass Tempering Division

Glass Association, National (NGA)

Glazing Industry Code Committee (GICC)

Insulating Glass Manufacturers Association/Alliance (IGMA)

Safety Glazing Certification Council (SGCC)

GOLF COURSES/TENNIS COURTS/RACING TRACKS

Golf Course Architects, American Society of (ASGCA)

Golf Course Builders Association of America (GCBAA)

Tennis Court & Track Builders Association, US (USTC&TBA)

GOVERNMENT ORGANIZATIONS

Academy of Engineering, National (NAE)

Academy of Science, National (NAS)

Architectural & Transportation Barriers Compliance Board, US (USATBCB)

Building Research Board (NIBS)

Building Sciences, National Institute of (NIBS)

Consumer Product Safety Commission (CPSC)

Environmental Protection Agency (EPA)

Federal Construction Council (NSF)

General Services Administration (GSA)

Highway Research Board (NIBS)

Science Foundation, National (NSF)

Occupational Safety & Health Administration (OSHA)

Public Buildings Service (GSA)

Postal Service, US (USPS)

GUNITE/SHOTCRETE

Gunite/Shotcrete Contractors Association (GSGA)

GYPSUM/PLASTER/STUCCO

Gypsum Association (GA)

Lath & Plaster, International Institute for (IILP)

Lime Association, National (NLA)

Stucco Manufacturers Association (SMA)

H

HAZARDOUS MATERIALS

Packaging, labeling, handling & transportation of hazardous materials (AAR/HM)

HOSPITALS

American Hospital Association (AHA)

HOTELS & LODGINGS

American Hotel & Lodging Association (AHLA)

HOUSING

Healthful housing (APHA)

HYGIENE

Industrial hygiene (AIHA)

Industrial hygiene (ACGH)

I

INDUSTRIAL PARKS

National Association of Industrial & Office Parks (NAIOP)

INSPECTION/INSPECTORS

Boiler & Pressure Vessel Inspectors, National Association of (NABPVI)

Construction Inspectors Association, American (ACIA)

Electrical Inspectors, International Association of (IAEI)

INSTRUMENTATION

Instrumentation, Systems & Automation (ISA)

INSULATION

Cellulose Insulation Manufacturers Association (CIMA)

Insulated Steel Door Institute (ISDI)

Insulation Contractors Association of America (ICAA)

Insulation Association, National (NIA)

Insulation Manufacturers Association, North American (NAIMA)

Perlite Institute (PI)

Polyisocyanurate Insulation Manufacturers Association (PIMA)

Sealed Insulating Glass Manufacturers Association (SIGMA)

INSURANCE

American Insurance Association (AIA)

   Workers' Compensation Digest, Annual

Factory Mutual Research Group (FMRG)

Underwriters Laboratory (UL)

IRRIGATION

Irrigation Association (IA)

   Irrigation systems for landscaping

American Society of Irrigation Consultants (ASIC)

L

LABORATORIES

Independent Laboratories, American Council of (ACIL)

Clinical Laboratory Standards, National Committee for (NCCLS)

LADDERS

American Ladder Institute (ALI)

LANDSCAPING/NURSERIES

Nursery & Landscape Association, American (ANLA)

Landscape Architects, American Society of (ASLA)

Associated Landscape Contractors of America (ALCA)

LAND USE

Urban Land Institute (ULA)

LATH & PLASTER

Lath & Plaster, International Institute for (IILP)

LIGHTING/ILLUMINATION

Illuminating Engineering Society of North America (IESNA)

Lighting Association, American (ALA)

Lighting Designers, Industrial Association of (IALD)

LIGHTNING PROTECTION

Lightning Protection Institute (LPI)

Lightning Protection Association, United (ULPA)

Lightning Protection Institute (LPI)

LOCKS/DOOR CLOSERS

Access Systems Manufacturers Association, International Door & (IDASMA)

Builders Hardware Manufacturers Association (BHMA)

Door & Hardware Institute (DHI)

Locking devices, building security systems & equipment (ALA)

LOSS CONTROL

Requirements for approval & listing of equipment, materials, and services for loss control (FMRG)

M

MACHINERY

Machinery guards (ISEA)

MAPS & MAPPING

Agricultural Stabilization & Conservation Service (USDA)

Army Corps of Engineers (ACE)

Bureau of Land Management (BLM)

Defense Mapping Agency (DOD)

Federal Highway Administration (DOT)

Federal Power Administration (DOE)

Forest Service, US (USFS)

Geological Survey, US (USGS)

International Boundary Commission (IBC)

Library of Congress (LC)

Map & Chart Information System (USGS)

Mississippi River Commission (MRC)

Aeronautics & Space Administration, National (NASA)

Cartographic Information Center, National (USGS)

Geographic & Cartographic Research, Office of

Ocean Survey, National (NOS)

Oceanic & Atmospheric Administration, National (NOAA)

Charting & Geodetic Services, Office of

Soil Conservation Service (USDA)

Tennessee Valley Authority (TVA)

Water & Power Resources Service (WPRS)

MARBLE

Marble Institute of America (MIA)

MARINE CONSTRUCTION

Society of Naval Architects & Marine Engineers (SNAME)

Marine environments (NFPA)

MASONRY

Brick Industry Association (BIA)

Concrete Masonry Association, National (NCMA)

Masonry & Concrete Saw Manufacturers Institute (MCSMI)

Masonry Institute, International (IMI)

Lime Association, National (NLA)

MATERIALS HANDLING

Automated Storage/Retrieval Systems (AS/RS)

Below Hook Lifters Association (BHLA)

Hoist Manufacturers Institute (HMI) Material Handling Industry Association (MHIA)

Materials Handling Institute (MHI)

Structural Movers, International Association (IASM)

Web Sling & Tie Down Association (WSTDA)

MATERIALS SCIENCE

Materials Research Society (MRS)

Materials Technology Institute of the Chemical Processing Industries (MTICPI)

Metals & Ceramics Information Center (DOD)

Measurement Laboratory, National (NIST)

Thermophysical & Electronics Properties Information Analysis Center (NIST)

MECHANICAL ENGINEERING

Mechanical Engineering Unit (DOE)

Mechanical Engineers, American Society of (ASME)

METALS

Aluminum Association (AA)

Architectural Manufacturers Association, American (AAMA)

Architectural Metal Manufacturers, National Association of (NAAMM)

Cold Finished Steel Bar Institute (CFSBI)

Copper Development Association (CDA)

Corrugated Steel Pipe Association, National (NCSPA)

Ductile Iron Society (DIS)

Erectors Association, National (NEA)

Institute of Steel Construction, American (AISC)

Iron & Steel Institute, American (AISI)

Iron & Steel Engineers, Association of (AISE)

Lead Industries Association (LIA)

Metal Construction Association (MCA)

Metal Framing Manufacturers Association (MFMA)

Reinforcing Steel Institute, Concrete (CRSI)

Research Council on Structural Connections (RCSC)

Sheet Metal & Air Conditioning Contractors National Association (SMACCNA)

Steel Deck Institute (SDI)

Steel Door Institute (SDI)

Steel Joist Institute (SJI)

Steel Plate Fabricators Association (APFA)

Steel Manufacturers Association (SMA)

Steel Tank Institute (STI)

Steel Tube Institute of North America (STINA)

Steel Window Institute (SWI)

Structural Stability Research Council (SSRC)

Truss Plate Institute (TPI)

MONORAILS

Monorail Manufacturers Association (MMA)

N

NONDESTRUCTIVE TESTING

Nondestructive Testing Information Analysis Center (DOD)

American Society for Nondestructive Testing (ASNT)

NUCLEAR TECHNOLOGY

Radiation Protection & Measurements, National Council on (NCRPM)

Office of Nuclear Energy (DOE)

　　　Nuclear Data Center, National

　　　Nuclear Safety Information Center

　　　Radiation Shielding Information Center

NURSERY/LANDSCAPING

American Association of Nurserymen (AAN)

Landscape Association, National (NLA)

Nursery & Landscape Association, American (ANLA)

O

OCEANOGRAPHY

National Oceanographic Data Center (NOAA)

OFFICE PARKS

National Association of Industrial & Office Parks (NAIOP)

OPTICS

American Institute of Physics (AIP)

P

PAINTS/VARNISHES/COATINGS

Coatings Technology, Federation of Societies for (FSCT)

Lead-based paint information (EIA)

Paint & Coatings Association, National (NPCA)

Painting & Decorating Contractors of America (PDCA)

Pipe Coating Applicators, National Association of (NAPCA)

Protective Coatings, The Society for (SSPC)

PAVEMENT/PAVING

Asphalt Pavement Association, National (NAPA)

Asphalt Paving Technologies, Association of (AAPT)

Concrete Pavement Association, American (ACPA)

Pavements & Soil Trafficability Information Analysis Center (COE)

Paving Technologies, Association of Asphalt (AAPT)

PEST CONTROL

National Pest Control Association (NPCA)

PETROLEUM

American Petroleum Institute (API)

PIPE/PIPING & FITTINGS

Asbestos Cement Pipe Producers Association (ACPPA)

Cast Iron Soil Pipe Institute (CISPI)

Clay Pipe Institute, National (NCPI)

Concrete Pipe Association (CPA)

Concrete Pipe Association, American (ACPA)

Concrete Pressure Pipe Association, American (ACPPA)

Corrugated Steel Pipe Association, National (NCSPA)

Ductile Iron Pipe Research Association (DIPRA)

Fiberglass Tank & Pipe Institute (FTPI)

Mechanical Engineers, American Society of (ASME)

Pipe Coating Applicators, National Association of (NAPCA)

Pipe Fabrication Institute (PFI)

Pipe Fittings Association, American (APFA)

Pipe Line Contractors Association (PLCA)

Pipe Welding Bureau, National Certified (NCPWB)

Pipes, fittings & valves (AWWA)

Plastic Pipe & Fittings Association (PPFA)

Plastic Pipe Institute (PPI)

Piping Engineers & Designers, Society of (SPED)

Tube & Pipe Association International (TPAI)

Uni-Bell PVC Pipe Association (UBPPA)

PLANNING

Consulting Planners, American Society of (ASCP)

Planning Association, American (APA)

PLASTER/STUCCO

Gypsum Association (GA)

Lath & Plaster, International Institute for (IILP)

PLASTICS

Polyurethane Industry, Alliance for the (API)

Composite Materials Association, Suppliers of Advanced (SACMA)

Composites Institute (CI)

Plastic Pipe & Fittings Association (PPFA)

Plastic Pipe Institute (PPI)

Plastics Technical Evaluation Center (ARDC)

Polyurethane Foam Association (PFA)

Polyurethane Manufacturers Association (PMA)

Plastics Engineers, Society of (SPE)

Plastics Industry, Society of the (SPI)

Uni-Bell PVC Pipe Association (UBPPA)

Vinyl Institute (VI)

Vinyl Siding Institute (VSI)

PLUMBING/PLUMBING FIXTURES

Mechanical Engineers, American Society of (ASME)

Plumbing Engineers, American Society of (ASPE)

Plumbing & Drainage Institute (PDI)

Plumbing-Heating-Cooling Contractors National Association (PHCCNA)

Plumbing Manufacturers Institute (PMI)

Plumbing Research Laboratory (NIST)

Sanitary Engineers, American Society of (ASSE)

Valve Manufacturers Association of America (VMAA)

POLLUTION CONTROL
Local Air Pollution Control Officials, Association of (ALAPCO)

Mechanical Engineers, American Society of (ASME)

Paper Industry for Air & Stream Improvement, National Council of (NCPIASI)

Waste Management Association, Air & (AWMA)

PORCELAIN ENAMEL
Porcelain Enamel Institute (PEI)

PORTS/HARBORS
Society of Marine Port Engineers (SMPE)

POWER GENERATION & DISTRIBUTION SYSTEMS
Distribution Contractors Association (DCA)

District Energy Association, International (IDEA)

Edison Electric Institute (EEI)

Edison Illuminating Companies, Association of (AEIC)

Electric Power Research Institute (EPRI)

Electrical Apparatus Service Association (EASA)

Electrical Generating Systems Association (EGSA)

Electrical Inspectors, International Association of (IAEI)

Electrical Testing Association, InterNational (NETA)

Insulated Cable Engineers Association (ICEA)

Mechanical Engineers, American Society of (ASME)

Power Engineers, National Association of (NAPE)

Solar Contractors, National Association of (NASC)

Utility Contractors Association, National (NUCA)

PRESSURE VESSELS
Mechanical Engineers, American Society of (ASME)

Boiler & Pressure Vessel Inspectors, National Association of (NABPVI)

Pressure Vessel Manufacturers Association (PVMA)

Uniform Boiler & Pressure Vessel Laws Society (UBPVLS)

PROCESS EQUIPMENT
Process Equipment Manufacturers Association (PEMA)

PRODUCTIVITY
Productivity improvement through the applications of industrial engineering techniques (IIE)

PROJECT MANAGEMENT
Project Management Institute (PMI)

PROPANE GAS

Transportation and distribution of liquefied petroleum gas (NPGA)

PUBLIC WORKS

American Public Works Association (APWA)

PUMPS/PUMPING

Concrete Pumping Association, American (ACPA)

Contractors Pump Bureau (CPB)

Shallow well water system pumps, deep well water system pumps & deep well submersible pump motors; hydropneumatic tank volumes (WSC)

Submersible Wastewater Pump Association (SWPA)

Sump & Sewage Pump Manufacturers Association (SSPMA)

Wells & well pumps, water storage tanks & water meters (AWWA)

Q
QUALITY CONTROL

American Society for Quality (ASQ)

R
RADIATION

National Council of Radiation Protection & Measurements (NCRPM)

RADON GAS

Radon gas information (EIA)

RAILWAYS

American Railway Engineering & Maintenance of Way Association (AREMWA)

REFRACTORIES

Refractories Institute (RI)

REFRIGERATION

Ammonia Refrigeration, International Institute of (IIAR)

Refrigeration Institute, Air Conditioning & (ARI)

    Commercial Refrigeration Manufacturers Division

Refrigerating & Air Conditioning Engineers, American Society of Heating, (ASHRAE)

Refrigeration Engineers & Technicians Association (RETA)

REHABILITATION

Rehabilitation Engineering Society of North America (RESNA)

ROOFING

Asphalt Roofing Manufacturers Association (ARMA)

Roof Deck Contractors Association, National (NRDCA)

Roofing Contractors Association, National (NRCA)

Roof Coatings Manufacturers Association (RCMA)

Roof Consultants Institute (RCI)

Single Ply Roofing Institute (SPRI)

Tile Roofing Manufacturers Association, National (NTRMA)

ROADS

Highway design, construction, and maintenance; construction materials (ARTBA)

ROPE

Cordage Institute (CI)

S

SAFETY & HEALTH

Safety Engineers, American Society of (ASSE)

    Confined spaces

    Eye protection

    Fall protection equipment

    Railings & stairways, workplace (ASSE)

Health & safety of workers in the workplace (AIHA)

Industrial Safety Equipment Association (ISEA)

Performance standards (AAI)

Property losses, injuries & damages to health & environment (AISG)

Radiation Protection & Measurement, National Council on (NCRPM)

National Safety Council (NSC)

National Safety Management Society (NSMS)

Safety & health (AAI)

Safety & health procedures for construction sites (AGC)

Safety Glazing Certification Council (SGCC)

SAFETY INSTRUMENTS

Industrial safety and health instruments (ISEA)

SANITATION/HYGIENE

Governmental Industrial Hygienists, American Conference of (ACGIH)

Industrial Hygiene Association, American (AICHA)

Portable Sanitation Association International (PSAI)

Public Health Association, American (APHA)

SCAFFOLDS/SCAFFOLDING/SHORING/FORMING

Scaffold Contractors Association (SCA)

Scaffold Industry Association (SIA)

Scaffolding, Shoring & Forming Institute (SSFI)

SCREENS

Screen Manufacturers Association (SMA)

SEALANTS/WATERPROOFING

Sealant Council, Adhesive & (ASC)

Sealant, Waterproofing & Restoration Institute (SWRI)

SECURITY/INDUSTRIAL

Central Station Alarm Association (CSAA)

Industrial Security, American Society for (ASIS)

Security Industry Association (SIA)

SENSIOMETRY

SHOCK & VIBRATION

Shock & Vibration Information Center (USN)

    Shock Wave Data Center

Vibration Institute (VI)

SIGNAGE/SIGNALS

Municipal Signal Association, International (IMSA)

SOFTWARE

Software, Data & Analysis Center for (USAF)

Reliability Analysis Center (USAF)

SOIL MECHANICS

Soil Mechanics Information Analysis Center (SMIAC)

SOLAR ENERGY/POWER

Solar Contractors, National Association of (NASC)

Solar Energy Research Institute (SERI)

    Daylighting Laboratory

Solar Energy Society, American (ASES)

Solar Heating & Certification Corporation (SHCC)

STONE

Building Granite Quarries, National (NBGQ)

Building Stone Institute (BSI)

Indiana Limestone Institute of America (ILIA) Stone Industries, Allied (ASI)

STORAGE/RETRIEVAL

Automated Storage/Retrieval Systems (ASRS)

STRUCTURAL CONNECTIONS

Structural Connections, Research Council on (RCSC)

STRUCTURES

Structural evaluation (NIST)

Structures Laboratory (COE)

Tri-Directional Test Facility (NIST)

SWIMMING POOLS/SPAS

Spa & Swimming Pool Institute, National (NSSPI)

Suggested ordinances & recommendations for public swimming pools (APHA)

T

TANKS

Tank & Pipe Institute, Fiberglass (FTPI)

Tank Institute, Steel (STI)

Underground storage tanks information (EIA)

TECHNICAL PUBLICATIONS/GOVERNMENT

Technical Information Service, National (NTIS)

Government Printing Office, US (USGPO)

TENNIS COURTS/RACE TRACKS/GOLF COURSES

Golf Course Builders Association of America (GCBAA)

US Tennis Court & Track Builders Association (USTC&TBA)

TERRAZZO/MOSAIC

Terrazzo & Mosaic Association, National (NTMA)

TESTING

Nondestructive Testing, American Society for (ASNT)

Testing & Materials, American Society for (ASTM)

Tri-Directional Test Facility (NIST)

THERMODYNAMICS

Thermodynamics Research Center (NIST)

TILE

Ceramic Tile Institute of America (CTIA)

Materials & Methods Standardization Association (MMSA)

Terrazzo & Mosaic Association, National (NTMA)

Tile Council of America (TCA)

Tile Roofing Manufacturers Association, National (NTRMA)

TIME MEASUREMENT MANAGEMENT

Methods Time Management (MTM)

TOXIC HAZARDS
Carbon Dioxide Information Center (EPA)
Chemical Effects Information Center (EPA)
Hazardous Materials Information Center (EPA)
Toxicology Data Bank (EPA)
   Toxicology Information Response Center

TUBE/TUBING & FITTINGS
Tube & Pipe Association International (TPAI)
Tube Institute of North America, Steel (STINA)

U
UNDERGROUND CONSTRUCTION
Underground Construction Association, American (AUCA)

V
VACUUM
Measuring techniques, flanges & fittings on vacuum equipment (AVS)

VALVES/FITTINGS
Manufactured Standardization Society of the Valve & Fittings Industry (MSSVFI)
Mechanical Engineers, American Society of (ASME)

VENTILATION
Industrial Ventilation Manual of recommended practices (ACGH)
Ventilation Institute, Home (HVI)

VIBRATION/SHOCK
Vibration & Noise Testing, Wind System
   Solar Energy Research Institute (SERI/DOE)
Vibration Information Center, Shock & (USN)
   Shock Wave Data Center
Vibration Institute (VI)

W
WALLS
Ceilings & Interior Systems Construction Association (CISCA)
Gypsum Association (GA)
Vinyl Siding Institute (WSC)
Wall & Ceiling Industries International, Association of (AWCII)
WATER
Groundwater Research, National Center for (EPA)

Water Conservation Laboratory, US (USDA)

Water Data Exchange, National (USGS)

Water Data Storage & Retrieval System (USGS)

Water Quality Association (WQA)

Water Quality & Watershed Research Laboratory (USDA)

Water Quality Systems, Center for (EPA)

Water System Council (WSC)

Water Works Association, American (AWWA)

WASTEWATER

Sedimentation Laboratory, USDA (USDA)

Standard methods for examination of water & wastewater (APHA)

Water Environment Federation (WEF)

WATERPROOFING/DAMPNESS-PROOFING

Waterproofing & Restoration Institute, Sealant (SWRI)

WEATHER/CLIMATE

National Weather Service (NWS)

WELDING

Pipe Welding Bureau, National Certified (NCPWB)

Resistance Welder Manufacturers Association (RWMA)

Welding Research Council (WRC)

Welding Society, American (AWS)

WINDOWS/DOORS

Architectural Manufacturers Association, American (AAMA)

Door & Access Systems Manufacturers International (DASMI)

Door & Hardware Institute (DHI)

Window & Door Manufacturers Association (WDMA)

Window Institute, Steel (SWI)

WIRE/WIRE ROPE

Wire Fabricators Association (WFA)

Wire Producers Association, American (AWPA)

Wire Rope Fabricators, Associated (AWRF)

Wire Rope Technical Board (WRTB)

Woven Wire Products Association (WWPA)

WOOD/TIMBER/LUMBER

Architectural Woodwork Institute (AWI)

Cedar Shake & Shingle Bureau (CSSB)

Engineered Wood Association, The (APA)

Forest & Paper Association, American (AFPA)

Forest Products Laboratory (USDA)

Forest Products Society (FPS)

Hardboard Association, American (AHA)

Hardwood Lumber Association, National (NHLA)

Hardwood Manufacturers Association (HMA)

Hardwood Plywood & Veneer Association (HPVA)

Maple Flooring Manufacturers Association (MFMA)

Oak Flooring Manufacturers Association, National (NOFMA)

Redwood Association, California (CRA)

Southern Cypress Manufacturers Association (SCMA)

Southern Forest Products Association (SFPA)

Timber Products Manufacturers Association (TPMA)

Timber Construction, American Institute of (AITC)

Wood Flooring Association, National (NWFA)

Wood Preservers Association, American (AWPA)

Wood Preservers Institute, American (AWPI)

Wood Component Manufacturers Association (WCMA)

Wood Molding & Millwork Producers Association (WMMPA)

Wood Truss Council of America (WTCA)

WORKPLACE DESIGN

Visual Display Terminal (VDT)

Workplace design (HFS)

A

AA—Aluminum Association

AABC—Associated Air Balance Council

AACC—American Automation Control Council

AACE—Association for the Advancement of Cost Engineering

AAMA—American Architectural Manufacturers Association

AAPT—Association of Asphalt Paving Technologies

AASHTO—American Association of State Highway & Transportation Officials

ABC—Associated Builders & Contractors

ABMA—American Boiler Manufacturers Association

ACCA—Air Conditioning Contractors of America

ACI—American Concrete Institute

ACGIH—American Conference of Governmental Industrial Hygienists

ACEC—American Council of Engineering Consultants

ACIA—American Construction Inspectors Association

ACIL—American Council of Independent Laboratories

ACPA—American Concrete Pavement Association

ACPA—American Concrete Pipe Association

ACPA—American Concrete Pumping Association

ACPA—Asbestos Cement Pipe Producers Association

ACPPA—American Concrete Pressure Pipe Association

ACS—American Ceramic Society

ADC—Air Diffusion Council

ADDA—American Design Drafting Association

ADSC/IAFD—ADSC: The International Association of Foundation Drilling

AEE—Association of Energy Engineers

AEG—Association of Engineering Geologists

AEIC—Association of Edison Illuminating Companies

AEMA—Asphalt Emulsion Manufacturers Association

AFMA—American Fiber Manufacturers Association

AFPA—American Forest & Paper Association

AGA—American Galvanizers Association

AGA—American Gas Association

AGC—Associated General Contractors

AHA—American Hardboard Association

AHA—American Hospital Association

AHAM—Association of Home Appliance Manufacturers

AInA—American Institute of Architects

AIA/NA—Asbestos Information Association/North America

AICHAW—American Institute for Conservation of Historic & Artistic Works

AIChE—American Institute of Chemical Engineers

AIHA—American Industrial Hygiene Association

AIP—American Physics Institute

AIBD—American Institute of Building Design

AISC—American Institute of Steel Construction

AISE—Association of Iron & Steel Engineers

AITC—American Institute of Timber Construction

AIA—American Insurance Association

AISI—American Iron & Steel Institute

ALCA—Associated Landscape Contractors of America

ALA—American Lighting Association

ALA—Associated Locksmiths of America

ALAPCO—Association of Local Air Pollution Control Officials

ALI—American Ladder Institute

AMCA—Air Movement & Control Association

ANLA—American Nursery & Landscape Association

ANSI—American National Standards Institute

APA—American Planning Association

APA—American Plywood Association/The Engineered Wood Association

APA—Architectural Precast Association

APFA—American Pipe Fittings Association

APHA—American Public Health Association

API—Alliance for the Polyurethane Industry

API—American Petroleum Institute

APPA—Association of Higher Education Facilities Officers

APWA—American Public Works Association

AREMWA—American Railway Engineering & Maintenance of Way Association

ARI—Air Conditioning & Refrigeration Institute

ARTB—American Road & Transportation Builders Association

AEMA—Asphalt Emulsion Manufacturers Association

AI—Asphalt Institute

ARMA—Asphalt Roofing Manufacturers Association

ASA—Acoustical Society of America

ASAE—American Society of Agricultural Engineers

ASC—Adhesive Sealing Council

ASC—Associated Specialty Contractors

ASCC—American Society of Concrete Contractors

ASCE—American Society of Civil Engineers

ASCP—American Society of Consulting Planners

ASFE—Association of Engineering Firms Practicing in Geosciences

ASGCA—American Society of Golf Club Architects

ASHE—American Society for Healthcare Engineering

ASHRAE—American Society of Heating, Refrigeration & Air Conditioning Engineers

ASI—Allied Stone Industries

ASID—American Society of Interior Designers

ASIC—American Society of Irrigation Consultants

ASIS—American Society for Industrial Security

ASLA—American Society of Landscapes Architects

ASME—American Society of Mechanical Engineers

ASNT—American Society for Nondestructive Testing

ASPE—American Society of Plumbing Engineers

ASQ—American Society for Quality

ASTM—American Society for Testing & Materials

ASSE—American Society of Safety Engineers

ASSE—American Society of Sanitary Engineers

ASES—American Solar Energy Society

ASRS—Automated Storage & Retrieval Systems/APA

AUCA—American Underground-Construction Association

AWCI—Association of the Wall & Ceiling Industries

AWEA—American Wind Energy Association

AWI—Architectural Woodwork Institute

AWMA—Air & Waste Management Association

AWPA—American Wire Producers Association

AWPA—American Wood-Preservers' Association

AWPI—American Wood Preservers Institute

AWRF—Associated Wire Rope Fabrication

AWS—American Welding Association

AWWA—American Water Works Association

B

BHLA—Below-Hook Lifters Association

BHMA—Builders Hardware Manufacturers Association

BIA—Brick Industry Association

BOMA—Building Owners & Managers Association

BSI—Building Stone Institute

BIFMA—Business & Institutional Furniture Manufacturers Association

C

CAGI—Compressed Air & Gas Institute

CBMA—Certified Ballast Manufacturers Association

CDA—Copper Development Association

CEFPI—Council of Educational Facility Planners International

CEMA—Conveyor Equipment Manufacturers Association

CETA—Cleaning Equipment Trade Association

CFESA—Commercial Food Equipment Service Association

CFSBI—Cold Finished Steel Bar Institute

CGA—Compressed Gas Association

CI—Combustion Institute

CI—Composites Institute

CI—Cordage Institute

CIMA—Construction Industry Manufacturers Association

CISCA—Ceilings & Interior Systems Construction Association

CISPI—Cast Iron Soil Pipe Institute

CLFMI—Chain Link Fence Manufacturers Institute

CMAA—Crane Manufacturers Association of America

CPA—Composite Panel Association

CPA—Concrete Pipe Association

CPB—Contractors Pump Bureau

CPMB—Concrete Plant Manufacturers Bureau

CRA—California Redwood Association

CRI—Carpet & Rug Institute

CRMA—Commercial Refrigeration Manufacturers Association

CRSI—Concrete Reinforcing Steel Institute
CRSTIAC—Cold Regions Science & Technology Information Analysis Center
CSAA—Central Station Alarm Association
CSDA—Concrete Sawing & Drilling Association
CSI—Construction Specifications Institute
CSSB—Cedar Shake & Shingle Bureau
CTI—Cooling Tower Institute
CTIA—Ceramic Tile Institute of America

D

DASMA—Door & Access Systems Manufacturers Association
DCA—Distribution Contractors Association
DFI—Deep Foundation Institute
DHI—Door & Hardware Institute
DIPRA—Ductile Iron Pipe Research Association
DIS—Ductile Iron Society

E

EASA—Electrical Apparatus Service Association
EBA—Environmental Business Association
EEI—Edison Electric Institute
EERI—Earthquake Engineering Research Institute
EGSA—Electrical Generating Systems Association
EIA—Environmental Information Association
EJMA—Expanded Joint Manufacturers Association
EMI—Equipment Manufacturers Institute
EPRI—Electric Power Research Institute
ESCSI—Expanded Shale Clay & Slate Institute

F

FCI—Fluid Controls Institute
FEMA—Fire Equipment Manufacturers Association
FEMA—Foot Equipment Manufacturers Association
FEMSA—Fire & Emergency Manufacturers & Services Association
FMRG—Factory Mutual Research Group

FPS—Forest Products Society

FRCA—Fire Retardant Chemicals Association

FSA—Fluid Sealing Association

FSCT—Federation of Societies for Coatings Technology

FAMA—Fire Apparatus Manufacturers' Association

FSSA—Fire Suppression Systems Association

FTPI—Fiberglass Tank & Pipe Institute

G

GAMA—Gas Appliance Manufacturers Association

GANA—Glass Association of North America

GCBAA—Golf Course Builders Association of America

GICC—Glazing Industry Code Committee

GSCA—Gunite/Shotcrete Contractors Association

GA—Gypsum Association

H

HAI—Helicopter Association International

HEBEM—Horizontal Earth Boring Equipment Manufacturers

HEI—Heat Exchange Institute

HEIAC—Hydraulics Engineering Information Analysis Center

HFES—Human Factors & Ergonomics Society

HI—Hydraulics Institute

HI—Hydronics Institute

HMA—Hardwood Manufacturers Association

HMI—Hoist Manufacturers Institute

HPVA—Hardwood Plywood & Veneer Association

HTI—Hand Tools Institute

HTMA—Hydraulic Tool Manufacturers Association

HVI—Home Ventilation Institute

I

IA—Irrigation Association

IAIA—International Association for Impact Assessment

IAEI—International Association of Electrical Inspectors

IALD—Industrial Association of Lighting Designers

IAPMO—International Association of Plumbing & Mechanical Officials

IASM—International Association of Structural Movers

ICAA—Insulation Contractors Association of America

ICC—International Code Council

ICEA—Insulated Cable Engineers Association

ICPA—International Cast Polymer Association

ICPS—International Coalition for Procurement Standards

ICRI—International Concrete Repair Institute

IDA—International Desalination Association

IDA—International Door Association

IDEA—International District Energy Association

IDRC—International Development Research Council

IECA—International Erosion Control Association

IEEE—Institute of Electrical & Electronics Engineers

IES—Illuminating Engineering Society

IES—Institute of Environmental Sciences

IETA—International Electrical Testing Association

IFAI—Industrial Fabrics Association International

IFI—Industrial Fasteners Institute

IFMA—International Facility Management Association

IGGA—International Grooving & Grinding Association

IHEA—Industrial Heating Equipment Association

IIAR—International Institute of Ammonia Refrigeration

IIDA—International Interior Design Association

IIE—Institute of Industrial Engineers

IILP—International Institute for Lath & Plaster

ILIA—Indiana Limestone Institute of America

IME—Institute of Makers of Explosives

IMI—International Masonry Institute

IMSA—International Municipal Sign Association

INCE—Institute of Noise Control Engineers

INMM—Institute of Nuclear Materials Managers

IPA—Institute for Polyacrylate Absorbents

ISAS—Instrumentation, Systems & Automation Society

ISDI—Insulated Steel Door Institute

ISEA—Industrial Safety Equipment Association

ISNTA—International Staple, Nail & Tool Association

ISPE—International Society for Pharmaceutical Engineering

ISSA—International Slurry Surfacing Association

ITA—Instrumentation Testing Association

ITE—Institute of Transportation Engineers

L

LIA—Laser Institute of America

LIA—Lead Industries Association

LICA—Land Improvement Contractors of America

LMPS—Lift Manufacturers Product Section

LPI—Lightning Protection Institute

M

MCAA—Mechanical Contractors Association

MCSMA—Masonry & Concrete Saw Manufacturers Institute

MFMA—Maple Flooring Manufacturers Association

MFMA—Metal Framing Manufacturers Association

MHIA—Material Handling Industry Association

MIA—Marble Institute of America

MHI—Manufactured Housing Institute

MMA—Monorail Manufacturers Association

MMSA—Materials & Methods Standardization Association

MRS—Materials Research Society

MSSVFI—Manufactured Standardization Society of the Valve & Fittings Industry

MTICPI—Materials Technology Institute of the Chemical Processing Industry

N

NAAMM—National Association of Architectural Metal Manufacturers

NAEC—National Association of Elevator Contractors

NACM—National Association of Chain Manufacturers

NADC—National Association of Demolition Contractors

NAHB—National Association of Home Builders

NAIMA—North American Insulation Manufacturers Association

NAIOP—National Association of Industrial & Office Properties

NAPAC—National Association of Pipe Coating Applicators

NAPE—National Association of Power Engineers

NASC—National Association of Solar Contractors

NARI—National Association of the Remodeling Industry

NBBPVI—National Board of Boiler & Pressure Vessel Inspectors

NBGQA—National Building Granite Quarries Association

NBFAA—National Burglar & Fire Alarm Association

NCCLS—National Committee for Clinical Laboratory Standards

NCPI—National Clay Pipe Institute

NCPWB—National Certified Pipe Welding Bureau

NCMA—National Concrete Masonry Association

NCPA—National Paint & Coatings Association

NCPO/ASI—National Council of the Paper Industry for Air & Stream Improvement

NCRPM—National Council on Radiation Protection & Measurements

NCSBCS—National Conference of States on Building Codes & Standards

NCSPA—National Corrugated Steel Pipe Association

NEA—National Erectors Association

NEMA—National Electrical Manufacturers Association

NECA—National Electrical Contractors Association

NEBB—National Environmental Balancing Bureau

NEHA—National Environmental Health Association

NEI—National Elevator Industry

NFBA—National Frame Builders Association

NFSA—National Fire Sprinkler Association

NFPA—National Fire Protection Association

NFPA—National Fluid Power Association

NGA—National Glass Association

NHLA—National Hardwood Lumber Association

NIA—National Insulation Association

NIBS—National Institute of Building Sciences

NLA—National Landscape Association

NLA—National Lime Association

NOFMA—National Oak Flooring Manufacturers Association

NPA—National Parking Association

NPCA—National Pest Control Association

NPCA—National Precast Concrete Association

NPGA—National Propane Gas Association

NQPC—National Quartz Producers Council

NRCA—National Roofing Contractors Association

NRMCA—National Ready Mixed Concrete Association

NRDCA—National Roof Deck Contractors Association

NSC—National Safety Council

NSMS—National Safety Management Society

NSDJA—National Sash & Door Jobbers Association

NSA—National Slag Association

NSAE—National Society of Architectural Engineers

NSSGA—National Stone, Sand & Gravel Association

NSWMA—National Solid Waste Management Association

NSPI—National Spa & Pool Institute

NTCA—National Tile Contractors Association

NTMA—National Terrazzo & Mosaic Association

NUCA—National Utility Contractors Association

NWFA—National Wood Flooring Association

P

PCA—Portland Cement Association

PCI—Preccast/Prestressed Concrete Institute

PDCA—Painting & Decorating Contractors of America

PDI—Plumbing & Drainage Institute

PEI—Porcelain Enamel Institute

PEMA—Process Equipment Manufacturers Association

PFA—Polyurethane Foam Association

PFI—Pipe Fabrication Institute

PHCCNA—Plumbing-Heating-Cooling Contractors National Association

PI—Perlite Institute

PIMA—Polyisocyanurate Insulation Manufacturers Association

PLCA—Pipe Line Contractors Association

PMA—Polyurethane Manufactures Association

PMI—Plumbing Manufacturers Institute

PPFA—Plastic Pipe & Fittings Association

PPI—Plastic Pipe Institute

PSAI—Portable Sanitation Association International

PTI—Post-Tensioning Institute

PVMA—Pressure Vessel Manufacturers Association

R

RCI—Roof Consultants Institute

RCMA—Roof Coatings Manufacturers Association

RCRC—Reinforced Concrete Research Council

RMA—Rubber Manufactures Association

RCSC—Research Council on Structural Connections

RESNA—Rehabilitation Engineering Society of North America

RETA—Refrigeration Engineers & Technicians Association

RFCI—Resilient Floor Covering Institute

RWMA—Resistance Welder Manufacturers Association

S

SACMA—Suppliers of Advanced Composite Materials Association

SAE—Society of Automotive Engineers

SAVE—Society of American Value Engineers

SCA—Scaffold Contractors Association

SCMA—Southern Cypress Manufacturers Association

SES—Standards Engineering Society

SDI—Steel Deck Institute

SDI—Steel Door Institute

SFPA—Southern Forest Products Association

SFPE—Society of Fire Protection Engineers

SGCC—Safety Glazing Certification Council

SHCC—Solar Heating & Certification Corporation

SIA—Scaffold Industry Association

SIA—Security Industry Association

SIGMA—Sealed Insulating Glass Manufacturers Association

SJI—Steel Joist Institute

SMA—Screen Manufacturers Association

SMA—Steel Manufacturers Association

SMA—Stucco Manufacturers Association

SMACCNA—Sheet Metal & Air Conditioning Contractors National Association

SMPE—Society of Marine Port Engineers

SOEH—Society for Occupational & Environmental Health

SPC—The Society for Protective Coatings

SPE—Society of Plastics Engineers

SPED—Society of Piping Engineers & Designers

SPFA—Steel Plate Fabrication Association

SPI—Society of the Plastics Industry

SPRI—Single Ply Roofing Institute

SSA—Seismological Society of America

SSFI—Scaffolding Shoring & Framing Institute

SSPMA—Sump & Sewage Pump Manufacturers Association

SSRC—Structural Stability Research Council

STI—Steel Tank Institute

STI—Steel Tube Institute

SWI—Steel Window Institute

SWPA—Submersible Wastewater Pump Association

SWRI—Sealant, Waterproofing & Restoration Institute

T

TAPPI—Technical Association of the Pulp & Paper Industry

TCA—Tile Council of America

TCMA—Technical Ceramics Manufacturers Association

TCTBA—Tennis Court & Track Builders Association

TEMA—Tubular Exchange Manufacturers Association

TMMB—Truck Mixer Manufacturers Bureau

TPAI—Tube & Pipe Association International

TPI—Truss Plate Institute

TPMA—Timber Products Manufacturers Association

TRI—The Refractories Institute

TRMI—Tubular Rivet & Machine Institute TUCA—Tilt-Up Concrete Association

U

UL—Underwriters Laboratories

UBPPA—Uni-Bell PVC Pipe Association

UBPVLS—Uniform Boiler & Pressure Vessel Laws Society

ULA—Urban Land Institute

ULPA—United Lightning Protection Association

USAEWES—US Army Engineers Waterway Experiment Station

USITT—US Institute of Theatre Technology

V

VMAA—Valve Manufacturers Association of America
VI—Vibration Institute
VI—Vinyl Institute
VSI—Vinyl Siding Institute

W

WAI—Wire Association International
WCMA—Wood Component Manufacturers Association
WDMA—Window & Door Manufacturers Association
WEF—Water Environment Federation
WRTB—Wire Rope Technical Board
WFA—Wire Fabricators Association
WMMPA—Wood Molding & Millwork Producers Association
WQA—Water Quality Association
WRC—Welding Research Council
WRI—Wire Reinforcement Institute
WSC—Water Systems Council
WSTDA—Web Sling & Tie Down Association
WTCA—Wood Truss Council of America
WWPA—Woven Wire Products Association

A

Abrasive Engineers Society (AES) ,

144 Moore Road

Butler, PA 16001

Tel: (724) 282-6210

Fax: (724) 234-2376

Web: *www.abrasiveengineering.com*

Theodore L. Glese, Business Manager

> Develops standards for abrasives through an ANSI Committee; promoted industry-wide standards.

Acoustical Society of America (ASA)

Two Huntington Quadrangle #1NO1

Melville, NY 11747-4502

Tel: (516) 576-2360

Fax: (516) 576-2377

Web: *www.asa.aip.org*

Charles Schmidt, Executive Director

> Develops and publishes standards & specifications & methods of measuring and testing in the fields of physical acoustics, including architectural acoustics & mechanical shock & vibration; psychological & physiological acoustics, including shock & vibration with regard to biological safety, tolerance & comfort; and acoustical, environmental & occupational noise.

Adhesive & Sealant Council (ASC)

7979 Old Georgetown Road #500

Bethesda, MD 20814-2429

Tel: (301) 986-9700

Fax: (301) 986-9795

Web: *www.ascouncil.org*

Larry Sloan, President

Air & Waste Management Association (AWMA)

One Gateway Center 3rd Floor

420 Duquesne Boulevard

Pittsburg, PA 1522-1435

Tel: (412) 232-3444

Fax: (412) 232-3450

Web: *www.awma.org*

Richard Scherr, Executive Director

Works through other organizations to develop standards for:

Air Cleaning Equipment, ANSI Z-105;

Domestic Gas-Fired Incinerators, ANSI Z-21;

Incinerators, ANSI Z-228;

Installation of Oil Burners and Oil Burning Equipment, ANSI Z-91.

Publishes:

Air purity—Manual of Methods of Ambient Air Sampling Analysis

Air Conditioning & Refrigeration Institute (ARI)

4100 N Fairfax Drive #20

Arlington VA 22203

Tel: (703) 524-8800

Fax: (708) 528-3816

Web: *www.ari.org*

William G. Sutton, President

Develops equipment standards, covering:

Physical and operating characteristics of equipment and components;

Procedures for testing equipment to determine performance and operating characteristics;

Rating standards for converting data into general statements of capacity and performance;

Application standards specifying acceptable installation criteria, including initial selection of equipment.

Air Conditioning Contractors of America (ACCA)

2800 Shirlington Road #200

Arlington, VA 22206

Tel: (703) 575-4477

Fax: (703) 575-4449

Web: *www.acca.org*

Paul T. Stalknecht, President/CEO

Develops procedures and standards for residential and commercial heating and air conditioning system design, load calculation, and equipment selection. (Standards are specifically prepared for use by non-engineering system designers, although also used by engineers and others.)

Air Distributing Institute (ADI)

4415 W Harrison Street #242-C

Hillside, IL 60162

Tel: (708) 449-2933

Fax: (708) 449-0837

Web: *www.adi.org*

Patricia H. Keating, General Manager

Develops production distribution and use standards for pipe, duct, and fittings for warm-air heating and air conditioning systems.

Produces a numerical data system for identifying association member products.

Publishes: Simplified practices and recommendations

Air Movement & Control Association International (AMCA)

30 W University Drive

Arlington Heights, Il 60004-1893

Tel: (708) 394-0150

Fax: (708) 253-0088

Web: *www.amca.org*

Barbara L. Morrison, Executive Director

Develops standards to:

Measure the performance of all air moving devices and the sound power of this equipment, as well as air curtains and industrial ceiling fans, drive arrangements, sizes, classification for spark resistant construction, operating limits for centrifugal fans, and inlet box positions for centrifugal fans.

Develops testing procedures that are adopted as standards and used as a basis for rating the industry's products.

Aluminum Anodizers Council (AAC)

1000 N Rand Road #214

Wauconda, IL 60084

Tel: (847) 526-2010

Fax: (847) 526-3998

Web: *www.anodizing.org*

Gregory T. Rajsky, President

Develops anodized aluminum color standards for architectural applications.

Aluminum Association (AA)

1525 Wilson Boulevard #600

Arlington, VA 22209

Tel: (703) 358-2960

Fax: (793) 358-2961

Web: *www.aluminum.org*

J. Stephen Larkin, President

> Develops, publishes, and disseminates standards, technical data, and industry statistics for aluminum and aluminum alloy products, including extruded and tubular items, aluminum finishes, aluminum structures, and mold castings.

American Architectural Manufacturers Association (AAMA)

1827 Walden Office Square #550

Schaumburg, IL 60173-5774

Tel: 847-303-5664

Fax: 847-303-5774

Web: *www.aamanet.org*

Richard G. Walker, Executive Vice President

> Develops standards for aluminum prime windows and doors and sliding glass doors; energy balance calculating procedures and recommended test methods; and coatings and finishes for storm windows and doors, aluminum siding, hardware, and sealants.

American Association for Laboratory Accreditation (AALA)

5301 Buckeystown Pike #350

Frederick, MD 21704

Tel: (301) 644-3248

Fax: (301) 662-2974

Web: *www.a2la.org*

Peter S. Unger, President

> Accredits testing laboratories on a voluntary basis, developing criteria for each field of testing with the use of national standards, including acoustical, biological, chemical, construction materials, electrical, environmental, geotechnical, mechanical, non-destructive, and thermal.

> Develops standards for testing laboratories, including acoustical, construction materials, electrical, environmental, geotechnical, mechanical, non-destructive, thermal, and others.

> Special programs include asbestos, metals, metal fasteners, paint, radon, thermal insulation materials, windows and doors, and others.

> Accredits testing laboratories and inspection agencies on the basis of technical competence.

American Boiler Manufacturers Association (ABMA)

8221 Old Courthouse Road #207

Vienna, VA 22182-3839

Tel: (703) 356-7177

Fax: (703) 356-4543

Web: *www.abma.com*

W. Randall Rawson, President

Maintains a Technical Standards Committee.

Publishes: Lexicon of industry terminology, coal analysis, water quality, steam quality, and accessory product definitions

American Chain Association (ACA)

6724 Lone Oak Boulevard

Naples, FL 34109-6834

Tel: (239) 514-3441

Fax: (239) 514-3470

Web: *www.americanchaingassn.org*

Works through other organizations to develop standards for dimensions of rollers, silent engineering steel and malleable iron chains, sprockets and wheels, and recommended power capacity and speed for these chains.

American Coal Ash Association (ACAA)

15200 E. Girard Avenue #3050

Aurora, CO 80014-3955

Tel: (720) 870-7897

Fax: (720) 870-7889

Web: *www.acca-usa.org*

Erast Borissoff, Executive Director

American Composites Manufacturers Association (ACMA)

1010 N Glebe Road #450

Arlington, VA 22201

Tel: (703) 525-0511

Fax: (703) 525-0743

Web: *www.acmanet.org*

Melissa Henriksen, Executive Director

Works through other organizations to develop standards.

American Concrete Institute (ACI)

388800 Country Club Drive

Farmington, Hills, MI 48331

Tel: (248) 848-3700

Fax: (248) 848-3701

Web: *www.aci-int.org*

William R. Tolley, Executive Vice President

Develops codes, specifications, and standard practices related to the whole structure, rather than for basic materials and standard components.

American Concrete Pavement Association (ACPA)

1010 Massachusetts Avenue NW

Washington, DC 20001

Tel: (202) 842-1010

Fax: (202) 842-2022

Web: *www.pavement.com*

Gerald F. Voight, President/CEO

Prepares guide specifications on concrete pavement construction, fast track concrete paving, rehabilitation, resurfacing, and restoration.

On request, provides recommendations regarding concrete pavement design and construction.

American Concrete Pipe Association (ACPA)

222 Las Colinas Boulevard #641

Irving, TX 75039-5423

Tel: (972) 506-7216

Fax: (972) 506-7682

Web: *www.concretepipe.org*

Matt Childs, President

Works through other organizations to develop standards for precast concrete products such as non-reinforced pipe for sewers, culverts, drain tile, and irrigation; reinforced circular, arch, and elliptical pipes; box sections and manholes for sewers and culverts; reinforced circular pipes for low-head pressure systems; perforated pipes; joints, jointing materials, and resilient connectors for pipes to structure connections; plant test methods; and design of pipe and box sections, including determination of loads, stresses, and required structural strength.

Conducts research and publishes technical and industry information.

American Concrete Pressure Pipe Association (ACPPA)

11800 Sunrise Valley Drive #309

Reston, VA 20191-5302

Tel: (703) 391-9135

Fax: (703) 391-9136

Web: *www.acppa.org*

David Prosser

Works through other organizations to develop standards. Manufacturing standards cover reinforced concrete pressure pipe, reinforced concrete cylinder pipe, pretensioned concrete cylinder pipe, and prestressed concrete cylinder pipe.

American Conference of Governmental Industrial Hygienists (ACGH)

1330 Kemper Meadow Drive #600

Cincinnati, OH 45240-1634

Tel: (513) 742-2020

Fax: (513 242-3355

Web: *www.aegih.org*

Jack Heusser, Executive Secretary

> Develops industrial hygiene, airborne contaminants, Threshold Limit Values, and industrial ventilation and annually revises the Threshold Limit Value recommended on airborne contaminants and physical agents in the workplace.
>
> Publishes:
>
> The Industrial Ventilation Manual of Recommended Practices

American Council of Independent Laboratories (ACIL)

1629 K Street NW #400

Washington, DC 20006-1633

Tel: (202) 887-5872

Fax: (202) 887-0021

Web: *www.acil.org*

John Walsh Cassedy, Executive Director

> Works through other organizations to develop standards.
>
> Publishes:
>
> Recommended Requirements for Independent Laboratory Qualification (Manual of Practice encompassing a quality control system for personnel and equipment evaluations as well as calibration and standardization of the system).

American Electroplaters & Surface Finishers Society (AESFS)

3660 Maguire Boulevard #250

Orlando, FL 32803-3075

Tel: (407) 281-6441

Fax: (407) 281-6446

Web: *www.aesf.org*

John Bednerik, Executive Director

> Works through other organizations to develop standards.
>
> Maintains a formal representation on ASTM and ANSI committees.

American Fiber Manufacturers Association (AFMA)

1530 Wilson Boulevard #690

Arlington, VA 22209

Tel: (703) 875-0432

Fax: (703) 875-0907

Web: *www.fibersource.com*

Paul T. O'Day, President

> Works through other organizations to develop standards concerned with flammability of textile products, including home furnishing items, such as carpets, draperies, and upholstered furniture, as well as apparel; and flammability testing procedures, such as the Carpet Flooring Radiant Panel Test Method.

American Foundry Society (AFS)

1695 N Penny Lane

Schaumberg, Il 60173-4555

Tel: (708) 824-0181

Fax: (708) 824-7848

Web: *www.afsinc.org*

Jerry Call, Executive Vice President

> Develops standards under ANSI.

> Develops and disseminates technical information regarding metallurgy, melting, core making, molding, sand casting, and control of both internal and external environment of foundries.

American Galvanizers Association (AGA)

6881 S Holly Circle #108

Centennial, CO 80012-1145

Tel (720) 554-0900

Fax: (720) 554-0909

Web: *www.galvanizeit.org*

Philip G. Rahrig, Executive Director

> Works through other organizations to develop coating standards for hot dip galvanized (zinc-coated) steel products such as fasteners, castings, forgings, structural shapes, tanks, fencing, piping, grating, reinforcing bars, and structural plate; and specifications for galvanizing and corrosion protection.

American Gas Association (AGA)

400 N Capital Street #450

Washington, DC 20001

Tel: (202) 824-7000

Fax: (202) 824-7115

Web: *www.aga.org*

David N. Parker, President/CEO

> Participates in developing national standards, including residential gas appliances and accessories; commercial and industrial gas equipment; gas displacement meters; and the installation of gas piping and appliances, including their venting.

> Coordinates review and updating of the National Fuel Gas Code;

> Certifies gas equipment complying with applicable national gas standards.

American Helicopter Society International (AHS)

217 N Washington Street

Alexandria, VA 22314-2538

Tel: (703) 684-6777

Fax: (703) 739-9279

Web: *www.vtol.org*

Morris E. Flater, Executive Director

> Works through other organizations to develop standards covering acoustics, aircraft design, avionics and systems, propulsion, commercial operators, dynamics, handling qualities, crew stations and human factors, test and evaluation, and other factors.

American Hospital Association (AHA)

One N. Franklin

Chicago, IL 60606-3421

Tel: (312) 422-3000

Fax: (312) 422-4796

Web: *www.aha.org*

Richard J. Davidson, President

> Works through other organizations to develop codes and standards related to:
>
> Hospital planning, design, construction, engineering;
>
> Equipment supplies;
>
> Facility management;
>
> Fire and life safety;
>
> Infection control;
>
> Environmental issues.

American Hotel & Lodging Association (AHLA)

1201 New York Avenue NW #600

Washington, DC 20005-3931

Tel: (202) 289-3100

Fax: (202) 289-3106

Web: *www.ahma.com*

Joseph A. McInerney, President/CEO

> Works through other organizations to develop standards covering safety and protection from fire, toxicity, and smoke generation in hotels and motels; to ensure safe use of elevators, dumbwaiters, and escalators; and to find solutions to problems of toxicity and smoke generation.
>
> Publishes:
>
> USA Standards Safety Code for Elevators, Dumbwaiters, and Escalators
>
> Recommended Practices for the Inspection of Elevators

American Industrial Hygiene Association (AIHA)

2700 Prosperity Avenue #250

Fairfax, VA 22031

Tel: (703) 849-8888

Fax: (703) 207-3561

Web: *www.aiha.org*

Steven Davis, Executive Director

> Promotes the study and control of environmental stresses in or from the work place of its products in relation to the health or well-being of workers and the public.
> Publishes:
> American Industrial Hygiene Association Journal (monthly) and the Synergist (annual)

American Institute of Chemical Engineers (AIChE)

Three Park Avenue

New York, NY 10016-5991

Tel: (212) 591-7338

Fax: (212) 591-8888

Web: *www.aiche.org*

John A. Sofranko, Executive Director

> Develops standards and works through other organizations to develop acceptable codes and standards in the chemical engineering field.

American Institute of Physics (AIP)

One Physics Ellipse

College Park, MD 20740-3843

Tel: (301) 209-3100

Fax; (301) 209-0843

Web: *www.aip.org*

Mark Brodsky, Executive Director/CEO

American Institute of Steel Construction (AISC)

One E Wacker Drive #700

Chicago, IL 60601-1802

Tel: (312) 670-2400

Fax: (312) 670-5403

Web: *www.aisc.org*

H. Louise Gurthet, President

> Publishes:
> The AISC Specification for the Design, Fabrication, and Erection of Structural Steel for Buildings; the Manual of Steel Construction; the AISC Code of Standard Practice; and a number of specifications for materials, products, and assemblies used in steel framed structures.

American Institute of Timber Construction (AITC)

7012 S Revere Parkway #140

Centennial, CO 80112-3932

Tel: (303) 792-9559

Fax: (303) 792-0669

Web: *www.aitc-glulam.org*

R. Michael Caldwell, Executive Vice President

> Develops industry standards related to structural glued laminated timber and heavy timber construction.

American Insurance Association (AIA)

1130 Connecticut Avenue NW–10th Floor

Washington, DC 20036

Tel: (202) 828-7100

Fax: (202) 293-1219

Web: *www.aiadc.org*

Marc F. Racicet, President

> Works through other organizations to develop standards covering:
>
> Reduction and control of life and property losses, injuries, and damages to health and the environment;
>
> Fire protection, nuclear, chemical, and environmental concerns;
>
> Construction and construction safety;
>
> Personnel safety in the workplace;
>
> Products, including boilers and machinery, among other concerns.
>
> Publishes:
>
> Workers' Compensation Digest (annual)

American Iron & Steel Institute (AISI)

1140 Connecticut Avenue NW #705

Washington, DC 20036

Tel: (202) 452-7100

Fax: (202) 463-6573

Web: *www.steel.org*

Andrew G. Sharkey, III, President/CEO

> Develops design specifications for cold-formed steel structural members and for light-gage cold-formed stainless steel structural members.

American Ladder Institute (ALAI)

401 N Michigan Avenue

Chicago, IL 60611-4267

Tel: (312) 644-6610

Fax: (312) 527-6705

Web: *www.americanladderinstitute.org*

Ron Pietrzak, Executive Director

Develops standards to promote uniform design, manufacturing, and safe use of ladders, stages, temporary scaffolding, mobile scaffolds, ladder towers, and telescopic work platforms; portable metal, portable wooden, portable reinforced plastic, and fixed and rolling ladders; and ladder accessories.

American Lighting Association (ALA)

2050 Stemmons Freeway #10046

PO Box 420288

Dallas, TX 75342-0288

Tel: (214) 698-9898

Fax: (214) 698-9899

Web: *www.americanlightingassoc.com*

Richard D. Upton, Managing Director

Works through other organizations to develop standards for lighting fixtures, portable lamps, lamps (bulbs), and lighting accessories.

American Lumber Standards Committee (NIST)

National Institute of Standards & Technology/DOC

PO Box 210

Germantown, MD 20874

Tel: (301) 972-1700

Fax: (301) 540-8004

Web: *www.alsc.org*

Thomas D. Searles, Executive Vice President

Sets the standards under which virtually all lumber is produced in the United States and Canada.

Reviews and approves rules submitted by agencies to assure they conform to the American Lumber Standards requirements.

Reviews and approves grading agencies.

American Monument Association (AMA)

4719 Reed Road #364

Columbus, OH 43143-1150

Tel: (614) 461-5852

Fax: (614) 461-1497

Web: *www.ama.org*

Pennie L. Sable, Executive Director

Quarries, fabricators, and dealers of memorial and monument stone.

American National Standards Institute (ANSI)

1819 L Street NW #600

Washington, DC 20036

Tel: (202) 293-8020

Fax: (202)293-9287

Web: *www.ansi.org*

S. Joseph Bhatia, President/CEO

11 West 42nd Street–13th Floor

New York, NY 10036

Tel: (212) 642-4900

Fax: (212) 398-0023

Web: *www.ansi.org*

Manuel Peralta, President

> Does not develop standards.
>
> Coordinates development of voluntary national standards in the United States by qualified technical and professional societies, trade associations, and other groups.
>
> Approves the standards as American National Standards.
>
> Manages & coordinates US participation in non-governmental international standards developing organizations. Maintains interface with government at all levels on standards-related matters.

American Nursery & Landscape Association (ANLA)

1000 Vermont Avenue NW #300

Washington, DC 20005-4914

Tel: (202) 789-2900

Fax: (202) 789-1893

Web: *www.anla.org*

Robert J. Dolibois, Executive Vice President

> Develops grades and standards for trees, shrubs, roses, vines, bulbs, tubers, and forest seedlings, including height, caliper, root size, root ball, container size, and various other standardized means of describing nursery plants.

American Pipe Fittings Association (APFA)

201 Park Washington Court

Falls Church, VA 22046

Tel: (703) 538-1786

Fax: (703) 241-5623

Web: *www.apfa.com*

Clay D/Tyeryar, Executive Director

> Works through other organizations to develop standards for pipe fittings and other products such as hangers and supports.

American Public Health Association (APHA)

800 I Street NW

Washington, DC 20001

Tel: (202) 777-2742

Fax: (202) 777-2534

Web: *www.apha.org*

George Benjamin, Executive Director

> Develops standards of procedures, personnel qualifications, and practices.
> Publishes:
> Standard Methods for Examination of Water & Wastewater
> Standards for Healthful Housing
> Suggested Ordinances and Recommendations Covering Public Swimming Pools
> Standard Methods for the Microbiological Examination of Ambient Air
> Other publications where standards are included

American Public Works Association (APWA)

2345 Grand Boulevard #300

Kansas City, MO 64108-2641

Tel: (816) 472-6100

Fax: (816) 472-1610

Web: *www.apwa.net*

Richard H. Sullivan, Executive Director

> Adapted standard Pavement Condition Index, with the US Army Corps of Engineers, for use on streets & standardized visual inspection for built-up roofs.
> Develops standards for implementation of Geo-Basic Information Systems for local governments and utilities.

American Road & Transportation Builders Association (ARTBA)

1219 28th Street NW

Washington, DC 20007-3712

Tel: (202) 289-4434

Fax: (202) 289-4435

Web: *www.artba.org*

T. Peter Ruane, President/CEO

> Develops standards covering highway design, construction, and maintenance; construction materials; and equipment.

American Society for Non-destructive Testing (ANSI)

1771 Arlingate Lane

PO Box 28518

Columbus, OH 43228-0518

Tel: (614) 274-6003

Fax: (614) 274-6899

Web: *www.anst.org*

Wayne Holliday, Executive Director

> Develops recommended practices for non-destructive testing, including radiography, ultrasonics, eddy current, leak testing, neutron radiography, magnetic particle, liquid penetrant, and acoustic emission.
>
> Works with other organizations to develop and review codes & standards for the inspection of conventional & nuclear power plants & other industry products.
>
> Offers Level III examinations in radiography, ultrasonics, eddy current, leak testing, neutron radiography, magnetic particle, liquid penetrant, and acoustic emission examinations.

American Society for Quality (ASQ)

611 E Wisconsin Avenue

PO Box 3005

Milwaukee, WI 53201-3005

Tel: (414) 272-8575

Fax: (414) 272-1734

Web: *www.asq.org*

Paul E. Borawski, Executive Director

> Develops standards covering quality control, quality assurance, quality systems, quality management, and sampling & inspection.

American Society of Civil Engineers (ASCE)

1801 Alexander Bell Drive

Reston, VA 20191-4400

Tel: (703) 295-6000

Fax: (703) 295-6222

Web: *www.asce.org*

Patrick J. Natale, P. E., Executive Director

> Develops standards in such areas as:
>
> Steel Deck and Concrete Diaphragm Standard;
>
> Pile Foundation Standard;
>
> Structural Applications for Steel Cables for Buildings Standard;
>
> Minimum Design Loads for Buildings and Other Structures (formerly ANSI A58.1);
>
> Design of Steel Transmission Towers Standard;
>
> Stainless Steel Cold-Formed Standard;
>
> Design Loads on Structures during Construction Standard, among others.

American Society of Heating, Refrigerating & Air Conditioning Engineers (ASHRAE)

1791 Tullie Circle NE

Atlanta, GA 30329-2305

Tel: (404) 636-8400

Fax: (404) 321-5478

Web: *www.ashrae.org*

Jeff Littleton, Executive Vice President/Secretary

Develops:

Standards for heating, refrigeration, air conditioning, ventilation systems, energy conservation, and environmental quality;

Specifications for methods of testing for rating equipment, ventilation levels for indoor air quality, and conditions for indoor comfort;

Offers a uniform method of testing for rating purposes;

Suggests safe practices in designating and installing equipment.

American Society of Mechanical Engineers (ASME)

Three Park Avenue

New York, NY 10016-5990

Tel: (212) 591-7000

Fax: (212) 591-7674

Web: *www.asme.org*

Virgil R. Carter, FAIA, Executive Director

Develops standards that are processed through ANSI covering:

Screw threads, bolts, nuts, rivets, and other fasteners;

Valves, pipe fittings, and plumbing fixtures;

Cranes, conveyors, and related equipment.

Publishes:

The Boiler and Pressure Vessel Code, a definitive compilation of safety and performance requirements for power and heating boilers, nuclear reactors and power plants, and pressure vessels

Performance Test Codes that define accepted methods of determining performance and efficiency for a wide range of equipment and systems, from safety valves and gas turbines to fuels, incinerators, and centrifugal pumps

Safety codes for elevators and escalators and related material handling equipment

American Society of Plumbing Engineers (ASPE)

8614 W Cartalpa Avenue #107

Chicago, IL 60605-1116

Tel: (773) 693-2773

Fax: (773) 695-9007

Web: *www.aspe.org*

Stanley M. Wolfson, Executive Director

> Works through other organizations to develop standards.

> Provides advisory service to builders, architects, and property owners in preparing plumbing drawings and concise specifications.

American Society of Safety Engineers (ASSE)

1800 E Oakton Street

Des Plaines, IL 60018-2187

Tel: (708) 692-4121

Fax: (708) 296-3769

Web: *www.asse.org*

Fred Forman, Executive Director/Secretary

> Develops standards and works through other organizations to develop standards covering such areas as eye protection, confined spaces, workplace railings and stairways, and fall protection equipment.

American Society of Sanitary Engineering (ASSE)

901 Canterbury Road #4

Westlake, OH 44145

Tel: (440) 835-3040

Fax: (440) 835-3488

Web: *www.asse-plumbing.org*

Shannon Corcoran, Executive Director

> Develops performance standards for plumbing system components, providing a tool for measuring quality and effectiveness of products, including backflow prevention devices, pressure regulators, water hammer arresters, water mixing and shower control valves, antisiphon hydrants, and other devices that directly affect public health and safety.

American Sports Builders Association (ASBA)

101 Mariners Drive

Ormond Beach, FL 32176-2372

Tel: (512) 858-9890

Fax: (512) 858-9892

Web: *www.sportsbuilders.org*

Carol T. Hogan, Executive Director

> Develops standards for design and construction of tennis courts, game courts, and running tracks, including court and track surface materials, fencing, lighting systems, and court accessories.

Publishes:

Tennis Court & Running Track Guide Specifications

Series of technical bulletins on tennis courts and tracks covering dimensions (with metric equivalents), windscreens, site investigation, site preparation, earthwork drainage, and base/court construction

Guidelines for reconditioning fast-dry tennis courts, tennis court orientation, and soil sterilization

Color finish systems for tennis courts and resurfacing of asphalt courts

American Water Works Association (AWWA)

6666 W Quincy Avenue

Denver, CO 80235-3098

Tel: (303) 794-7711

Fax: (303) 794-2461

Web: *www.awwa.org*

Jack Hoffbuhr, Executive Director

Develops standards for a variety of pipes, fittings, valves, wells, pumps, water treatment chemicals, water storage tanks, water meters & procedures for installation and use of these products.

Publishes:

Standard Methods for the Examination of Water and Wastewater (190 laboratory tests developed jointly with the American Public Health Association & Water Environment Federation.)

American Welding Society (AWS)

550 NW LeJuene Road

Miami, FL 33126

Tel: (305) 443-9353

Fax: (305) 443-7559

Web: *www.aws.org*

Roy Shook, Executive Director

Develops standards such as codes, specifications, and recommended practices covering four broad categories of welding:

Fundamentals, including metric practice, symbols, testing, filler metals, safety, and health;

Processes, including resistance welding, thermal spraying, brazing, soldering, oxy-fuel, ARC, friction, and high energy;

Inspection, including methods, mechanical testing, and qualification of welders and procedures;

Industrial applications of welding, including structural, water tanks, sheet metal, piping and tubing, and machinery.

American Wire Producers Association (AWPA)

801 N Fairfax Street #211

Alexandria, VA 22314-1750

Tel: (703) 299-4434

Fax: (703) 299-9233

Web: *www.awpa.org*

Kimberly A. Korbel, Executive Director

> Develops standard manuals for round and flat shaped wires, including spring wire, rope wire, and stapling wire.

American Wood Preservers Association (AWPA)

PO Box 388

Selma, AL 36702

Tel: (334) 874-9800

Fax: (334) 874-9008

Web: *www.awpa.com*

Colin McGown, Executive Vice President

> Works through other organizations to develop standards for treated wood.

American Wood Preservers Institute (AWPI)

12100 Sunset Hills Road #120

Reston, VA 20190

Tel: (703) 204-0500

Fax: (703)

Web: *www.preservedwood.com*

Parker Brugge, President

> Develops standards and specifications for wood preservatives and their introduction into the materials to be preserved, including preservatives, treatment of commodities, analysis methods, and conversion tables.

APA-The Engineered Wood Association (APA)

7011 South 19th Street

Tacoma, WA 98466

Tel: (253) 565-6600

Fax: (253) 565-7265

Web: *www.apawood.org*

David Rogoway, President

> Develops standards encompassing engineering design, manufacturing, and application of plywood and other structural-use panels.

> Develops performance criteria for qualification of structural panels in accordance with their end use.

Appalachian Hardwood Manufacturers Association (AHMA)

PO Box 427

High Point, NC 27261

Tel: (919) 885-8315

Fax: (919) 886-8865

Web: *www.appalachianwood.org*

Mark A. Barford, President

Architectural Engineering Institute (AEI)

(Affiliate of ASCE)

1801 Alexander Bell Drive

Reston, VA 20191-4400

Tel: (703) 295-6300

Fax: (703) 295-6222

Web: *www.aeinstitute.org*

Patricia S. Brown, Director

Architectural Precast Association (APA)

8710 Winkler Road #8

Ft. Meyers, FL 33910

Tel: (239) 454-6989

Fax: (239) 454-6787

Web: *www.archprecast.org*

Fred L. McGee, Executive Director/CEO

> Develops standards for precast concrete panels.
>
> Prepares the guide Specifying Precast Concrete Panels and the CSI Specification Series 03410, in conjunction with the Construction Specifications Institute.

Architectural Woodwork Institute (AWI)

1952 Isaac Newton Square West

Reston, VA 20190

Tel: (703) 733-0600

Fax: (703) 733-0584

Web: *www.awinet.org*

Judith B. Durham, Executive Vice President

> Develops standards for the fabrication of architectural woodwork (also called millwork); and for cost accounting, estimating, detailing, and billing of architectural woodwork.
>
> Publishes:
>
> Quality Standards for Architectural Woodwork and Guide Specifications for Architectural Woodwork

Asbestos Cement Pipe Producers Association (ACPPA)

1745 Jefferson Davis Highway #509

Arlington, VA 22202

Tel: (703) 560-2980

Fax: (703) 560-2981

Web: *www.acppa.org*

Robert J. Pigg, President

> Works through other organizations to develop standards covering asbestos cement water and sewer pipe, and special applications.

Asbestos Information Association/North America (AIANA)

1235 Jefferson Davis Highway #509

Arlington, VA 22202

Tel: (703) 979-1150

Fax: (703) 979-1152

Web: *www.aiana.org*

Robert J. Pigg, President

> Develops standards on health and safety aspects of asbestos and its use.

Asphalt Emulsion Manufacturers Association (AEMA)

3 Church Circle #250

Annapolis, MD 21401

Tel: (410) 267-0023

Fax: (410) 267-7546

Web: *www.aema.org*

Michael R. Krissoff, Executive Director

> Develops a series of recommended performance guidelines for the manufacture of emulsified asphalt, and the proper use of asphalt emulsions, slurry seals, and seal coats in construction.

Asphalt Institute (AI)

Asphalt Institute Building

2696 Research Park Drive

PO Box 14052

Lexington, KY 40511

Tel: (606) 288-4960

Fax: (606) 288-4999

Web: *www.asphaltinstitute.org*

Gerald S. Triplett, President

> Develops Asphalt Institute Guidelines, many of which are subsequently processed as ASTM and AASHTO standards.

Asphalt Roofing Manufacturers Association (ARMA)

1156 15th Street NW #900

Washington, DC 20005

Tel: (202) 207-0917

Fax: (202) 223-9741

Web: *www.asphaltroofing.org*

Russell K. Snyder, Executive Vice President

> Works through other organizations to develop standards covering asphalt roofing products, including asphalt shingles, roll goods, and allied roofing products; and coordinates industry standard activities to assure recommended application practices adhere to building code requirements.

Associated Air Balance Council (AABC)

1518 K Street NW #503

Washington, DC 20005

Tel: (202) 737-0202

Fax: (202) 638-4833

Web: *www.aabchq.com*

Kenneth M. Sufka, Executive Director

> Develops standards for testing and balancing air handling systems and AABC National Standards—a performance standard for Total System Balancing.

Associated General Contractors of America (AGC)

2300 Wilson Boulevard

Arlington, VA 22200

Tel: (703) 548-3118

Fax: (703) 548-3119

Web: *www.agc.org*

> Works through other organizations to develop standards covering fields, such as safety & health procedures for construction sites, contract documents for use by contractors & owners for a wide range of contractual variations, federal procurement regulations, and training & competency of on-site construction workers & supervisors.

Associated Locksmiths of America (ALA)

3500 Easy Street

Dallas, TX 75247-6414

Tel: (214) 819-9733

Fax: (214) 819-9736

Web: *www.aloa.org*

Charles W. Gibson, Jr., Executive Director

> Develops standards for locking devices, building security systems, and other equipment.

Association for Iron & Steel Technology (AISI)

186 Thorn Hill Road

Warrendale, PA 15086

Tel: (724) 776-6040

Fax: (724) 776-1880

Web: *www.aist.org*

Ronald E. Ashburn, Executive Director

Advances the technical development, production, processing, and application of iron and steel.

Develops standards for the steel industry, including:

DC Mill Motor Standards;

AC Mill Motor Standards;

Standard for Machine Surface Finishes;

Alloy Steel Chain and Alloy Steel Chain Slings for Overhead Lifting;

Specifications for Design of Ladle Hooks;

Design of Hot Metal Ladles;

Specifications for Design and Construction of Mill Buildings;

New Steel Pressure-Containing Components for Blast Furnace Installers, among others.

Association of American Railroads/Hazardous Materials (AAR/HM)

50 F Street NW

Washington, DC 20001-1564

Tel: (202) 639-2100

Fax: (202) 639-2558

Web: *www.aar.org*

Edward R. Hamberger, President

Develops standards pertaining to covering:

Packaging, labeling, handling, and transportation of hazardous materials; Specifications, standards, and recommended practices dealing with railroad mechanical equipment, communications and signal systems, among other railroad standard needs.

Association of Edison Illuminating Companies (AEIC)

PO Box 2641

600 North 18th Street

Birmingham, AL 35291-0992

Tel: (205) 250-2530

Fax: (205) 250-2540

Web: *www.aeil.org*

Robert Huffman, Executive Director

Develops standards relating to the electric utility industry.

Prepares and publishes specifications for high voltage underground cable design used in the industry.

Association of Engineering Geologists (AEG)

PO Box 460518

Denver, Co 80246

Tel: (303) 757-2926

Fax: (303) 757-2969

Web: *www.aegweb.org*

Becky Roland, Chief of Staff Secretary

> Develops standards, including code provisions for development of floodplains and tidal marshlands; and standard map symbols for use by all states and counties.

Association of Equipment Manufacturers (AEM)

(Formerly CIMA)

6737 N. Washington Street #2400

Milwaukee, WI 53214-5647

Tel: (414) 272-0943

Fax: (414) 272-1170

Web: *www.aem.org*

Dennis J. Slater, President

> Develops standards in areas of safety, health, and environmental performance for construction equipment, including criteria for machine safety, protective devices, noise characteristics, and so forth, as opposed to engineering standards that dictate equipment design.

Association of the Wall & Ceiling Industries-International (AWCI)

803 W Broad Street #600

Falls Church, VA 22046-3108

Tel: (703) 534-8300

Fax: (703) 534-8307

Web: *www.awci.org*

Steven A. Etkin, Executive Vice President

> Develops proprietary standards and works through other organizations to address standardization of materials, systems, and application/installation procedures for asbestos abatement, acoustic systems, carpentry, coatings, demountable partitions, exterior insulation and finish systems, fireproofing, flooring systems, lathing, furring, plastering, texturing, insulation, light-gage steel framing.

ASTM International (ASTM)

(American Society for Testing & Materials)

100 Barr Harbor Drive

PO Box C700

West Conshohocken, PA 19428-2959

T: (610) 832-9500

Fax: (610) 832-9500

Web: *www.astm.org*

James A. Thomas, President

> Develops standards on characteristics & performance of materials, products, systems & services, including classifications, guides, practices, specifications, terminology & test methods. Standards cover iron, steel & non-ferrous metals; construction; paints & related coatings; textiles; plastics; rubber; electrical insulation; water & environmental technology; nuclear, solar & geothermal energy; general methods & instrumentation; and other materials, products, and methodologies.

International Coalition for Procurement Standards/ASTM (ICPS)

> Works through other organizations to develop standards, specifications, and test methods that do not exist currently.

AVS Science & Technology Society (AVS)

120 Wall Street, 32nd Floor

New York, NY 10005

Tel: (212) 248-0200

Fax: (212) 248-0245

Web: *www.avs.org*

Yvonne Towse, Administrative Director

> Develops standards for nomenclature, measuring techniques & such items as flanges & fittings on vacuum equipment.

B

Brick Industry Association (BIA)

11490 Commerce Park Drive #300

Reston, VA 20191-1525

Tel: (703) 620-0010

Fax: (703) 620-3928

Web: *www.gobrick.org*

Richard Jennison, President

> Develops standards involving or related to Brick Masonry, including:
> Building Code Requirements for Masonry Structures (ACI 530, ASCE 5);
> Specifications for Masonry Structures (ACI 530.1, ASCE 6);
> ASTM—
> Mortar for Unit Masonry (C-12)
> Manufactured Masonry Units (C-15)
> Paint and Related Coatings and Materials (D-1)
> Fire Testing (E-5)

Performance of Building Constructions (E-6)

Building Seismic Safety Council (NFPA).

Conducts research for the development of new standards dealing with masonry design and applications.

Builders Hardware Manufacturers Association (BHMA)

355 Lexington Avenue–17th Floor

New York, NY 10017-6603

Tel: (212) 297-2122

Fax: (212) 370-9047

Web: *www.buildershardware.com*

Peter S. Rush, Executive Director

Develops standards for builders hardware, including locks, door closers, and exit devices, among other products.

Building Owners & Managers Association International (BOMA)

1201 New York Avenue NW #300

Washington, DC 20005

Tel: (202) 408-2662

Fax: (202) 326-6377

Web: *www.boma.org*

Chamberlain, Executive Vice President

Develops standards covering safety for power operated platforms and equipment used for exterior and interior building maintenance, energy conservation, and methods for measuring floor space in office buildings.

Business & Institutional Furniture Manufacturers Association (BIFMA)

2680 Horizon Drive SE #A-1

Grand Rapids, MI 49546-7500

Tel: (616) 285-3463

Fax: (616) 285-3765

Web: *www.bifma.org*

Thomas Reardon, Executive Director

Develops standards for the design and testing of office and institutional furniture, including tests for office chairs, lateral and vertical files, desks, lounge furniture, and panel systems furniture.

C

California Redwood Association (CRA)

(*Division, Redwood Inspection Services*)

405 Enfrente Drive #200

Novato, CA 94949

Tel: (868) 225-7339

Fax: (415) 382-8531

Web: *www.calredwood.org*

Christopher Grover, President

> Develops standards and specifications for Grades of California Redwood Lumber.
>
> Adopts standard specifications for grades, sizes, patterns, and grade marks for redwood lumber; planing-mill products; and special purpose uses for redwood lumber, including tank stock, stadium seat stock, foundation sills, structural grades, structural glue laminating grades, and miscellaneous products such as railroad ties, cooling tower material, and shingles and shakes.

Carpet & Rug Institute (CRI)

PO Box 2048

310 Holiday Avenue

Dalton, GA 30722-2048

Tel: (706) 278-3176

Fax: (706) 278-8835

Web: *www.carpet-rug.com*

Werner Brau, President

> Works through other organizations to develop standards for testing various components or characteristics of carpets and rugs.

Cast Iron Soil Pipe Institute (CISPI)

5959 Shallow Ford Road #419

Chattanooga, TN 37421

Tel: (423) 892-0137

Fax: (423) 892-0817

Web: *www.cispi.org*

William H. LeVan, Executive Vice President

> Develops standards for cast iron soil pipe and fittings, testing, and evaluation, including setting dimensions and specifications that provide interchangeability between all manufacturers' pipes and fittings.

Cedar Shake & Shingle Bureau (CSSB)

PO Box 1178

Suma South, WA 98295-1178

Tel: (674) 820-7700

Fax: (674) 800-0266

Web: *www.cedarbureau.org*

Lynne Christensen, President/CEO

> Develops and revises standards relating to the quality, packaging, and application of shakes and shingles.

Inspects shake and shingle mills and issues labels for product identification by complying mills.

Inspects and labels shakes and shingles manufactured from species other than red cedar, under the auspices of the Wood Shake and Shingle Association, an in-house subsidiary.

Ceilings & Interior Systems Construction Association (CISCA)

1500 Lincoln highway #202

St. Charles, IL 60174-2386

T: (630) 584-1919

F: (630) 584-2003

Web: *www.cisca.org*

Bonny Luck, Executive Director

Works through other organizations to develop standards for acoustical tile and lay-in panel ceilings, including:

ASTM Standard Specification for Metal Suspension Systems for Acoustical Tile and Lay-in Panel Ceilings (ASTM C635-69);

Standard Recommended Practice for Installation of Metal Ceiling Suspension Systems for Acoustical Tile and Lay-in Panels (ASTM C636-69);

Recommended Standards for Seismic Restraint of Direct-Hung Suspended Ceiling Assemblies.

Cellulose Insulation Manufacturers Association (CIMA)

136 S Keowee Street

Dayton, OH 45402

Tel: (937) 222-2462

Fax: (937) 222-5794

Web: *www.cellulose.org*

Daniel Lea, Executive Director

Works through other organizations to develop standards that apply to cellulose insulation

Certifies compliance with CPSC Interim Safety Standard 16 CFR Part 1209 and ASTM C-739 for initial certification.

Monitors and documents continuing compliance with fire, corrosion, and settled density sections of ASTM C-739 and FTC "R-Value-Rule" (16 CFR Part 460).

Chain Link Fence Manufacturers Institute (CLFMI)

10015 Columbia Road #B-215

Columbia, MD 21046

Tel: (301) 596-2583

Fax: (301) 596-2594

Web: *www.chainlinkinfo.org*

Mark Levin, Executive Vice President

> Develops standards for fencing specifications.

> Publishes:

> A product manual which includes ASTM standards

Chlorine Institute (CI)

1300 Wilson Boulevard

Rosslyn, VA 22209

Tel: (703) 741-5760

Fax: (703) 741-6068

Web: *www.chlorineinstitute.org*

Kathleen Shaver

> Works through other organizations to develop standards concerning the safe manufacturing, transportation, and use of chlorine and caustic soda.

> Publishes:

> Literature and drawings of equipment as guidelines and recommended practices for handling chlorine, caustic soda, and caustic potash

Cleaning Equipment Trade Association (CETA)

7691 Central Avenue NE #201

Fridley, MN 55432-3541

Tel: (763) 786-9200

Fax: (763) 786-7775

Web: *www.ceta.org*

Carol Waieleski, Managing Director

> Develops standards for safe use of cleaning equipment, including water blasters, industrial cleaning machines, and steam cleaners.

Cold Formed Parts & Machine Institute (CFPMI)

25 North Broadway

Tarrytown, NY 10591-3201

Tel: (914) 332-0040

Fax: (914) 332-1541

Web: *www.cfpmi.org*

Richard C. Byrne, Secretary

> Develops standards covering rivets and rivet setting machines.

> Distributes Metric Dimensional Standards for General Semi-Tubular Rivets.

> Publishes: Metric and inch engineering standards

> Safety standards for use of rivet setting machines.

Commercial Refrigeration Manufacturers Association (CRMA)

(Affiliate of ARI)

4100 N Fairfax Drive #200

Arlington, VA 22203

Tel: (703) 524-8800

Fax: (703) 528-3816

Web: *www.ari.org*

William G. Sutton, President

Develops standards for refrigerated display cases and cabinets, food service refrigerators, and sectional cooling rooms.

Compliance Board (CB)

(Formerly: Architectural & Transportation Barriers Compliance Board)

1111 18th Street NW #501

Washington, DC 20036

Tel: (202) 653-7834

Web: *www.access-board.gov*

Information Officer: Paul Beatty, Office of Technical and Information Services

Develops and revises:

Minimum Guideline Requirements for Accessible Design

Publication serves as a basis for the Uniform Federal Accessibility Standards (UFAS) developed by the federal government's standard-setting agencies: the General Services Administration, Department of Defense, Department of Housing & Urban Development, and the US Postal Service.

Composite Panel Association (CPA)

(Absorbed American Hardboard Association)

18922 Premier Court

Gaithersburg, MD 20879-1574

Tel: (301) 670-0604

Fax: (301) 840-1252

Web: *www.pbmdf.com*

Thomas A. Julia, President

Develops standards for hardboard, prefinished hardboard paneling, hardboard siding, and fiberboard products.

Publishes: Specifier's Guide to Particleboard and Medium-Density Fiberboard

Compressed Air & Gas Institute (CAGI)

1300 Sumner Avenue

Cleveland, OH 44115-2851

Tel: (215) 241-7333

Fax: (216) 241-0105

Web: *www.cagi.org*

John H. Addington, Executive Vice President

Develops standards, including:

Performance statements that identify parameters for performance evaluation of centrifugal compressors;

Test standard for rating compressed air dryers;

Test code for sound measurement of pneumatic equipment, ANSI S5.1.

Compressed Gas Association (CGA)

4221 Walney Road, 5th Floor

Chantilly, VA 20151

Tel: (703) 788-2700

Fax: (703)961–1831

Web: *www.cganet.com*

Carl T. Johnson, President

Develops standards for safety and methods of handling, transporting, and storing gases; and technical specifications pertaining to the compressed gas and related product and service industries, including the medical fields of anesthesia and respiration.

Publishes: Handbook of Compressed Gases and pamphlets that contain a description of the used gases and give in detail the safest methods for handling and storing gases

Concrete Reinforcing Steel Institute (CRSI)

933 N Plum Grove Road

Schaumburg, IL 60173-4758

Tel: (708) 517-1200

Fax: (708) 517-1206

Web: *www.crsi.org*

Susan O'Sullivan, Financial Administrator

Develops standards on bar supports, placing reinforcing bars, concrete joist construction, detailing reinforced concrete, and splicing reinforcing steel.

Concrete Sawing & Drilling Association (CSDA)

1101 Danka Way North #1

St. Petersburg, FL 33716

Tel: (727) 577-5004

Fax: (727) 577-5012

Web: *www.csda.org*

Patrick A. O'Brien, Executive Director

Develops safety standards for use of masonry and concrete saws.

Developed the ANSI Safety Code for the Construction, Use, and Care of Gasoline Powered, Hand Held, Portable, Abrasive, and Cutting Off Machines.

Construction Specifications Institute (CSI)

99 Canal Center Plaza

Alexandria, VA 22314-1791

Tel: (703) 684-0300

Fax: (703) 684-0465

Web: *www.csinet.org*

Karl F. Borgstrom, Executive Director

Develops standards for the language and format of construction specifications; as well as format, organization, and coordination of the contents of the Project Manual for a construction project.

Develops SPEC-DATA II, an information retrieval system & an automated computerized system for specification text manipulation, adaptable to all types of master specification programs.

Publishes:

Manual of Practice providing techniques, procedures, and formats for the preparation and organization of construction documents

MASTERFORMAT that provides a uniform system for filing product information and other technical data

SPECTEXT, a 440 section library of master guide specifications for construction projects prepared in accordance with CSI recommended practices

SPECTEXT II, for smaller or less complex projects

Contractors Pump Bureau (CPB)

111 E Wisconsin Avenue #1000

Milwaukee, WI 53202-4806

Tel: (414) 272-0943

Fax: (414) 272-1170

Web: *www.aem.org*

Russell E. Hutchinson, Director, Technical & Safety Services

Develops standards for self-priming centrifugal, trash, diaphragm, and electrically driven submersible pumps used in the construction industry.

Developed the Certified Performance Seal used by manufacturers.

Conveyor Equipment Manufacturers Association (CEMA)

6724 Lone Oak Boulevard

Naples, FL 34109-6834

Tel: (239) 514-3441

Fax: (239) 514-3470

Web: *www.cemanet.org*

Robert A. Reinfried, Executive Vice President

> Develops standards for design, manufacture, and application of conveying machinery and component parts.

Cooling Technology Institute (CTI)

PO Box 73383

Houston, TX 77273

Tel: (281) 583-4087

Fax: (281) 537-1721

Web: *www.cti.org*

Virginia A. Manser, Administrator

> Develops standards including:
>
> Recommended grades, grading rules, and allowable design stresses for redwood lumber;
>
> Methods and instrumentation determining water cooling capability of mechanical draft towers;
>
> Recommended material, manufacturing limitations, design requirements, and allowable loads for timber fasteners.

Copper Development Association (CDA)

260 Madison Avenue

New York, NY 10016-2401

Tel: (212) 251-7200

Fax: (212) 251-7234

Web: *www.copper.org*

Andrew G. Kireta, Sr., President/CEO

Cordage Institute (CI)

994 Old Eagle School Road #11019

Wayne, PA 19087-1866

Tel: (610) 971-4854

Fax: (610) 971-9859

Web: *www.ropecord.com*

Rovert H. Ecker, Executive Director

> Develops standards for hard fiber and synthetic rope and twines.
>
> Advises engineers, users, and consumers on technical aspects cordage, twines, and ropes.
>
> Publishes:
>
> Technical data, including Quality Control-Minimum Standards
>
> Specifications for Natural and Man-made Fiber Ropes
>
> Standard Test Methods for Synthetic Fiber Ropes

Bend Tests Made on Natural and Synthetic Fiber Ropes

Cordage and Rope Definitions; Standard Terminations for Testing

General Rope Usage; among others

International Cast Polymer Association (ICPA)

435 N Michigan Avenue #1717

Chicago, IL 60611-4067

Tel: (312) 644-0828

Fax: (312) 644-8557

Edward L. Kawala, Executive Director

Develops standards for cultured marble products, including lavatories, bathtubs, shower receptors, water closets, and flat stocks.

D

Deep Foundations Institute (DFI)

326 Lafayette Avenue

Hawthorne, NJ 07506

Tel: (973) 423-4030

Fax: (973) 423-4031

Web: *www.dfi.org*

G. Robert Compton, Jr., Executive Director

Develops standards and codes covering the investigations, installation, materials, inspections & equipment used for deep foundations, including caissons, drilled shafts, sheet piling & slurry walls.

Door Access Systems Manufacturers Association International

1300 Sumner Avenue

Cleveland, O 44115-2851

Tel: (216) 241-7333

Fax: (216) 241-0105

Web: *www.dasma.com*

John H. Addington, Executive Director

Works through other organizations to develop standards, including Minimum Standard for Heavy Duty Industrial and Commercial Draw Bar Type Electrically Powered Door Operators;

Cooperates with UL in developing UL 325—Standard for Safety for Door, Drapery, Gate, and Window Operators and Systems (in cooperation with UL).

Door & Hardware Institute (DHI)

14150 Newbrook Street

Chantilly, VA 22251-2223

Tel: (703) 222-2010

Fax: (703) 222-1410

Web: *www.dhi.org*

Jerry Heppes, Executive Director

> Develops standards for preparation of standard steel doors and frames for builders and architectural hardware.

Ductile Iron Pipe Research Association (DIPRA)

245 Riverchase Parkway East #O

Birmingham, AL 35244

Tel: (205) 402-8700

Fax: (205) 402-8730

Web: *www.dipra.org*

Troy F. Stroud, President

> Works through other organizations to develop product standards pertaining to ductile iron pipe, including manufacturing, design, installation, joints, coatings, linings, fittings, and other appurtenances.

Ductile Iron Society (DIS)

28938 Lorain Road #202

North Olmstead, OH 44070-4014

Tel: (216) 734-8040

Fax: (216) 734-8182

Web: *www.ductile.org*

John V. Hall, Executive Director

E

Electrical Apparatus Service Association (EASA)

1331 Baur Boulevard

St. Louis, MO 63132

Tel: (314) 993-2220

Fax: (314) 993-1269

Web: *www.easa.com*

Linda J. Raynes, President/CEO

> Develops standards and limited warranties for the electrical apparatus sales and service industry that cover the mechanical and electrical aspects of repair, rebuilding, and testing electro-mechanical equipment, including single and polyphase AC induction motors, DC motors and generators, transformers (liquid and dry types), hermetic motors, and hand power tools.
>
> Develops set of electrical safety standards.

Electrical Generating Systems Association (EGSA)

1650 S. Dixie highway #500

Boca Raton, FL 33432-7462

Tel: (561) 750-5575

Fax: (561) 395-8557

Web: *www.egsa.org*

Jalane Kellogh, Executive Director

> Develops standards and specifications covering the generation, transmission, storage, and control of electrical energy not directly supplied by the public utility companies.

Environmental Industry Association (EIA)

4301 Connecticut Avenue NW #300

Washington, DC 20008

Tel: (202) 244-4700

Fax: (202) 966-4818

Web: *www.evasns.org*

Bruce J. Parker, President/CEO

Environmental Information Association, The (EIA)

6735 Wisconsin Avenue #306

Chevy Chase, MD 20815-6112

Tel: (301) 961-4999

Fax: (301) 961-3094

Web: *www.eia-usa.org*

Kelly Rutt, Manager of Communications

> Works through other organizations to develop industry standards in asbestos management.

> Provides balanced information about asbestos & other issues, including environmental site assessments, lead-based paint, radon gas, indoor air quality, and underground storage tanks.

Expanded Shale, Clay & Slate Institute (ESSI)

2225 E Murray Holladay Road #102

Salt Lake City, UT 84117

Tel: (801) 272-7070

Fax: (801) 272-3377

Web: *www.escsi.org*

John P. Ries, Managing Director

> Develops standards.

Publishes:

Guide Specifications for Structural Lightweight Concrete

Members' products meet requirements of Standard Specification for Lightweight Aggregates for Structural Concrete, ASTM C330

Expansion Joint Manufacturers Association (EJMA)

25 North Broadway

Tarrytown, NY 10591-3201

Tel: (914) 332-0040

Fax: (914) 332-1541

Web: *www.ejma.org*

Richard C. Byrne, Secretary

Develops standards covering joints for piping systems.

F

Federation of Societies for Coatings Technologies (FSCT)

492 Norristown Road

Blue Bell, PA 19422-2350

Tel: (215) 940-0777

Fax: (215) 940-0292

Web: *www.coatingstech.org*

Robert F. Zieglaer, Executive Vice President

Works through other organizations to develop standards covering development, manufacture, and use of coatings, including paints, varnishes, and printing inks, among other materials.

Fiberglass Tank & Pipe Institute (FTPI)

11150 S Wilcrest Drive #101

Houston, TX 77099-4343

Tel: (281) 568-4100

Fax: (281) 568-4343

Web: *www.fiberglasstankandpipe.com*

Sullivan D. Curran, Executive Director

Fluid Controls Institute (FCI)

1300 Sumner Avenue

Cleveland, OH 44115-2851

Tel: (216) 241-7333

Fax: (216) 241-0105

Web: *www.fluidcontrolsinstitute.org*

John H. Addington, Executive Secretary

Develops standards for fluid control and fluid conditioning, including:

Modulating service control valves;

Fluid clarification equipment, such as strainers, separators, and filters;

Pressure and temperature gauges;

Pressure, temperature, and volumetric regulators;

Process control switches;

Related equipment;

Silent check valves;

Solenoid valves;

Steam traps.

Food Processing Machinery & Supplies Association (FPMSA)

200 Daingerfield Road

Alexandria, VA 22314-2800

Tel: (703) 684-1080

Fax: (703) 548-6563

Web: *www.processfood.com*

Nancy Janssen, Executive Director

Works through other organizations to develop standards for manufacturing machinery and providing services and supplies for the canning, freezing, and food processing industry.

Forest Products Society (FPS)

2801 Marshall Court

Madison, WI 53705-2295

Tel: (608) 231-1361

Fax: (608) 231-2152

Web: *www.forestprod.org*

Carol Lewis, Executive Vice President

Works through other organizations to develop standards for wood by-products.

Forging Industry Association (FIA)

LTV Building #300

25 Prospect Avenue W

Cleveland, OH 44115-1040

Tel: (216) 781-6260

Fax: (216) 781-0102

Web: *www.froging.org*

Charles H. Hagerman, Executive Vice President

Develops standards and coordinates forging industry safety and product standards.

Publishes: Guidelines for Tolerances for Hot Forged Impression Die Forgings; Hammer, Press, and Upsetter; Tolerance Precision Aluminum Forgings; Allowances and Tolerances for Seamless Rolled Rings

G

Gas Appliance Manufacturers Association (GAMA)

2107 Wilson Boulevard #600

Arlington, VA 22201

T: (703) 525-7060

F: (703) 525-6790

Web: *www.gamanet.org*

Jack W. Klimp, President

Works through other organizations to develop standards covering:

Residential, commercial, and industrial gas appliances and equipment;

Gas, electric, heat pump, and oil water heaters;

Gas- and oil-fired central furnaces;

Equipment used in the production, transmission, and distribution of natural gas.

Gas Processors Association (GPA)

6526 East 60th Street

Tulsa, OK 74145-902

Tel: (918) 493-3872

Fax: (918) 493-3875

Web: *www.gasprocessors.com*

Mark Sutton, Executive Director

Develops:

Standards and product specifications for natural gas liquids (propane, butane, natural gasoline, and so forth), principally for large intercompany industrial custody transfer;

Standards for plant design and storage facilities for gas and liquids;

Specifications for consumer products LP Gas.

Glass Association of North America (GANA)

2945 SW Wanamaker Drive #4

Topeka, KS 66614-5321

Tel: (785) 271-0208

Fax: (785) 271-5321

Web: *www.glasswebsite.com*

Stanley L. Smith, Executive Vice President

Glass Industry Code Committee, Division of GANA (GICC)

2945 SW Wanamaker Drive A

TOPEKA, KS 66614

Tel: (785) 271-0208

Fax: (785) 271-0166

Web: *www.glazingcodes.org*

Gypsum Association (GA)

810 First Street NE #510

Washington, DC 20002

Tel: (202) 289-5440

Fax: (202) 289-3707

Web: *www.gypsum.org*

Michael Gardner, Executive Director

Develops standards on the application and uses of gypsum products.

Provides advisory services on the life-safety aspects of fire protection, including:

GA-216, Recommended Specifications for the Application and Finishing of Gypsum Board;

GA-600, Fire Resistance and Sound Control Design Manual.

H

Hand Tools Institute (HTI)

25 North Broadway

Tarrytown, NY 10591-3201

Tel: (914) 332-0040

Fax: (914) 332-1541

Web: *www.hti.org*

Richard C. Byrne, Executive Director

Develops standards covering the performance, design, and safety of hand tools.

Hardwood Manufacturers Association (HMA)

400 Penn Center Boulevard #530

Pittsburg, PA 15235

Tel: (412) 829-0770

Fax: (412) 829-0844

Web: *www.hardwood.org*

Susan M. Regan, Executive Vice President

Works through other organizations to develop standards for southern hardwood lumber and hardwood products.

Heat Exchange Institute (HEI)

1300 Sumner Avenue

Cleveland, OH 44115-2851

Tel: (216) 241-7333

Fax: (216) 241-0105

Web: *www.heatexchange.org*

John H. Addington, Secretary-Treasurer

> Develops standards concerning steam surface condensers, closed feedwater heaters, power plant heat exchangers, liquid ring vacuum pumps, and steam jet ejectors.

Helicopter Association International (HAI)

1635 Prince Street

Alexandria, VA 22314-2818

Tel: (703) 683-4646

Fax: (703) 683-4745

Web: *www.rotor.com*

Matthew Zuccaro, President

> Works through other organizations to develop standards for safety, test, performance, and environment affecting helicopter design or operation and heliport construction, and codes involving heliport/helicopter fire protection and crash/rescue services.

> Assists community planners and heliport developers in communities and city business districts, including heliports for public, hospital, off-shore, private, and personal uses.

Human Factors & Ergonomics Society (HFES)

PO Box 1369

Santa Monica, CA 90406-1369

Tel: (213) 394-1811

Fax: (213) 394-2410

Web: *www.hfes.org*

Lynn Strother, Executive Administrator

> Develops standards on Visual Display Terminal (VDT) workplace design through ANSI Safety & Health Management Board.

Hydraulic Institute (HI)

Nine Sylvan Way

Parsippany, NJ 07054-3802

Tel: (973) 267-9700

Fax: (973) 267-9055

Web: *www.pumps.org*

Robert K. Asdal, Executive Director

Develops standards for four categories of pumps: centrifugal, vertical, reciprocating, and rotary.

Provides information on:

Classes, types, and nomenclature;

Ratings;

Test codes;

Applications;

Installation, operation, and maintenance;

Measurement of airborne sound from pumping equipment and construction materials.

Publishes: *The Engineering Data Book*

Hydronix Institute (HI)

(Division of Gas Appliances Manufacturers Association)

2107 Wilson Boulevard #600

Arlington, VA 22201

Tel: (908) 464-8200

Fax: (908) 464-7818

Web: *www.gamanet.org*

Janine Brady, Office Manager

Develops standards for testing heating boilers, comfort radiation equipment, and immersion water heaters, and for establishing their ratings and installation criteria.

Assists other organizations in developing standards for residential and commercial buildings, hot water heating, steam, piping and system design criteria, residential cooling, panel heating, and snow melting.

I

Indiana Limestone Institute of America (ILIA)

Stone City National Bank Building #400

Bedford, IN 47421

Tel: (812) 275-4426

Fax: (812) 279-8682

Web: *www.iliai.com*

Jim Owens, Executive Director

Develops standards on limestone, recommended practices, grades, colors, and finishes and all technical data required for specifying, detailing, fabricating, and erecting Indiana limestone.

Industrial Fabrics Association International (IFAI)

1801 Country Road B West

Roseville, MN 55113-4061

Tel: (612) 222-2508

Fax: (612) 631-9334

Web: *www.ifai.com*

Stephen M. Warner, President

> Develops standards ranging from fabric structures to truck cover tarpaulins, including:
>
> Architectural Fabric Structures ASI-77, setting requirements for the materials, design, construction, and erection of structures;
>
> CPAI-CLI, standard classifications and test methods for woven, coated, or laminated polyolefins, or both;
>
> CPAI-63, a quality assurance standard for domestic cotton tarpaulins;
>
> CPAI-79, which includes a listing of standard test methods for coated and laminated fabrics.

Industrial Fasteners Institute (IFI)

1717 East 9th Street #1105

Cleveland, OH 44114

Tel: (216) 241-1482

Fax: (216) 241-5901

Web: *www.industrial-fasteners.org*

Robert J. Harris, Managing Director

> Develops standards for bolts, nuts, screws, rivets, and all types of special industrial fasteners and technical practices for use of various fasteners.
>
> Publishes:
>
> *Fastener Standards Book*
>
> *Metric Fastener Standards*

Industrial Perforators Association (IPA)

5157 Deerhurst Crescent Circle

Boca Raton, FL 33486

Tel: (561) 447-7511

Fax: (561) 447-7511

Web: www.iperfor.org

Delores Morris, Executive Secretary

> Works through other organizations to develop standards for industrial perforated metals, including screens, punched plate, and other perforated materials; published by ASTM Committee E-29.

Industrial Truck Association (ITA)

1750 K Street NW #460

Washington, DC 20006

Tel: (202) 296-9880

Fax: (202) 296-9884

Web: *www.indtrk.org*

William J. Montwieler, Executive Director

Develops standards covering powered industrial trucks, tractors, and forklifts and their major components.

Publishes:

Manual of Recommended Practices for safety and efficiency in the design, manufacturing, and use of industrial trucks and equipment

Institute of Clean Air Companies (ICAC)

(Formerly Industrial Gas Cleaning Institute)

1730 M Street NW #206

Washington, DC 20036-4535

Tel: (202) 457-0911

Fax: (202) 331-1388

Web: *www.icac.com*

Dave Foerster, Executive Director

Institute of Electrical & Electronics Engineers (IEEE)

3 Park Avenue, 17th Floor

New York, NY 10016-5997

Tel: (212) 419-7900

Fax: (212) 752-4929

Web: *www.ieee.org*

Jeffrey W. Raynes, Executive Director

Develops standards on a variety of topics, including electrical safety, commercial and industrial power systems, communications, and computer languages and software engineering.

Institute of Environmental Sciences & Technology (IES)

5005 Newport Drive #506

Rolling Meadow, IL 60008-3841

Tel: (847) 255-1561

Fax: (847) 255-1699

Web: *www.iest.org*

Julie Kendrick, Executive Director

Works through other organizations to develop:

Standards, specifications & recommended practices;

Simulation, testing & contamination control techniques;

Design criteria for equipment operation.

Publishes:

Journal of the Institute of Environmental Sciences & Technology

Institute of Industrial Engineers (IIE)

3577 Parkway Lane #200

Norcross, GA 30092

Tel: (770) 449-0460

Fax: (770) 441-3295

Web: *www.iienet.org*

John Powers, Executive Director

> Develops standards for improving productivity through the applications of industrial engineering techniques.

Institute of Makers of Explosives (IME)

1120 19th Street NW #310

Washington, DC 20036-3605

Tel: (202) 429-9280

Fax: (202) 293-2420

Web: *www.ime.org*

J. Christopher Ronay, President

> Develops standards relating to safety in the transportation, storage, handling, and use of commercial explosive materials.

Insulated Cable Engineers Association (ICEA)

PO Box 1568

Carrollton, GA 30117

Tel: (770) 830-0569

Fax: (770) 830-0501

Web: *www.icea.net*

Executive Director

> Develops standards electrical power, control, instrumentation, communications, and portable cables.

Insulating Glass Manufacturers Alliance (IGMA)

1500 Bank Street #300

Ottawa, ON, Canada K1H 1B8

Tel: (613) 233-1510

Fax: (613) 482-9436

Web: *www.igmaonline.org*

Contact: Public Information

> Develops standards of insulating glass quality (durability, longevity, and so forth) and voluntary performance standards (ratings, recommendations, and the like.

International Association of Electrical Inspectors (IAEI)

901 Waterfall Way #602

Richardson, TX 75080-3855

Tel: (214) 235-1455

Fax: (214) 235-3855

Web: *www.iaei.org*

James W. Carpenter, Executive Director/CEO

Works through other organizations to develop standards for the safe use of electrical materials, devices, and appliances.

Promotes the uniform understanding and application of the National Electrical Code, as well as other electrical codes and standards.

International Association of Foundation Drilling (IAFD)

Pacific Center 1

14180 Dallas Parkway #510

Dallas, TX 75254

Tel: (214) 343-2091

Fax: (214) 343-2584

Web: *www.adsc-iafd.com*

International Association of Plumbing & Mechanical Officials (IAPMO)

5001 E Philadelphia

Ontario, CA 91761

Tel: (909) -472-4100

Fax: (909) 472-4150

Web: *www.iapmo.org*

G. P. Chaney, Executive Director

Develops standards and works through others to develop standards for conventional plumbing products.

Promulgates both installation and material standards for plumbing in the mobile home and recreational vehicle industry.

International Brotherhood of Electrical Workers (IBEW)

900 Seventh Street NW

Washington, DC 20001

Tel: (202) 833-7000

Fax: (202) 728-7676

Web: *www.ibew.org*

Edwin D. Hill, International President

Works through other organizations to develop standards.

Represents workers in all branches of the electrical industry.

International Cast Polymer Association (ICPA)

1010 N Glebe Road

Arlington, VA 22201

Tel: (703) 525-0320

Fax: (703) 525-0743

Web: *www.icpa-hq.org*

Missy Hericksen, Executive Director

International Code Council (ICC)

5203 Leesburg Pike #600

Falls Church, VA 22041

Tel: (703) 931-4533

Fax: (703) 379-1546

Web: *www.iccsafe.org*

James Lee Witt, CEO

Developed the International Building Codes (IBC).

Absorbed the three former Model Codes in 2003:

Building Officials and Code Administrators International;

International Conference of Building Officials;

Southern Building Code Congress International.

International District Energy Association (IDEA)

125 Turnpike Road #4

Westborough, MA 01581-2841

Tel: (508) 366-9339

Fax: (508) 366-0019

Web: *www.districtenergy.org*

Rob Thornton, President

Develops standards, including:

Liquid Thermal Meter Standard

Steam Thermal Meter Standard

Insulated Piping for

District Heating & Cooling

Publishes:

IDHCA Code for Steam Metering

District Heating Handbook—guidelines that references US standards in *Principles of Economical Heating Unwin Chart* of losses in steam piping systems

International Grooving & Grinding Association (IGGA)

12573 State Route 9-W

West Coxsackie, NY 12192-1709

Tel: (518) 731-7450

Fax: (518) 731-7490

Web: *www.igga.net*

John H. Roberts, Executive Director

Grooving and diamond grooving of highways, airport runways, municipal streets, rural roads, parking areas, sidewalks, industrial floors, and other surfaces constructed with Portland cement concrete or asphalt concrete.

Works with other organizations to develop standards and specifications.

Promotes the best practices in the texturing of pavement and pavement systems.

International Institute of Ammonia Refrigeration (IIAR)

110 N Glebe Road #250

Arlington, VA 22201

Tel (703) 312-4200

Fax: (703) 312-0065

Web: *www.iiar.org*

M. Kent Anderson, President

Develops standards for proper and safe use of ammonia as a refrigerant, including Equipment Design and Installation of Ammonia Mechanical Refrigeration Systems (ANSI/IIAR 74-2).

International Masonry Institute (IMI)

42 East Street

Annapolis, MD 21401

Tel: (410) 280-1305

Fax: (301) 261-2855

Web: *www.imiweb.org*

Joan B. Calambokids, President

Works through other organizations to develop standards.

Formed through a joint trust agreement between the Mason Contractors Association of America and the International Union of Bricklayers and Allied Craftsmen.

International Safety Equipment Association (ISEA)

1901 N Moore Street #808

Arlington, VA 22209

Tel: (703) 525-1695

Fax: (703) 528-2148

Web: *www.safetyequipment.org*

Daniel K. Shipp, President

Works through other organizations to develop standards covering emergency eyewash and safety shower, eye and face protection, fall protection, head protection, hearing protection, industrial first aid, industrial safety and health instruments, industrial warning devices, machinery guards, respiratory protection, safety cans, and safety wearing apparel.

International Sign Association (ISA)

707 N Saint Asaph Street

Alexandria, VA 22314

Tel: (703) 836-4012

Fax: (703) 836-8353

Web: *www.signs.org*

Losri M. Anderson, President/CEO

International Staple, Nail & Tool Association (ISNTA)

512 W Burlington Avenue #203

LaGrange, IL 60525-2245

Tel: (708) 482-8138

Web: (708) 482-8186

Web: *www.isanta.org*

John Kurtz. Executive Vice President

> Develops standards on tool design and operation, and guidelines on performance testing of fastened connections, including nails, staples, and other fasteners, power fastening, and pneumatic fastening.

Irrigation Association, The (IA)

6540 Arlington Boulevard

Falls Church, VA 22042-6638

Tel: (703) 536-7080

Fax: (703) 536-7019

Web: *www.irrigation.org*

Henry Lamb, Executive Vice President

> Develops standards for irrigation systems for landscaping.

L

Laser Institute of America (LIA)

13501 Integrity Drive #128

Orlando, FL 32826

Tel: (407) 380-1553

Fax: (407) 380-5588

Web: *www.laserinstitute.org*

Peter M. Baker, Executive Director

> Develops standards for the Safe Use of Lasers.

> Publishes:

> Guides to hazard control measures for industry and health care facilities, and all personnel involved with lasers in various applications

Lightning Protection Institute (LPI)

PO Box 64506

Tel: (816) 233-0140

Fax: (816) 676-0093

Web: *www.lightning.org*

Bud Van Stickle, Executive Director

> Develops standards covering all materials and components that might be under stress while a lightning protection system is conducting lightning current.

> Covers metals from the standpoint of durability under weathering and possible damage from corrosion, physical impact, or reaction with dissimilar metals.

M

Manufactured Housing Institute (MHI)

2101 Wilson Boulevard #610

Arlington, VA 22201-3062

Tel: (703) 558-0400

Fax: (703) 558-0401

Web: *www.manufacuredhousing.com*

Chris S. Stinebert, President

> Works through other organizations to develop standards.

> Advises the US Department of Housing & Urban Development in maintenance/ proponency of the Federal Manufactured Home Construction & Safety Standards and Procedural Enforcement Regulations (24CFR 3280, 3282, and 3283).

Manufacturers Standardization Society of the Valve & Fittings Industry (MSSVFI)
Monorail Manufactures Association (MMA)

127 Park Street NE

Vienna, VA 22180-4602

Tel: (703) 281-6613

Fax: (703) 281-6671

Web: *www.mss-hq.com*

Robert O'Neill, Executive Director

Maple Flooring Manufacturers Association (MFMA)

60 Revere Drive #500

Northbrook, IL 60062

Tel: (847) 480-9138

Fax: (847) 480-9282

Web: *www.maplefloor.org*

John R. Waxman, Executive Director

Develops standards.

Establishes and enforces uniform grades and standards of Northern Maple hard-wood flooring.

Establishes grading rules for hard maple, beech, and birch flooring.

Adopts specifications for heavy duty and gymnasium-type floor finish products.

Marble Institute of America (MIA)

2890 Clemens Road #100

Cleveland, OH 44145-1166

Tel: (440) 250-9222

Fax: (440) 250-9223

Web: *www.marble-institute.org*

Garis F. Distelhorst, Executive Vice President

Works through other organizations to develop standards for dimension stone, including marble, granite, limestone, sandstone, slate, bluestone, and quartzite.

Publishes: A design manual

Materials & Methods Standards Association (MMSA)

PO Box 350

Grand Haven, MI 49417-0350

Tel: (231) 799-8000

Fax: (231) 799-8850

Web: *www.mmsa.ws*

Harvey J. Powell, President

Develops standards of quality and performance of materials and methods for instal-lation and use of ceramic tiles.

Material Handling Industry of America (MHIA)

8720 Red Oak Boulevard #201

Charlotte, NC 28217-3992

Tel: (704) 676-1190

Fax: (704) 676-1199

Web: *www.mhia.org*

John B. Nofsinger, CEO

Works through other organizations to develop standards covering material handling equipment used in plants, plant-yards, piers, terminals, and warehouses.

Mechanical Contractors Association of America (MCAA)

1385 Piccard Drive

Rockville, MD 20850-4340

Tel: (301) 869-5800

Fax: (301) 990-9690

Web: *www.mcaa.org*

John R. Noble, Executive Vice President/CEO

> Works through other organizations to develop standards related to heating, ventilating, air conditioning (HVAC), plumbing, piping, welding, safety, and other construction-related topics.

Metal Building Contractors & Erectors Association (MBCEA)

PO Box 499

Shawnee Mission, KS 66201

Tel: (913) 432-3800

Fax: (913) 432-3803

Web: *www.mbcea.org*

Angela M. Cruse, Executive Director

Metal Building Manufacturers Association (MBMA)

1300 Sumner Avenue

Cleveland, OH 44115-2851

Tel: (216) 241-7333

Fax: (216) 241-0105

Web: *www.mbma.com*

Charles M. Stockinger, General Manager

> Develops standards covering methods used in application of design loads, recommended minimum thicknesses of steel used in manufacturing metal buildings, and other general recommendations for use by model code bodies in preparing or revising codes to ensure proper construction of metal buildings.

Metal Construction Association (MCA)

4700 W Lake Street

Glenview, IL 60025

Tel: (847) 347-4718

Fax: (877) 665-2234

Web: *www.metalconstruction.org*

Mark Engle, Executive Vice President

> Develops specifications.
>
> Publishes:
>
> Technical guidelines & specifications manuals

Metal Framing Manufacturers Association (MFMA)

401 N Michigan Avenue

Chicago, IL 60611

Tel: (312) 644-6610

Fax: (312) 321-4098

Web: *www.metalframingmfg.org*

Jack M. Springer, Executive Director

> Publishes:
>
> Guidelines for use of steel framing
>
> Standards Publication

Metal Powder Industries Federation (MPIF)

105 College Road E

Princeton, NJ 08540-6992

Tel: (609) 452-7700

Fax: (609) 987-8523

Web: *www.mpif.org*

C. James Trombino, Executive Director/CEO

> Develops standards in the field of powder metallurgy dealing with ferrous and non-ferrous materials, including self-lubricating bearings and industry practices.
>
> Issues safety standards for metal powder compacting presses with ANSI.

Metal Treating Institute (MTI)

1550 Roberts Drive

Jacksonville, FL 32250-3222

Tel: (904) 249-0448

Fax: (904) 249-0459

Web: *www.metaltreat.com*

M. Lance Miller, Vice President

Methods Time Measurement Association for Standards & Research (MTM)

1411 Peterson Avenue

Park Ridge, IL 60068

Tel: (708) 823-8320

Fax: (708) 823-2319

Web:

Dirk Rauglas, Executive Director

> Develops standards covering the methodology for deriving a time to perform a given manual task, including standardization data for clerical operations, works under the microscope & works in maintenance areas.

Monorail Manufacturers Association (MMA)

(Section of Material Handling Industry of America)

8720 Red Oak Boulevard #201

Charlotte, NC 28217-3992

Tel: (704) 676-1190

Fax: (704) 676-1199

Web: *www.mhia.org*

John B. Nofsinger, CEO

Develops standards covering overhead, underhung, material handling equipment, including monorails, stacker cranes, and underhung traveling cranes.

N

NACE International (NACE)

1440 S Creek Drive

Houston, TX 77087-6200

Fax: (281) 228-6300

Web: *www.nace.org*

Tony Keane, Executive Director

Develops performance standards and practices to guide producer and user industries.

Supplies information regarding the science and engineering of corrosion control and material selection.

Publishes:

Standards and practices on performance (resistance to corrosion) of offshore steel platforms, performance of cathodic protection systems, and performance of materials in corrosive environments.

National Association of Architectural Metal Manufacturers (NAAMM)

Eight S Michigan Avenue #1100

Chicago, IL 60603

Tel: (312) 532-0405

Fax: (312) 332-0706

Web: *www.naamm.org*

August L. Sisco, Executive Vice President

Develops, maintains, and improves technical standards of the industry, including metal stairs, metal stair railings, pipe railings, flagpoles, hollow metal doors and frames, metal bar grating, metal lath and plaster assemblies, and light-gage steel framing.

Maintains five active standards divisions;

Architectural Metal Products;

Flagpole;

Hollow Metal Manufacturers Association;

Metal Bar Grating;

Metal Lath/Steel Framing Association.

Provides technical information to architects and engineers.

National Association of Chain Manufactures (NACM)

PO Box 22681

Lehigh Valley, PA 18002-2268

Tel: (610) 691-8708

Fax: (610) 886-0695

Web: *www.nacm.info*

Donald Sayenza, Executive Director

> Works through other organizations to develop standards covering welded chain, weldless chain, and tire chains.

National Association of Industrial & Office Properties (NAIOP)

2201 Cooperative Way, 3rd Floor

Herndon, VA 20171-3034

Tel: (703) 904-7100

Fax: (703) 904-7942

Web: *www.naiop.org*

Thomas J. Bisacquino, Executive Vice President

> Works through other organizations to develop standards in the area of paved streets, utility systems for multiple users, setback or percentage coverage requirements, landscaping, off-street parking, & architectural control.

National Association of Pipe Coating Applicators (NAPCA)

Am South Bank Building #717

Shreveport, LA 71101-3673

Tel: (318) 227-2769

Fax: (318) 222-0482

Web: *www.napca.com*

Merritt B. Chastain, Jr., Managing Director

> Develops standards, specifications, and suggested procedures for pipe coating applications.

> Publishes:

> Pocket edition of *National Association of Pipe Coating Applicators Specifications Plant Coating Guide* (1987), which contains all current and revised specifications

National Association of Plumbing-Heating-Cooling Contractors (NAPMC)

1085 S Washington Street

Falls Church, VA 22142

Tel: (703) 237-8100

Fax: (703) 237-7442

Web: *www.phccweb.org*

Dwight L. Casey, Executive Vice President

> Works through other organizations to develop standards in the field of plumbing, hydronic heating, and hydronic cooling.

> Advances sanitation and sanitary laws and techniques in air conditioning.

Improves plumbing appliances and fixtures and heating and cooling equipment and parts.

Publishes:

National Standard Plumbing Code

National Board of Boiler & Pressure Vessel Inspectors (NBOBPVI)

1055 Crupper Avenue

Columbus, OH 43229

Tel: (614) 888-8320

Fax: (614) 888-0750

Web: *www.nationalboard.org*

Donald E. Tanner, Executive Director

Develops safety standards, codes, and uniform safety inspections, including:

National Board Inspection Code (1983);

National Board Boiler Blowoff

Equipment (1973);

Relieving Capacities of Safety Valves & Relief Valves.

National Building Granite Quarries Association (NBGQA)

1220 L Street NW #100-167

Washington, DC 20005

Tel: (800) 557-2848

Web: *www.nbgqa.com*

Kurt M. Swenson, Secretary

Develops standards.

Publishes:

Specifications for Architectural Granite, a listing of types of granite offered by members with products classified by color, name, quarry location, and quarrier

National Burglar & Fire Alarm Association (NBFAA)

2300 Valley View Lane #230

Irving, TX 75062

Tel: (214) 260-5479

Fax: (214) 260-5979

Web: *www.alarm.org.org*

Merlin J. Guilbeau, Executive Director

Works through other organizations to develop standards covering burglary alarms, fire alarms, security systems, and other alarm systems.

National Certified Pipe Welding Bureau (NCPWB)

1385 Piccard Drive

Rockville, MD 20850-4340

Tel: (301) 869-5800

Fax: (301) 990-9690

Web: *www.mcaa.org*

Stephanie Mills, Communications Coordinator

>   Works through other organizations to develop standards.

>   Conducts research and supplies information and data on welding department of the Mechanical Contractors Association of America, Inc.

National Clay Pipe Institute (NCPI)

N 3219 County Highway H

PO Box 759

Lake Geneva, WI 53147

Tel: (262) 248-9094

Fax: (262) 248-1564

Web: *www.ncpi.org*

Michael Van Dine, Corporate Engineer

>   Develops standards for Vitrified Clay Pipe and its installation, working through ASTM.

>   Publishes:

>   *Clay Pipe Engineering Manual* and technical brochures relating the use of Vitrified Clay Pipe in sanitary sewer systems

National Concrete Masonry Association (NCMA)

13750 Sunrise Valley Drive

Herndon, VA 20171

Tel: (703) 713-1900

Fax: (703) 713-1910

Web: *www.ncma.org*

Mark Hogan, President

>   Works through other organizations to develop standards.

>   Develops criteria for the proper use of concrete masonry products and concrete pavers and encourages their use.

NCSL International (NCSL)

(National Conference of Standards Laboratories)

2995 Wilderness Place #107

Boulder, CO 80301-5404

Tel: (303) 440-3339

Fax: (303) 440-3384

Web: *www.ncsli.org*

Craig Gulka, Business Manager

>   Develops standards of practice for laboratories concerned with the measurement of physical quantities, the calibration of standards and instruments.

National Conference of States on Building Codes & Standards (NCSBCS)

505 Huntmar Park Drive #210

Herndon, VA 20170

Tel: (703) 437-0100

Fax: (703) 481-3596

Web: *www.ncsbcs.org*

Robert C. Wible, Executive Director

> Works through other organizations to develop, update & maintain building codes & standards responsible for ANSI A225.1 Standard on Manufactured Housing Installations (Manufactured Home Sites, Communities, and Setups).

> Publishes:

> *Handbook of Building Codes*

National Corrugated Steel Pipe Association (NCSPA)

13140 Coit Road #320, LB 120

Dallas, TX 75240-5737

Tel: (972) 850-1907

Fax: (972) 490-4219

Web: *www.ncspa.org*

Jennifer Raney, Director of Operations

> Develops standards for use of corrugated steel pipe and plate in culverts, sewers, bridges, subdrains, and other drainage facilities.

National Council on Radiation Protection & Measurements (NCRPM)

7910 Woodmont Avenue #400

Bethesda, MD 20814-3095

Tel: (301) 907-8968

Web: *www.ncrponline.org*

D. A. Schauer, Information Contact

National Demolition Association (NDA)

(Demolition Contractors)

16 N Franklin Street #203

Doylestown, PA 18901-3536

Tel: (215) 348-4949

Fax: (215) 348-3536

Web: *www.demolitonassociation.com*

Michael R. Taylor

National Electrical Contractors Association (NECA)

Three Bethesda Metro Center #1100

Bethesda, MD 20814-5330

Tel: (301) 657-3110

Fax: (301) 215-4500

Web: *www.neca.org*

John M. Grau, CEO

Develops standards and works through other organizations to develop standards for electrical equipment and materials and methods of their installation.

National Electrical Manufacturers Association (NEMA)

1300 N 17th Street #1752

Rosslyn, VA 22209

Tel: (703) 841-3200

Fax: (703) 841-5900

Web: *www.nema.org*

Evan Gaddis, President

Develops standards dealing with the safety of electrical equipment and apparatus used for the generation, transmission, distribution, and utilization of electrical power.

National Elevator Industry (NEI)

1677 County Road 64

PO Box 838

Salem, NY 12865-0838

Tel: (518) 854-3100

Fax: (518) 854-3257

Web: *www.neil.org*

Edward A. Donoghue, Secretary

Develops and maintains standards and safety codes covering elevators, dumbwaiters, escalators, and moving walks.

Develops requirements for the handicapped using vertical transportation, codes for personnel elevators, personnel and material hoists, model building codes, electrical codes, requirements for elevator fire doors, and metric codes.

National Electrical Testing Association (NETA)

106 Stone Street

Morrison, CO 80465

Tel: (303) 697-8441

Fax: (303) 697-8431

Web: *www.netaworld.org*

Mary R. Jordan, Executive Director

Develops standards and testing guidelines for electrical power transmission and utilization equipment, including Automatic Reclosures and Sectionalizers, Capacitors,

Circuit Breakers, Direct Current Systems, Disconnects, Emergency Systems, Fiber-Optic Cables, Ground Fault Systems, Instrument Transformers, Instrumentation, Metal Motor Control, Network Protectors, Outdoor Bus Structures, Power Cables, Power Transformers, Protective Relays, Rotating Machinery, Safety Equipment, Thermographic Testing, Short Circuit Studies and Overcurrent Coordination Studies, Surge Arrestors, Switchboard Assemblies, Switches, and Systems. Other specifications are based on ANSI, NEMA, and other industry consensus standards.

National Environmental Balancing Bureau (NEBB)

8575 Grovemont Circle

Gaithersburg, MD 20877

Tel: (301) 977-3698

Fax: (301) 977-9589

Web: *www.nebb.org*

Michael P. Dolim, Executive Vice President

Develops standards and works with other organizations to develop standards for testing, adjusting, and balancing (TAB) of environmental systems in buildings.

Develops manuals that provide a comprehensive set of systematic procedures representing the state-of-the-art of TAB work, including air/hydronic TAB, and sound and vibration measurement procedures for environmental systems in buildings.

National Environmental Health Association (NEHA)

720 S Colorado Boulevard, South Tower #970

Denver, CO 802-46-1925

Tel: (303) 756-9090

Fax: (303) 691-9490

Web: *www.neha.org*

Nelson E. Fabian, Executive Director

Develops standards for environmental health & protection of personnel in controlling environmental hazards.

Publishes:

State-of-the-art manual for on-site wastewater management

Various model ordinances such as a model ordinance for the regulation and certification of swimming pool service companies, and swimming pool technicians and apprentices

National Fastener Distributors Association (NFDA)

401 N Michigan Avenue #2200

Chicago, IL 60611

Tel: (312) 527-6671

Fax: (312) 673-6740

Web: *www.nfda-fastener.org*

Karen A. Hurley, Executive Vice President

Works through other organizations to develop standards on fasteners and manufacturing.

National Fluid Power Association (NFPA)

3333 N Mayfair Road #211

Milwaukee, WI 53222-3219

Tel: (414) 778-3344

Fax: (414) 778-3361

Web: *www.nfpa.com*

Linda Western, Executive Director

Develops standards covering dimensions, specifications, methods of testing or rating, terminology, symbols, and procedures for systems, as well as individual components, including fluid power cylinders, valves, pumps, motors, sealing devices, conductors, fittings, filters, fluids, servovalves, accumulators, and pneumatic logic devices.

National Fire Protection Association (NFPA)

One Batterymarch Park

Quincy, MA 02169-7411

Tel: (617) 770-3000

Fax: (617) 770-0700

Web: *www.nfpa.org*

Anthony R. O'Neill, Vice President/CEO

Develops standards covering electrical installations, flammable liquids, gases, life safety, and marine environments.

Publishes:

National Fire Codes covering protection, prevention, and suppression

Recommended practices, guides, and manuals

National Fire Sprinkler Association (NFSA)

PO Box 1000

Route 22 & Robin Hill Park

Patterson, NY 12563

Tel: (845) 878-4200

Fax: (845) 878-4215

Web: *www.nfsa.org*

John A. Viniello, President

Develops standards on fire protection of buildings, including design, installation, inspection, and maintenance of automatic sprinklers.

Works with ANSI in developing and revising code for pressure piping, pipe threads, and pipe flanges and fittings.

National Forest Products Association (NFPA)

1250 Connecticut Avenue NW #200

Washington, DC 20036

Tel: (202) 463-2700

Fax: (202) 463-2785

Web: *www.nfpa.gov*

Barry M. Cullen, President

> Develops and distributes recommended specifications, standards, and general construction data guides for the use of lumber and wood products, including structural design data, design values for wood construction, span tables for joists and rafters, design of wood frame structures, and permanent wood foundations.

National Glass Association (NGA)

8200 Greensboro Drive #302

McLean, VA 22102-3881

Tel: (703) 442-4890

Fax: (703) 442-0630

Web: *www.glass.org*

Philip J. James, President/CEO

National Hardwood Lumber Association (NHLA)

PO Box 34518

Memphis, TN 38184-0518

Tel: (901) 377-1818

Fax: (901) 382-6419

Web: *www.nhla.com*

Paul Houghland, Jr., Executive Manager

> Develops and maintains standards for grading hardwood lumber.

> Inspects, measures, and certifies hardwood lumber, cypress, and thin lumber.

North American Insulation Manufacturers Association (NAIMA)

99 Canal Center Plaza

Alexandria, VA 22314-1538

Tel: (703) 683-6422

Fax: (703) 549-4383

Web: *www.insulation.org*

Michele M. Jones, Executive Vice President

> Works through other organizations to develop standards and specifications referring to mineral wool insulation products, including thermal performance standards that will contribute to the conservation of energy.

North American Die Casting Association (NADCA)

241 Holbrook Drive

Wheeling, IL 60090

Tel: (847) 279-0001

Fax: (847) 279-0002

Web: *www.diecasting.org*

Daniel Twarog, President

> Works through other organizations to develop standards pertaining to the die casting industry, including safety and health, material testing, and environmental protection.

National Lime Association (NLA)

200 N Glebe Road #800

Arlington, VA 22203

Tel: (703) 243-5463

Fax: (703) 243-5489

Web: *www.lime.org*

Arlene Seeger, Executive Director

> Works through other organizations to develop standards and guidelines on using lime for steelmaking; water, sewage, and waste treatment; sulfur dioxide removal from flue gasses; stabilization for road and airfield construction; mortar and plaster; and other applications.
>
> Publishes: Guidelines for using lime; Water Supply and Treatment; Lime Handling, Application & Storage in Treatment
>
> Processes; Lime Stabilization
>
> Construction Manual—Flexible Pavement Design Guide
>
> Effective Use of Lime in Asphalt; Specifications for Lime and Its Uses in Plastering Stucco, Unit Masonry, and Concrete

National Propane Gas Association (NPGA)

1150 1st Street NW

Washington, DC 20036-4623

Tel: (202) 466-7200

Fax: (202) 466-7205

Web: *www.npga.org*

Richard Rolden, President/CEO

> Works through other organizations to develop standards pertaining to the production, transportation, and distribution of liquefied petroleum gas.

National Roof Deck Contractors (NRDC)

PO Box 1582

Westford, MA 01886-4996

Tel: (800) 217-7944

Web: *www.nrdca.org*

Hubert T. Dudley, Executive Director

Works through other organizations to develop standards pertaining to structural roof deck systems, including gypsum roof decks, built-up roofing, and so forth.

National Roofing Contractors Association (NRCA)

10255 W Higgins Road #600

Rosemont, IL 60018-5607

Tel: (847) 299-9070

Fax: (847) 299-1183

Web: *www.nrca.net*

William A. Good, Executive Vice President

Works with other organizations to develop standards for all roofing systems, materials, and application procedures, including asphalt, asbestos, coal tar pitch, elastic/plastic, slate, tile, metal, and wood roofs.

Publishes:

Roofing & Waterproofing Manual that provides recommended procedures, practices, and evaluative comments on roofing specifications, construction details, and roofing materials

National Safety Council (NSC)

444 N Michigan Avenue

Chicago, IL 60611

Tel: (312) 527-4800

Fax: (312) 527-9281

T. C. Gilchrest, President

Works through other organizations to develop standards.

Focuses on standards concerned with safety of products or systems & accident/injury record systems, including accident prevention, occupational health & traffic safety, among other areas.

National Sash & Door Jobbers Association (NSDJA)

10047 Robert Trent Jones Plaza

New Port Richey, FL 34655-4649

Tel: (727) 372-3665

Fax: (727) 372-2879

Web: *www.nsdja.com*

Rosalle Leone, Executive Director

Works through other organizations to develop standards related to windows and door products.

National Sanitation Foundation International (NSF)

PO Box 1468

NSF Building

3475 Plymouth Road

Ann Arbor, MI 48106

Tel: (312) 769-8010

Fax:

Web:

James G. Kendzel, Manager, Standards

Develops standards in public and environmental health.

Publishes:

List of available standards covering plastic piping systems, components & materials; swimming pool equipment; drinking water direct & indirect additives; plumbing components for mobile homes and recreational vehicles; water and wastewater treatment devices; and biohazard chemistry & flexible membrane liners; among other areas.

National School Supply & Equipment Association (NSSEA)

8330 Colesville Road #250

Silver Spring, MD 20910

Tel: (301) 495-0240

Fax: (301) 495-3330

Web: *www.nssea.org*

Tim Holt, Executive Vice President

Works through other organizations to develop standards covering school supplies and equipment, including auditoriums, theaters, classrooms, bleachers, seating, operable partitions, and play ground equipment.

Issues certification when operable and folding walls are tested for sound transmission loss in accordance with ASTM E90.

Endorses ASTM E557-77 standards for the application and installation of operable partitions.

Issues testing procedures for measuring sound transmission loss.

National Slag Association (NSA)

25 Stevens Avenue, Building A

Westlawn, PA 19609

Tel: (610) 670-0701

Fax: (610) 670-0702

Web: *www.nationalslagassociation.org*

Contact: Public Information

Works through other organizations to develop standards.

Cooperates actively with specification-writing organizations at national and state levels in formulating and revising aggregate specifications and in developing standards covering test procedures.

Conducts research dealing with aggregates and their end-use products in the association's laboratory, Youngstown, Ohio.

National Solid Wastes Management Association (NSWMA)

1730 Rhode Island Avenue #1000

Washington, DC 20036

Tel: (202) 659-4613

Fax: (202) 775-5917

Web:

Eugene J. Wingerter, Exec Director/CEO

> Develops safety standards primarily associated with the waste management industry, including procedures for the manufacturing, installation & operation of equipment & facilities used in refuse processing, collection & disposal.

National Stone Association (NSA)

1415 Elliot Place NW

Washington, DC 20007-2599

Tel: (202) 342-1100

Fax: (202) 342-0702

Web: *www.*

Robert G. Bartlett, President

> Works through other organizations to develop standards.

> Cooperates with national technical associations in standardizing specifications, test methods, and recommended practices involving the use of stone.

National Stone, Sand and Gravel (NSSGA)

1605 King Street

Alexandria, VA 22314

Tel: (703) 525-8788

www.nssga.org

Contact: Public Information

National Swimming Pool Foundation (NSPF)

10803 Gulfdale #300

San Antonio, TX 78216

Tel: (512) 525-1227

Fax:

Web:

Evelyn Robinson, Executive Director

National Terrazzo & Mosaic Association (NTMA)

201 N Maple Avenue #208

Purcellville, VA 20132

Tel: (540) 751-0930

Fax: (540) 751-0935

Web: *www.ntma.com*

George D. Hardy, Executive Director

Develops standards on terrazzo and mosaic, including various applications and grinding techniques.

Conducts research on installation methods.

Publishes:

Technical Data Book—contains standard national specifications for the installation of both cementitious and resinous terrazzo

National Water Well Association (NWWA)

6375 Riverside Drive

Dublin, OH 43017

Tel: (614) 761-1711

Fax: (614) 761-3446

Web:

Jay H. Lehr, EXEC DIR

Works through other organizations to develop standards for well construction and the sampling & monitoring of ground water resources.

National Wood Flooring Association (NWFA)

(Formerly National Oak Flooring Manufacturers Association)

111 Chesterfield Industrial Boulevard

Chesterfield, MO 63005

Tel: (636) 519-9663

Fax: (636) 519-9664

Web: *www.nwfa.org*

Edward S. Korczak, Executive Director/CEO

Works through other organizations to develop wood flooring standards.

National Wood Window & Door Association (NWWDA)

1400 E Touhy Avenue

Des Plaines, IL 60018

Tel: (708) 299-2000

Fax: (708) 299-1286

Web: *www.wooddoorspecialities.com*

John W. Shoemaker, Executive Vice President

Develops standards covering wood flush-doors, windows, sliding patio doors, and water repellent preservatives.

NCSL International (NCSL)

(National Conference of Standards Laboratories)

2995 Wilderness Place #107

Boulder, CO 80301-5404

Tel: (303) 440-3339

Fax: (303) 440-3384

Web: *www.ncsli.org*

Craig Gulka, Business Manager

> Develops standards of practice for laboratories concerned with the measurement of physical quantities, the calibration of standards and instruments.

P

Painting & Decorating Contractors of America (PDCA)

11960 Westlake Industrial Drive #201

St. Louis, MO 63146-3209

Tel: (314) 514-7322

Fax: (314) 514-9417

Web*: www.pdca.org*

Ian Horen, CEO

> Works through other organizations to develop standards of workmanship and safety in painting, decorating, drywall, wall covering, and coating industries.

1924 N Second Street

Harrisburg, PA 17102

Tel: (717) 238-9723

Fax: (717) 238-9985

Web: *www.perlite.org*

Denise Calabreze, Executive Director

> Develops standards, specifications, and test methods.
>
> Publishes:
>
> Test methods and related standards containing test methods for evaluating the quality of expanded perlite, and ASTM specifications applicable to perlite
>
> Standards for perlite products used in building industries
>
> Sponsors research leading to the standardization of specifications and methods of testing perlite and perlite products.

Pipe Fabrication Institute (PFI)

666 Fifth Avenue #325

New York, NY 10103

Tel: (514) 634-3434

Fax: (514) 634-9736

Web: *www.pfi-institute.org*

Guy Fortin, Executive Director

Develops standards and technical bulletins covering the design, fabrication, and erection of industrial high pressure/temperature piping systems to meet requirements of chemical plants and refineries, nuclear and fossil power stations, and ships.

Pipeline Contractors Association (PLCA)

1700 Pacific Avenue #4100

Dallas, TX 75201-4675

Tel: (214) 969-2700

Fax: (214) 969-2705

Web: *www.plca.org*

J. Patrick Teilborg, Managing Director-General Counsel

Works through other organizations to develop standards.

Reviews and revises American Petroleum Institute's Standard Welding Pipelines & Related Facilities *(API 1104).*

Plastic Pipe & Fittings Association (PPFA)

800 Roosevelt Road Building C #20

Glen Ellyn, IL 60137

Tel: (630) 858-6540

Fax: (630) 790-3095

Web: *www.ppfahome.org*

Richard Church, Executive Director

Plastics Pipe Institute (PPI)

1825 Connecticut Avenue NW #680

Washington, DC 20009

Tel: (202) 462-9067

Web: (202) 462-9779

Web: *www.plasticpipe.org*

Rich Gottwald, President

Develops standards for plastics pipe and related products.

Maintains a Hydrostatic Stress Board, which writes standard policies and procedures for forecasting the long-term strength of plastic piping products and plastics piping thermoplastic materials.

Issues listings of Hydrostatic Design Stress recommendations for thermoplastics materials. The Institute's Municipal and Industrial Division develops technical information, guides, and manuals related to the use of plastics piping for municipal and industrial applications.

Plumbing & Drainage Institute (PDI)

800 Turnake Street #300

North Andover, MA 01845

Tel: (978) 557-0721

Fax: (978) 557-0721

Web: *www.pdionline.org*

William C. Whitehead, Executive Director

> Develops standards for plumbing and drainage products, including backwater valves, hydrants, floor and roof drains, plumbing fixture supports, and cleanouts, among other products.

Polyurethane Manufacturers Association (PMA)

1123 N Water Street

Milwaukee, WI 58202

Tel: (414) 431-3094

Fax: (414) 276-7704

Web: *www.pmahome.org*

Jennifer Gelinskey, Associate Director

> Develops standards for physical test procedures suitable for use with solid polyurethane elastomers, standards for cast urethanes, and specifications for RIM processing of urethane.

Porcelain Enamel Institute (PEI)

PO Box 920220

Norcross, GA 30010

Tel: (770) 281-8980

Fax: (770) 281-8981

Web: *www.porcelainenamerl.com*

Cullenn L. Hackler, Executive Vice President

> Develops standards and specifications covering sanitary ware, plumbing fixtures, and other specialized porcelain products.

Portable Sanitation Association International (PSA)

7800 Metro Parkway #104

Bloomington, MN 55425

Tel: (612) 854-8300

Fax: (612) 854-7560

Web: *www.psai.org*

William F. Carroll, Executive Director

Portland Cement Association (PCA)

5420 Old Orchard Road

Skokie, IL 60077-1083

Tel: (708) 966-6200

Fax: (708) 966-8389

Web: *www.cement.org*

John P. Gleason, Jr., President

Works through other organizations to develop consensus standards and update existing standards to reflect the latest findings in scientific research and test programs in the fields of cement and concrete technology, advanced engineering developments in all areas of concrete design and construction, and results of structural investigations and field experiences in the uses of concrete.

Provides a range of services to the private and the public sectors of the economy that serves the needs of the construction community in the United States and Canada.

Post-Tensioning Institute (PTI)

8601 Black Canyoh Highway #103

Phoenix, AZ 85021

Tel: (602) 870-7540

Fax: (602) 870-7541

Web: *www.post-tensioning.org*

Theodore L. Neff, Executive Director

Works through other organizations to develop standards for post-tensioning materials and concrete construction.

Publishes:

ACI Standard Building Code

AASHTO Specifications for Highway Bridges

Guide Specifications for Post-Tensioning Materials

Recommendations for Grouping of Post-Tensioned Prestressed Concrete Members

Powder Actuated Tool Manufacturers Institute (PATMI)

1603 Boone's Lick Road

St. Charles, MO 63301

Tel: (636) 947-6610

Fax: (636) 946-3336

Web: *www.patmi.org*

James A. Borchers, Executive Director

Works through other organizations to develop standards for the safe use and effective application of powder actuated fastening systems and ancillary tools.

Power Sources Manufacturers Association (PSMA)

PO Box 418

Mendham, NJ 07945-0418

Tel: (973) 543-9660

Fax: (973) 543-6207

Web: *www.psma.com*

Joseph Horzepa, Executive Director

Develops technical standards for AC and DC power source systems and related components.

Power Tool Institute (PTI)

1300 Sumner Avenue

Cleveland, OH 44115-2851

Tel: (216) 241-7333

Fax: (216) 241-0105

Web: *www.powertoolinstitute.com*

Charles M. Stockinger, Executive Manager

Works through others to coordinate global product listing standards.

Sponsors programs to promote the safe use of power tools.

Precast/Prestressed Concrete Institute (PCI)

209 W Jackson Boulevard #500

Chicago, IL 60606

Tel: (312) 786-0300

Fax: (312) 786-0353

Web: *www.pci.org*

James G. Toscas, President

Develops standards and administers the Plant Certification Program that certifies a plant's capability to produce architectural precast and prestressed concrete of the highest quality.

Was recognized as a Quality Assurance Inspection Agency by the Council of American Building Officials (CABO).

Four Campus Boulevard

Newtown Square, PA 19073-3299

Tel: (610) 356-4600

Fax: (610) 356-4649

Web: *www.pmi.org*

Gregory Balastrero, CEO

Works through other organizations to develop standards for project management applications.

Property Casualty Insurers Association of America (PCIAA)

2600 River Road

Des Plaines, IL 60018-3286

Tel: (847) 297-7800

Fax: (847) 297-5064

Web: *www.pciaa.net*

Ernie Cziszar, President/CEO

Works through other organizations to develop safety and health standards.

Provides technical representatives to assist in formulating standards.

Urges the development of performance standards, where practicable.

R

Rack Manufacturers Institute (RMI)

(Affiliate of Material Handling Industry of America)

8720 Red Oak Boulevard #201

Charlotte, NC 28217-3992

Tel: (704) 676-1190

Fax: (704) 676-1199

Web: *www.mhia.org*

John B. Nofsinger, CEO

Publishes: Specification for the Design, Testing, and Utilization of Industrial Steel Storage Racks

Minimum Design Standards for Pallet Stacking Framer

Manual of Safety Practices

Stacker Rack Nomenclature

Railway Engineering Maintenance Suppliers Association (REMSA)

417 West Broad Street #203

Falls Church, VA 22046

Tel: (703) 241-8514

Fax: (703) 241-8589

Web: *www.remsa.org*

J. A. Meyerhoeffer, Executive Director

Railway Tie Association (RTA)

115 Commerce Drive #C

Fayetteville, GA 30214

Tel: (770) 460-5553

Fax: (770) 460-5573

Web: *www.rta.org*

Jim Gaunt, Executive Director

Develops standards for railway ties, cross ties, and switch ties.

Publishes:

Specifications for Cross Ties and Switch Ties

Wood Tie Fastener Performance Specifications

Resilient Floor Covering Institute (RFCI)

401 E Jefferson Street #102

Rockville, MD 20850

Tel: (301) 340-8580

Fax: (301) 343-7283

Web: *www.rfci.com*

Douglas Wiegand Managing Director

Develops standards for all types of floors and floor surfaces

Conducts programs for investigating fire safety of synthetic surfaces.

Resilient Floor Covering Institute (RFCI)

401 E Jefferson Street #102

Rockville, MD 20850

Tel: (301) 340-8580

Fax: (301) 340-7283

Web: *www.rfci.com*

Douglas Wiegard, Managing Director

Develops standards for tile and sheet vinyl products, including adhesives and installation, and maintenance.

Resistance Welder Manufactures Association (RWMA)

550 NW LeJeune Road

Miami, FL 33126

Tel: (305) 443-9353

Fax: (305) 492-7421

Web: *www.rwma.org*

Ray Shook, Contact

Develops standards covering resistance welding machines, electrode alloy materials, nomenclature, and components (controls, transformers, and the like).

Rubber Manufacturers Association (RMA)

1400 K Street NW #900

Washington, DC 20005

Tel: (202) 682-4800

Fax: (202) 682-4854

Web: *www.rma.org*

Donald B. Shea, President/CEO

Develops standards and specifications for hose, conveyor belting, power transmission belting, sealing products, molded and extruded products, protective linings, roll coverings, and coated materials.

Rubber Pavement Association (RPA)

1801 S Jentilly Lane #A-2

Tempe, AZ 85281-5738

Tel: (480) 517-9944

Fax: (480) 517-9959

Web: *www.rubberpavements.org*

Douglas Carlson, Executive Director

S

Safety Glazing Certification Council (SGCC)

PO Box 9

Henderson Harbor, NY 13651

Tel: (315) 646-2234

Fax: (351) 646-2297

Web: *www.sgcc.org*

John G. Kent, Administrative Manager

> Administers a safety glazing certification program operated in compliance with ANSI Practice for Certification Procedures and the Code of Federal Regulations.
>
> Publishes:
>
> Certified Products Directory, which lists all certified products, label requirements, and procedural guidelines for manufacturers seeking certification

Scaffolding Shoring & Forming Institute (SSFI)

1300 Sumner Avenue

Cleveland, OH 44115-2851

Tel: (216) 241-7333

Fax: (216) 241-0105

Web: *www.ssfi.org*

John H. Addington, Managing Director

> Develops standards for scaffolding, suspended powered scaffolding, shoring, and forming (none processed through ANSI).
>
> Establishes recommended criteria and inspection procedures for proper and safe use of scaffolding to support formwork in concrete construction.
>
> Provides recommended safety requirements for shoring concrete formwork and scaffolding including flying deck forms, rolling shore brackets, horizontal shoring beams, single post shores, and steel frame shoring.
>
> Provides recommended scaffolding erection procedures.

Screen Manufacturers Association (SMA)

2850 S Ocean Boulevard #114

Palm Beach, FL 33480-6205

Tel: (561) 533-0991

Fax: (561) 533-7466

Web: *www.smacentral.org*

Frank S. Fitzgerald, Executive Vice President

Develops standards and maintains testing procedures and specifications for metal screens, including window, patio, door, and porch, and solar screens.

Sealed Insulating Glass Manufacturers Association (SIGMA)

401 N Michigan Avenue

Chicago, IL 60611

Tel: (312) 644-6610

Fax: (312) 527-6640

Web: *www.sigmaonline.org*

J. Dollard Carey, Executive Vice President

Works with other organizations to develop standards covering insulation glass.

Sheet Metal & Air Conditioning Contractors' National Association (SMACNA)

4201 Lafayette Center Drive

Chantilly, VA 20151-1209

TeL: (703) 803-2980

Fax: (703) 803-3732

Web: *www.smacna.org*

John W. Sroka, Executive Vice President

Develops standards covering duct construction and architectural sheet metal.

Publishes:

Accepted Industry Practice for Industrial Duct Construction

Architectural Sheet Metal Manual

Ducted Electric Heat Guide for Air Handling Systems

Energy Conservation Guidelines

Energy Recovery Equipment and Systems Air-To-Air

Fibrous Glass Duct Construction Standards

Fire, Smoke, and Radiation Damper Guide for HVAC Systems

Guide for Steel Stack Design and Construction

Guidelines for Roof Mounted Outdoor Air-Conditioner Installation

HVAC Air Duct Leakage Test Manual

HVAC Duct Construction Standards—Metal and Flexible

HVAC Systems—Duct Design Tables and Charts

HVAC Systems—Applications

HVAC Systems—Testing, Adjusting and Balancing

Indoor Air Quality Manual

Installation Standards for Residential Heating & Air Conditioning Systems

Management Change Order Manual

Managers Guide for Welding

Rectangular Industrial Duct Construction Standards

Retrofit for Building Energy Systems and Processes

Round Industrial Duct Construction Standards

Thermoplastic Duct (PVC) Construction Manual Welding Guidelines/ Troubleshooting Chart

Standards Practice in Sheet Metal Work Environmental Systems Technology

Sound & Vibration in Environmental Systems

Procedural Standards for Measuring Sound & Vibration

Procedural Standard for Testing, Adjusting, and Balancing of Environmental Systems

Procedural Standards for Certified Testing of Cleanrooms

Testing, Adjusting, and Balancing Manual for Technicians

Society of Fire Protection Engineers (SFPE)

7315 Wisconsin Avenue 602E

Bethesda, MD 20814

Tel: (301) 718-2810

Fax; (301) 718-2242

Web: *www.sfpe.org*

David D. Evans, Executive Director

Works through other organizations to develop standards.

Society of Marine Port Engineers (SMPE)

PO Box 466

Avenel, NJ 07001-2402

Tel: (732) 381-7673

Fax: (732) 381-2046

Web: *www.smpe.org*

Benjamin A. Bailey, Secretary

Society of Naval Architects & Marine Engineers (SNAME)

601 Pavonia Avenue #400

Jersey City, NJ 07306-3881

Tel: (201) 798-4800

Fax: (201) 798-4975

Web: *www.sname.org*

Philip B. Kimball, Executive Director

Works through other organizations to develop standards & specifications pertaining to design, construction, maintenance & operation of off-shore & ocean bottom structures.

Society of the Plastics Industry (SPI)

1667 K Street NW #1000

Washington, DC 20006

Tel: (202) 974-5200

Fax: (202) 296-7005

Web: *www.plasticsindustry.org*

William R. Carteaux, President

> Develops standards for plastics products through ASTM, ANSI, and NSF. Two divisions of the society have their own standardization programs:
>
> Vinyl Siding Institute;
>
> Vinyl Window and Door Institute.

Solar Rating & Certification Corporation (SRCC)

1679 Clearlake Road

Cocoa, FL 32922-5703

Tel: (321) 638-1537

Fax: (321) 638-1010

Web: *www.solar-rating.org*

Jim Huggins, Technical Director

> Develops & implements solar industry certification programs for solar energy equipment, including solar collectors & solar water heating systems.
>
> Administers a laboratory accreditation program for independent test facilities evaluating solar components, subsystems & systems.

SSPC: The Society for Protective Coatings (SSPC)

40 24th Street, 6th Floor

Pittsburgh, PA 15222-4656

Tel: (412) 281-2331

Fax: (412) 281-9992

Web: *www.sspc.org*

William L. Shroup, Executive Director

> Develops standards for:
>
> Surface preparation, including hand and power tool cleaning, chemical cleaning, and all levels of blast cleaning; Visually evaluating surface appearance after cleaning;
>
> Paint application, including shop, field, and maintenance painting;
>
> Measuring paint film thickness;
>
> Painting systems, paints, and safety in paint applications;
>
> Visually evaluating degree of rusting on painted steel surfaces.
>
> Publishes:
>
> Guide for maintenance of repainting systems and paints

Standards Engineering Society (SES)

13340 S. W. 96th Avenue

Miami, FL 33176

T: (305) 971-4798

F: (305) 971-4799

Web: *www.ses-standards.org*

Dr. H. Glenn Ziegenfuss, Executive Director

    Promotes standardization, knowledge & use of national & international standards.

Steel Deck Institute (SDI)

PO Box 25

Fox River Grove, IL 60021-0025

Tel: (847) 458-4647

Fax: (847) 458-4648

Web: *www.sdi.org*

Steven A. Roelrig, Managing Director

    Develops standards.

    Publishes:

    SDI Design Manual for Composite Decks, Form Decks, and Roof Decks

    SDI Diaphragm Design Manual

    Deck Design Manual containing Specifications and Commentaries

    Code of Recommended Standard Practice, Roof Deck Construction, and Suggested Architect's Specifications

    SDI Standard Load Tables

    Roof Deck Fire Resistance Ratings

    Cantilever Criteria.

Steel Door Institute (SDI)

30200 Detroit Road

Cleveland, OH 44145-1967

Tel: (216) 899-0010

Fax: (216) 892-1404

Web: *www.steeldoor.org*

J. Jeffery Wherry, Managing Director

    Develops standards, including standardized specifications for steel doors and frames, standardized hardware locations and hardware preparations, building code improvements, and performance specifications.

Steel Founders Society of America (SFSA)

780 McArdle Drive Unit G

Crystal Lake, IL 60014

Tel: (815) 455-8240

Fax: (815) 455-8241

Web: *www.sfsa.org*

Raymond W. Monroe, Executive Vice President

> Develops standards for foundry raw materials and works through other organizations to develop standards for the manufacture and use of carbon and low- and high-alloy steel castings.

Steel Joist Institute (SJI)

3127 10th Avenue North Extension

Myrtle Beach, SC 29577-6760

Tel: (843) 626-1995

Fax: (843) 262-5565

Web: *www.steeljoist.org*

Perry Green, Technical Director

> Develops standards for design and construction methods for steel joists and standard specifications and load tables for Joist Girders (structural members).

> Steel Joist standards include Load Tables for Open Web, Longspan, and Deep Longspan Steel joists comprising K-Series, LH-Series, and DLH-Series.

Steel Manufacturers Association (SMA)

1150 Connecticut Avenue NW #715

Washington, DC 20036

Tel: (202) 296-1515

Fax: (202) 296-2506

Web: *www.steelnet.org*

Thomas A. Danjzec, President

> Works through other organizations to develop standards, primarily in the development of bar standards in billet, rail, and axle steel.

> Does not issue standards, but sponsors ASTM A616, A617 Rail & Axles Steel, Concrete Reinforcing Bars, and a Standards Specification for Hot Rolled Steel Fence Posts.

Steel Plate Fabricators Association (SPFA)

(Division of STI/SPFA)

570 Oakwood Road

Lake Zurich, IL 60047

Tel: (847) 428-8265

Fax: (847) 438-8766

Web: *www.spfa.org*

Wayne B. Geyer, Executive Vice President

Works through other organizations to develop standards for fabrication and erection of all types of weldable plate into pressure and non-pressure tanks, processing and storage vessels, heat exchangers, penstocks, weldments, and other industry products.

Steel Tank Institute (STI)

(Division of STI/SPFA)

570 Oakwood Road

Lake Zurich, IL 60047

Tel: (708) 438-8265

Fax: (708) 438-8766

Web: *www.steeltank.com*

Wayne B. Geyer, Executive Vice President

Develops standards for exterior corrosion protection of underground steel storage tanks and a limited number of recommended practices for both underground and aboveground storage.

Steel Window Institute (SWI)

1300 Sumner Avenue

Cleveland, OH 44115-2851

Tel: (216) 241-7333

Fax: (216) 241-0105

Web: *www.steelwindows.com*

John H. Addington, Executive Secretary

Develops standards and recommended specifications for steel windows.

Structural Board Association (SBA)

(Formerly Waferboard Association)

25 Valleywood Drive, Unit 27

Markham, ON, L3R 5-LR, Canada

Tel: (905) 475-1100

Fax: (905) 475-1101

Web: *www.osbguide.com*

Mark Angelini, President/CEO

Structural Insulated Panel Association (SIPA)

PO Box 1699

Gig Harbor, WA 98335

Tel: (253) 858-7472

Fax: (253-858-0272

Web: *www.sipa.org*

William Wachtler, Executive Director

Sump & Sewage Pump Manufacturers Association (SSPMA)

PO Box 647

Northbrook, IL 60065-0647

Tel: (647) 559-9233

Fax: (647) 559-9235

Web: *www.sspma.org*

Pamela W. Franzen, Managing Director

Develops standards covering design & performance criteria for domestic sump sewage & effluent pumps, component & accessory supplies.

Publishes:

Domestic Sump Effluent & Sewage Pump Standards that provide a uniform method of testing & rating, detailing minimum specifications for motors, nameplate data, service cords & control switches

T

Test Boring Association (TBA)

Five Mapleton Road #200

Princeton, NJ 08540

Tel: (609) 514-2660

Fax: (609) 514-2660

Web: *www.tba.org*

Patricia Zita, Managing Executive

Develops standards covering test boring and core drilling.

Tile Council of America (TCA)

100 Clemson Research Boulevard

Anderson, SC 29625

Tel: (864) 646-8453

Fax: (864) 646-2821

Web: *www.tileusa.com*

Eric Astrachan, Executive Director

Develops standards.

Annually publishes:

The guide specification Handbook for Ceramic Tile Installation, which covers all accepted ceramic tile installation methods, and references installations and material standards applicable to the methods

Tin Stabilizers Association (TSA)

100 N 20th Street, 4th Floor

Philadelphia, PA 19103

Tel: (215) 564-3484

Fax: (215) 564-2175

Web: *www.tinstabilizers.org*

John D. McGreevey, Executive Director

Works through other organizations to develop standards and specifications for tin ingots, tinplates, tin alloys, bearings, solders, pewter and tin, and tin alloy coatings.

Truss Plate Institute (TPI)

218 N Lee Street #300

Alexandria, VA 22314

Tel: (703) 683-1010

Fax: (703) 548-4399

Web: *www.tpinst.org*

Michael A. Cassidy, Executive Vice President

Develops standards for metal plate connected wood trusses, metal plate connected parallel chord wood trusses, and temporary bracing of metal plate connected wood trusses.

Provides an in-plant inspection service for manufacturers of metal plate connected wood trusses in accordance with the Uniform Building Code (UBC) Standards.

Tubular Exchanger Manufacturers Association (TEMA)

25 North Broadway

Tarrytown, NY 10591-3201

Tel: (914) 332-0040

Fax: (914) 332-1541

Web: *www.tema.org*

Richard C. Byrne, Secretary

Develops standards for shell and tube heat transfer equipment that clarify and expand material, thermal and physical properties of fluids, and other information related to various classes of exchangers for the chemical processing and petroleum refining industries.

U

Unified Abrasives Manufacturers Association (UAMA)

30200 Detroit Road

Cleveland, OH 44145-1967

Tel: (440) 899-0010

Fax: (440) 892-1404

Web: *www.uama.org*

J. Jeffery Wheery, Managing Director

Publishes:

V

Valve Manufacturers Association of America (VMAA)

1050 17th Street NW #701

Washington, DC 20036

Tel: (202) 331-8105

Fax: (202) 296-0378

Web: *www.vmi.org*

J. Stephen Larkin, President

Works through other organizations to develop standards for industrial valves and actuators used in construction, water, oil and gas, power, chemical, and process industries.

Vinyl Institute (VI)

1300 Wilson Boulevard #800

Arlington, VA 22209

Tel: (703) 741-5670

Fax: (703) 741-5672

Web: *www. vinylinfo.org*

Tim Burns, President

Vinyl Siding Institute (VSI)

1201 15th Street NW #220

Washington, DC 2005

Tel: (202) 587-5100

Fax: (202) 587-5127

Web: *www.vinylsiding.org*

Jerry Y. Huntley, President

Vinyl Window & Door Institute (VWDI)

1667 K Street NW #1000

Washington, DC 20006

Tel: (202) 974-5200

Fax: (202) 296-7005

Web: *www.plasticsindustry.org*

William R. Carteaux, President

Develops standards independent of SPI.

W

Water Environment Federation (WEF)

601 Wythe Street

Alexandria, VA 22314-1994

Tel: (708) 686-2406

Fax: (703) 686-2492

Web: *www.wef.org*

Quincalee Brown, Executive Director

> Works through other organizations to develop standards.

> Develops & publishes:

> Design, operation & maintenance literature on: wastewater collection & treatment; hazardous wastes sampling & collection; microbiology; disinfection; wetlands; air pollution & industrial wastes; sludge processing & handling; sewerage systems financing & regulations.

Water Quality Association (WQA)

(International Headquarter and laboratory)

4151 Naperville Road

Lisle, IL 60532-1088

Tel: (708) 505-0160

Fax: (708) 505-9637

Peter Censky, Executive Director

> Develops standards for household, commercial & portable exchange water softeners and household & commercial water filters.

> Certifies water softeners and filters complying with association standards.

Water Systems Council (WSC)

1101 30th Street NW

Washington, DC 20007

Tel: (202) 625-1587

Web: (202) 625-4363

Web: *www.wsc.org*

Kathleen Stanley, Executive Director

> Develops Testing and Rating Standards designed to supply the purchaser & user of automatic, electric water systems with accurate performance data & to assist in determining the proper application & selection of this equipment.

> Standards cover shallow well water system pumps, deep well water system pumps & deep well submersible pump motors, and hydropneumatic tank volumes.

Western Dredging Association (WDA)

PO Box 5797

Vancouver, WA 98668-5797

Tel: (360) 750-0209

Fax: (360) 750-1445

Web: *www.westerndredging.org*

Lawrence M. Patella, Executive Vice President

Provides dredging and marine engineering assistance covering North, Central, and South America.

Incorporates Central Dredging Association, Eastern Dredging Association, and World Organization of Dredging Associations.

Welding Research Council (WRC)

PO Box 1942

New York, NY 10156

Tel: (216) 653-3847

Fax: (216) 653-3854

Web: *www.foreignengineers.org*

Martin Prager, Executive Director

Wire Reinforcement Institute (WRI)

942 Main Street #300

Hartford, CT 06103

Tel: (800) 552-4976

Web: *www.wri.org*

Contact: Public Information

Works through other organizations to develop standards covering welded wire fabric, wire reinforcement, and wire products for the reinforcement of concrete and other construction materials.

Wire Rope Technical Board (WRTB)

801 N Fairfax Street #211

Alexandria, VA 22314-1757

Tel: (703) 299-8550

Fax: (703) 299-9233

Web: *www.wrtb.org*

Kimberly A. Korbel, Executive Director

Wood Moulding & Millwork Producers Association (WMMPA)

507 First Street

Woodland, CA 95695-4025

Tel: (530) 661-9590

Fax: (530) 661-9586

Web: *www.wmmpa.com*

Kellie Schroeder Executive Vice President

Develops standards, including the WM/Series Moulding patterns catalog of accurate, full-scale renderings of the most popular wood moulding profiles:

Exterior Wood Door Frames—WM 3-79;

Industry Standard 20-Minute Fire-Rated Wood Door Frames—WM 8-89;

Standard Certified Non-structural laminated or Finger-Jointed Wood—WM 5-81; Vinyl Wrapped Interior Moulding and Millwork Products Standard—WM 2-82; Wood Moulding Requirements—WM 4-85.

Wood Products Manufacturers Association (WPMA)

175 State Road East

Westminster, MA 01473-1208

Tel: (978) 874-5445

Fax: (978) 874-9946

Web: *www.wpma.org*

Philip A. Bibeau, Executive Director

Wood Truss Council of America (WTCA)

6300 Enterprise Lane

Madison, WI 53719

Tel: (608) 274-4849

Fax: (608) 274-3329

Web: *www.woodtruss.com*

Kirk Grundehl, Executive Director

Woven Wire Products Association (WWPA)

Newark Wire Works

1059 King George Post Road

Edison, NJ 08837

Tel: (732) 661-2001

Web: *www.wovenwire.org*

J. P. Spellman, President

Index